MW00770557

NARRATING HISTORY, HOME, AND DYASPORA

NARRATING HISTORY, HOME, AND DYASPORA

Critical Essays on Edwidge Danticat

Edited by Maia L. Butler,
Joanna Davis-McElligatt,
and Megan Feifer

Foreword by Nadège T. Clitandre
Afterword by Thadious M. Davis

University Press of Mississippi / Jackson

The University Press of Mississippi is the scholarly publishing agency of
the Mississippi Institutions of Higher Learning: Alcorn State University,
Delta State University, Jackson State University, Mississippi State University,
Mississippi University for Women, Mississippi Valley State University,
University of Mississippi, and University of Southern Mississippi.

www.upress.state.ms.us

The University Press of Mississippi is a member
of the Association of University Presses.

Copyright © 2022 by University Press of Mississippi
All rights reserved

First printing 2022
∞

Library of Congress Cataloging-in-Publication Data

Names: Butler, Maia L., editor. | Davis-McElligatt, Joanna, editor. |
Feifer, Megan, editor. | Clitandre, Nadège T., 1977– author of introduction, etc. |
Davis, Thadious M., 1944– author of introduction, etc.
Title: Narrating history, home, and dyaspora : critical essays on Edwidge Danticat /
edited by Maia L. Butler, Joanna Davis-McElligatt, and Megan Feifer ;
foreword by Nadège T. Clitandre, afterword by Thadious M. Davis.
Description: Jackson : University Press of Mississippi, 2022. |
Includes bibliographical references and index.
Identifiers: LCCN 2022008969 (print) | LCCN 2022008970 (ebook) |
ISBN 9781496839879 (hardback) | ISBN 9781496839886 (trade paperback) |
ISBN 9781496839893 (epub) | ISBN 9781496839909 (epub) |
ISBN 9781496839916 (pdf) | ISBN 9781496839923 (pdf)
Subjects: LCSH: Danticat, Edwidge, 1969—Criticism and interpretation. |
Haitian American authors—Criticism and interpretation. | American literature—
Haitian American authors—Criticism and interpretation. | LCGFT: Essays. |
Literary criticism.
Classification: LCC PS3554.A5815 Z78 2022 (print) | LCC PS3554.A5815
(ebook) | DDC 813/.54—dc23/eng/20220405
LC record available at https://lccn.loc.gov/2022008969
LC ebook record available at https://lccn.loc.gov/2022008970

British Library Cataloging-in-Publication Data available

To all the Haitians in the floating homeland.

CONTENTS

Part II. Welcoming Ghosts: Memory and Historicity

Part III. I Speak Out: Storytelling and Narrative Structure

Part IV. "Create Dangerously": Trauma, Resilience, and the Way Forward

ACKNOWLEDGMENTS

MAIA'S ACKNOWLEDGMENTS

I could not dream of better collaborators than Megan Feifer and Joanna Davis-McElligatt. The rich friendship Megan and I have shared, and the bonding over Danticat's work that led us to found the Edwidge Danticat Society, are a precious gift with many returns. I met Megan while we were both beginning our respective work on Danticat in Louisiana, where Jo was the director. Jo was the first Black woman appointed to the tenure track in the English department at the University of Louisiana at Lafayette, and I absolutely would not be the scholar I am today without her deep care and community building, my exposure to her cutting-edge research, and her encouragement as I developed my own research skills and writing voice. I am so grateful for our community of contributors to this collection; we persevered through many events of personal, community, and trans/national magnitude along our journey to completing this project. I am also lucky for the immense support of my family and writing community who have listened to me discuss my vision for this book over the past several years. Thank you, Carol Butler Hill, Amara Butler, Eileen Butler Cox, Oriana Bolden, Roderick Adams, Andrea Roberts, M. Yvonne Taylor, Krista Benson, April Petillo, Shylah Pacheco Hamilton, Rachel Afi Quinn, Eesha Pandit, Nicole Spigner, Jennifer Caroccio Maldonado, Tiffany Gilbert, Lanice Avery, and the so, so many fabulous emerging scholars of the #AcWri Collective. I am ever thankful for Nadège Clitandre and Thadious Davis, whose deep appreciation of Danticat's work inspires our own, and who are absolutely amazing models of what a life of the mind looks like when we remain committed to slow, thoughtful, and caring scholarship. I have great appreciation for my departmental colleagues at the University of North Carolina Wilmington for their ceaseless encouragement and celebration of my work, and to our College of Arts and Sciences for generous support of the project.

JOANNA'S ACKNOWLEDGMENTS

I am endlessly grateful for and to Maia L. Butler and Megan Feifer, whose vision, friendship, and perseverance made this book possible. We are in incalculable debt to our contributors, who kept the faith amid endless local and global trials: this book is the product of their love-labor. Nadège Clitandre and Thadious Davis are models of intellectual and professional generosity; this collection is stronger for their willingness to engage so thoroughly with the project. The Department of English at the University of North Texas provided me with crucial support in the form of a teaching release that made it possible for this project to be completed during the pandemic.

I would not have been able to complete this without the support of Colin Davis-McElligatt, my beautiful August, Don and Beth Davis, Daniel and Jenn Davis, Sara Chirchirillo, T. J. Tallie, Molly Freeman, Patricia Eamon, Priscilla Ybarra, Anna Hinton, Devin Garofalo, Jacqueline Vanhoutte, Haley Fedor, Shelley Ingram, and Maria Seger—thank you, thank you, thank you.

MEGAN'S ACKNOWLEDGMENTS

I am deeply grateful to Maia L. Butler and Joanna Davis-McElligatt for their tireless efforts, enduring commitment, and critical companionship. Much gratitude to our contributors for their exceptional patience and brilliant chapters. So very grateful for our board members, contributors, and members of the Edwidge Danticat Society, who believed in and supported this project from its inception. Thank you to Pallavi Rastogi, Solimar Otero, Katherine Henninger, Kumkum Sangari, Gwynne Kennedy, Gregory Jay, and Lenore Danies for encouraging my personal scholarship on Edwidge Danticat all these years. Finally, thank you to Edwidge Danticat, whose body of work inspires and shapes how we think about the world and our places in it.

FOREWORD

A Soulful Life at Work

NADÈGE T. CLITANDRE

> There, in that pale region, beneath that essential cover, the twin
> incompatibility of an oeuvre and madness is unveiled; it is the blind
> spot of each one's possibility, and of their mutual exclusion.
> —MICHEL FOUCAULT[1]

In 2018 I received tenure, and by the end of that year my monograph on Edwidge Danticat, the first of its kind, was published.[2] The process of arriving at these two most important events in my professional career to date was not exactly a descent into madness, but the moments of confusion, insecurity, uncertainty, and restlessness at times made me feel like I was getting close. In retrospect, the many years I have spent reading, teaching, and analyzing Danticat's work has led to a number of epiphanies at various phases of both my professional and my personal life. By the time I had completed my book on Danticat, I realized that I no longer examined her work as individual texts but as a collection of her life's work. I would from that point refer to her oeuvre. I would speak of her fictional and nonfictional texts in relation to each other. It's the reason why I developed the idea of the "echo chamber" as a theory of relation and analytical framework in my book. In the process of organizing Danticat's oeuvre by looking at its parts in relation to a whole, I had another epiphany. I was also sorting out and ordering my own life. I was beginning to ask questions about my own life work and the myriad ways in which Danticat's work has led me to a reconsideration of the meaning of an oeuvre not only in the literary sense but also in a spiritual sense.

I am writing this foreword to *Narrating History, Home, and Dyaspora: Critical Essays on Edwidge Danticat* having recently completed a coedited volume on Danticat with my esteemed colleague Jana Braziel.[3] I wanted to finish the collection before delving into the fifteen critical essays you are about to read. The fact that more collections of critical essays on Danticat are appearing at this moment is exciting and offers the opportunity for dynamic engagement between established scholars and more junior scholars working on this prolific writer. That editors are able to "collect" new articles on Danticat from scholars of various disciplines and fields is also indicative of Danticat's success and enduring influence. The first edited collection of critical essays devoted entirely to Danticat was published in 2010. The collection, *Edwidge Danticat: A Reader's Guide*, edited by Martin Munro, aims to examine the myriad intersecting contexts in which Danticat writes.[4] In 2019, a second collection, *Approaches to Teaching the Works of Edwidge Danticat*, edited by Celucien L. Joseph, Suchismita Banerjee, Marvin E. Hobson, and Danny M. Hoey Jr., was published; it focuses on pedagogical approaches to Danticat's work.[5] *Narrating History, Home, and Dyaspora* contributes to transdisciplinary work that points to new directions and emerging fields. It also advances more recent discussions about Danticat's activism and role as a public intellectual. Indeed, the collection is a delightful glance into the future of studies on Danticat. It gives me an opportunity to further reflect on what has evolved since I first picked up a copy of Danticat's first novel, *Breath, Eyes, Memory*, in the mid-1990s. I remember a time when I had to request permission to write my undergraduate thesis on Danticat because her work was not yet part of a canon of Caribbean literature and Black women's writings. She was at the beginning of her life work as a writer, and after reading *Breath, Eyes, Memory*, I was compelled to follow her work. I did not know then that this decision would shape my own life work.

What is it about the life work of Danticat that pulls me, and so many others, in? What is it about any writer's oeuvre that lures a scholar to engage with the work? The writer and psychotherapist Thomas Moore, whose work I started reading to avoid a possible descent into madness as a tenure-track assistant professor, states in his 2008 book *A Life at Work: The Joy of Discovering What You Were Born to Do*: "To be grafted to soul means to be open to the life that pools deep inside you, allowing it to coalesce into a career or other kind of work. Your choice of work flows from who you are—from your interests, tastes, hopes, and values. As you work, you feel that you are doing something consonant with your nature. You aren't working against yourself, not contradicting the person you are."[6] Reading Danticat's work feels very much like that. Her oeuvre helps you to understand that what you see as contradictions may in fact be the parts of yourself that you are piecing together in your life journey toward a sense of wholeness, whatever that means to you. It reminds you that your fragments are your own and at the same time something even greater than you. It helps you reflect on the complex dimensions of the human mind and at the same time foregrounds the marvelous simplicity of everyday life. If madness, as Michel Foucault writes, is "the absence of an oeuvre," perhaps Danticat is my elixir against madness. One thing is abundantly clear to me now: I am so grateful to have her as my guide toward the lifework that I am learning to cultivate and perceive as an oeuvre in its own right.

Shortly after obtaining tenure in 2018, I also had a chance to connect with Edwidge while I was enjoying summer vacation with my husband in Miami. We met at a restaurant near Little Haiti. We spent quite a bit of time talking about gentrification in South Florida. But we also briefly talked about her work, and the work of a new generation of Haitian writers. I remember vividly noticing the joy on her face when I asked about her new projects. I remember thinking she has the tranquility and gratitude that I imagine some people have when they have found their calling. I thought: she leads a soulful life, and perhaps a life less fragmented.

NOTES

1. Michel Foucault, "Madness, the Absence of an Oeuvre," in *History of Madness*, ed. Jean Khalfa (Abingdon, Oxon., England: Routledge, 2006), 541–49.

2. Nadège T. Clitandre, *Edwidge Danticat: The Haitian Diasporic Imaginary* (Charlottesville: University of Virginia Press, 2018).

3. Jana Evans Braziel and Nadège T. Clitandre, eds., *The Bloomsbury Handbook to Edwidge Danticat* (London: Bloomsbury Academic, 2021).

4. Martin Munro, ed., *Edwidge Danticat: A Reader's Guide* (Charlottesville: University of Virginia Press, 2010).

5. Celucien L. Joseph, Suchismita Banerjee, Marvin E. Hobson, and Danny M. Hoey Jr., eds., *Approaches to Teaching the Works of Edwidge Danticat* (New York: Routledge, 2019).

6. Thomas Moore, *A Life at Work: The Joy of Discovering What You Were Born to Do* (New York: Broadway Books, 2008), 28.

NARRATING HISTORY, HOME, AND DYASPORA

INTRODUCTION

MAIA L. BUTLER, JOANNA DAVIS-McELLIGATT, AND MEGAN FEIFER

"My country," Edwidge Danticat writes, "is one of uncertainty."[1] Danticat's country in this instance is neither Haiti, the nation she left at age twelve, nor the United States, the empire to which she moved and where she lives now. Rather, she clarifies, her country is the tenth department, "the floating homeland, the ideological one, which joined all Haitians living outside of Haiti, in the *dyaspora*."[2] The Haitian Creole term *dyaspora* is polysemous, referring all at once to the scattering of Africans in the course of the Atlantic slave trade, the ecological and political exile of Haitians from the island, and the floating homeland inhabited by exiled and immigrant Haitians around the globe. Dyaspora thus identifies simultaneous belonging to the place and community from which one has been exiled, and to the distinct communities forged out of the experience of that exile—indeed, as the Haitian journalist Jean Dominique explains to Danticat, "*dyaspora* are people with their feet planted in both worlds."[3] To *be* a dyaspora, then, is to embody the fundamental precarity of double-belongingness; to belong and not belong is to be a cotemporal denizen of both Haiti and the United States, to be at home and in exile at the same time. For Danticat and the hundreds of thousands of Haitians who live as exiles and immigrants, life in dyaspora registers the instability of home and place, the intricate relations between history as it is both experienced and remembered, and the inherent complexity of nation and national identity. In all of her work, from essays to interviews, novels to children's books, documentaries to editorials, Danticat has investigated the experiences of Haitians at home and in dyaspora, carefully exploring how they endure and survive the trauma of ongoing ecological catastrophe, government instability, and financial insecurity.

As Nadège T. Clitandre has explained, Danticat's diasporic imaginary encourages readers to confront and grapple with past and present constructions of nation, homeland, and dyaspora. Danticat's writing from the tenth department, Clitandre argues, not only forges new narratives of national identity, national and diasporic histories, and constructions of home and dyaspora but makes up an archive that successfully (re)imagines "old and new narratives of homeland and articulations of home as both geographical spaces that can be mapped and symbolic places that are imagined."[4] Although Danticat's reenvisioning of the complexity of national belonging and being-in-dyaspora is informed by her own experiences in specific places, such as Port-au-Prince and Miami, her work is also deeply concerned with the condition of inclusion and belonging for all peoples of the African diaspora; Danticat locates herself within both the Black diaspora and the Haitian dyaspora. In an interview in *Callaloo*, a scholarly and creative journal dedicated to publishing the Black arts, Danticat aligns herself with "writers from the entire African Diaspora," including Richard Wright, Toni Morrison, Zora Neale Hurston, or "her Afro-Mexican or Afro-Brazilian or Haitian equivalent."[5] The writer in diaspora/dyaspora, Danticat explains, "to borrow from Toni Morrison's Nobel lecture[,] knows what it is 'to live at the edge of towns that cannot bear' our company, hamlets that need our labor but want our children banned from their schools, villages that want our sick shut out from their hospitals, big cities that want our elderly, after a lifetime of impossible labor, to pack up and go off somewhere else to die."[6] In Danticat's formulation, the Black experience in diaspora is the immigrant's experience in another country; to be Black, she explains, is to always already exist in a form of exile. Wright's childhood self in *Black Boy*, Morrison's Sethe, Hurston's Janie, and Danticat's Sophie can be said, then, to function as contemplations on similar phenomena attending Black life: ostracism, dispersion, exclusion, survival, presence, persistence. Indeed, Danticat makes it plain that her work is a celebration and exploration of the lives of "all of us exiles, émigrés, refugees, migrants, nomads, immigrants, citizens, half-generation, first-generation, American, Haitian, Haitian American, men, women, and children living in the United States and elsewhere."[7] By providing an ongoing record of the experiences, memories, and narratives of the displaced and often voiceless, the writer in dyaspora functions for their community as an oracle, a journalist, a storyteller, a truth seeker, and an artist.

Known for her novels and collections of short fiction such as *Breath, Eyes, Memory* (1994), *Krik? Krak!* (1995), and *Claire of the Sea Light* (2013), Danticat is also a writer of nonfiction, including her memoir *Brother, I'm Dying* (2007) and essay collection *Create Dangerously: The Immigrant Artist at Work* (2010). Yet Danticat is increasingly known for her work as a public intellectual and her editorial writing for the *New York Times*, the *New Yorker*, and *Harper's Magazine*. Her literary experimentation in form continues to expand, and examples include a novel-in-stories in *The Dew Breaker* (2004), books for children such as *Mama's Nightingale: A Story of Immigration and Separation* (2015), and editorial work for the anthology series *Haiti Noir* (2011, 2013). Furthermore, Danticat has demonstrated a commitment to oral and visual storytelling mediums, important to a nation with low rates of literacy, including television, radio, and film. In order to best analyze the scope of Danticat's cultural work at the axes of home and nation, dyaspora, and historicity, the essays in this collection draw our attention to a wide range of her intellectual and artistic oeuvre.

The chapters in this collection address the function, space, and place of homes, and the representation of nationalisms and post- and transnationalisms; and tease out the tensions inherent in the confluences of past and present in Danticat's literature. Each contributor considers, in various ways, how Danticat's writing, anthologizing, and storytelling trace, map, (re)construct, and develop alternative histories and historiographies, narratives of nation building and national belonging, and conceptions of home and homelands. The contributors to this collection read Danticat's visionary work as resistant to colonial narratives, which depict a poverty-stricken and diseased Haitian choreography in opposition to a stalwart United States. Danticat's fiction and nonfiction establishes Haitian resistance to US ascendancy as a communal undertaking, iterated over and over again by her fictional characters, in her accounts of her own life experiences, and in her critical expositions. Edwidge Danticat's literary representations, astute political commentary, and personal investment in activism at the axis of witnessing and testifying to violence have exigent transnational dimensions, and are vital to comprehending and imagining new radical futures. In our current global moment, marked as it is by increasing anti-immigrant sentiment, border anxiety and containment, and rampant ecological volatility, Danticat's contributions to public discourse, art, and culture deserve sustained and critical attention. It is our hope that scholars, public intellectuals, and students of literature who are interested in literature of the African diaspora will find these essays useful, and that they will find studies of Danticat's work a necessary indictment of statelessness, racialized and gendered state violence, and the persistence of political and economic margins. We have sought to include the work of both emerging and established scholars who are invested in taking stock of Danticat's activism and her role as a public intellectual. In various ways, the contributors to this collection attend to Haiti's prominent role in the socioeconomic, cultural, and political development of the United States, and explore how and why US imperialism and Haitian resistance has been omitted from classroom curricula, literary and historical canons, and US public memory.

Narrating History, Home, and Dyaspora is composed of fifteen critical essays examining the fiction, nonfiction, essays, and activism of Edwidge Danticat. The book is organized in four parts. The first part, "Another Country: Nation and Dyaspora," includes four chapters engaged in conversation with Danticat's construction and negotiation of nation, both Haiti and the United States; the broader dyaspora; and her own, her family's, and her fictional characters' places within them. Maria Rice Bellamy's opening chapter, "From Her 'Little Middle Place': Edwidge Danticat's Identity and Poetics," establishes the history of Danticat's and her family's liminal position between the United States and Haiti through geography, language, and the complex double bind of being subject to racist/xenophobic treatment and economic difficulties, as well as the myth of the model immigrant. Reading *Brother, I'm Dying, After the Dance: A Walk through Carnival in Jacmel, Haiti* (2002), and *Create Dangerously*, Bellamy highlights Danticat's effort to build an imaginary homeland as a means of reconciling dyasporic in-betweenness. Joyce White's chapter, "*Lòt Bò Dlo*, the Other Side of the Water: Examining the Kongo Cosmogram in Danticat's *The Farming of Bones*," draws dyasporic connections between trauma and the rebuilding of self, community, and history through the Kongo cosmogram. White's close reading of *The Farming of Bones* (1998) examines how the novel applies cosmological and ontological frameworks in order to comprehensively revise Haitian national histories. Building on this, Olga Blomgren's chapter, "'Cast *Lòt Bò Dlo*, Across the Seas': Re/Writing Home and Nation in Edwidge Danticat's *Create Dangerously: The Immigrant Artist at Work*," stakes a claim for the archipelagic thinking Danticat offers as a means of reimagining nation, history, and home. Blomgren argues that immigrant mobilities and transit prove fruitful grounds for rethinking national and spatial relationships. Finally, Gwen Bergner's piece, "*Lòt Bò Dlo* and the Spatial Relations of Dyaspora," highlights the ways in which Danticat enacts Haitian spiritual traditions and vernacular phrases in her short story cycle *The Dew Breaker* (2004) in order to mediate, across time and space, an aesthetic that ultimately creates an epistemic perspective of migration.

Part 2, "Welcoming Ghosts: Memory and Historicity," delves into the ever-present specter of history and memory, two prominent themes found throughout Danticat's work. From origin stories to broader Haitian histories, this section addresses the underlying traumas involved when remembering the past and its relationship to the present moment. In her chapter "Writing Amerindian Ayiti: Edwidge Danticat's Reclaimed Memory and Shifting Homes," Erika Serrato calls attention to Danticat's syncretic recording of Amerindian origin stories alongside Haitian histories and experiences.

Through a close reading of the young adult novel *Anacaona: Golden Flower, Haiti, 1490* (2005), Serrato highlights the ways in which the foundational mythos of Hispaniola's autochthonous populations deeply inform Haitian histories. Tammie Jenkins's "Intertextually Weaving a Home-Place: Viewing the Past as Present in *Breath, Eyes, Memory* and *Untwine*" explores the intertextual connections between Danticat's ancestral and acquired narratives and the diasporic experiences of Black people, particularly women, in the New World. Jenkins's insightful reading of *Breath, Eyes, Memory* and *Untwine* (2015) poses an essential argument regarding Danticat's move to syncretize Haitian culture, social narratives, and family traditions within Black diasporic discourses. Next, Shewonda Leger's chapter "*Untwine*: Navigating Memories through Healing and Self-Definition" employs Sara Ahmed's theory of reorientation as a frame to consider how *Untwine* uses the main character's struggle to draw a clear relationship between Haitian cultural identity and historical narratives. Leger argues that the main character's trauma, and subsequent working-through, help readers understand the value of reflecting on past memories as a means of healing and self-definition. Akia Jackson's "Collecting and Releasing Embodied Memories: Redefining Shame in Edwidge Danticat's *Breath, Eyes, Memory*" concludes this section with an insightful reading of the novel's emphasis on the matrilineal generational traumas that link history and memory. Jackson's innovative analysis of *Breath, Eyes, Memory* critically examines the familial shame that textures Haitian politics and impacts the suffering of women on a macro level in the country, further nuancing the paradoxes involved when recollecting history.

The third part, "I Speak Out: Storytelling and Narrative Structure," continues the critical conversation regarding the imperative to speak, paying particular attention to the narrative form in which such telling occurs. Laura Dawkins's piece "'The Listening Gets Too Loud': The Reader's Task in Edwidge Danticat's *Brother, I'm Dying*," hones in on Danticat's attentiveness to the role of the reader in *Brother, I'm Dying*. Dawkins suggests that the reader is charged with the task, via a reciprocal intimacy, of engaging actively with a multilayered text—a text that fundamentally reshapes the memoir into a narrative space for collective political action. In "Reading Edwidge Danticat's Essays in Light of Her Fiction: Diaspora, Ethics, Aesthetics," Lucía Stecher and Thomás Rothe offer a comprehensive overview of the formal and discursive aspects prevalent in several of Danticat's literary projects. Through a close reading of Danticat's fiction and nonfiction, Stecher and Rothe illustrate the ethical and aesthetic modalities through which the author navigates speaking up as a member of the Haitian dyaspora. Cécile Accilien's chapter, "Home, Exile, Language, and the Paratext in *Anacaona: Golden Flower* and

Mama's Nightingale: A Story of Immigration and Separation," examines the paratextual elements found in two of Danticat's young adult novels. In doing so, Accilien highlights the ways in which Danticat embeds her own migratory story into the form of both texts. Jennifer Lozano's "'Quietly, Quietly': Thinking and Teaching the Global South through Edwidge Danticat's Intertextual Writing, Reading, and Witnessing" brings the section to a close. Through her analysis of Danticat's *Create Dangerously*, Lozano poses the argument that Danticat's textual witnessing, through a diasporic consciousness and "intertextual" framework, functions as a larger guide for a Global South analytic and pedagogy.

The fourth and final section of the collection, "'Create Dangerously': Trauma, Resilience, and the Way Forward," contends with Haitians' activism and community building in the face of eroding citizenship, and the political and ecological climate of Haiti and its dyaspora. In "Edwidge Danticat: The Ethics of Disobedient Writing," Isabel Caldeira argues that Danticat is one of several contemporary writers-as-citizens, offering their talent as authors and courage as activists to defend freedom and citizenship in a political climate in which democratic practices are eroding. Caldeira considers how citizenship implies both rights and duties, the former to protect against coercive state power and political tyranny. Metaphors for dividing lines (river and ocean, ridge and mountain: *The Farming of Bones, Krik? Krak!*, *The Dew Breaker*); and for connections (bridge, home, generations, twins: *The Farming of Bones, Krik? Krak!, Create Dangerously, Untwine*) guide Caldeira's analysis of the ways Danticat's work functions a form of dissidence and dissent—an ethical and artistic response to the other (the subaltern) in defense of the rights of freedom and citizenship. Delphine Gras's chapter, "More than a Phrase: Fighting Silence and Objectification in Danticat's *Claire of the Sea Light*," explores how Danticat, an author who sees herself as one of the "storytellers of the world,"[8] deploys the art of the griot, retracing Haiti's forgotten history and bringing the novel's characters together to redefine what it means to be Haitians in the twenty-first century. This chapter shows that, just as Danticat's characters are connected to one another in sometimes surprising ways, so is Haiti connected to the rest of the world—both as a result of the long-standing effects of neo/colonialism and in the ways this island nation faces global threats of the present and future, such as climate change. Finally, in "Black Butterflies: Survival, Transformation, and the Invention of Home in Edwidge Danticat's Fiction and Nonfiction," Marion Christina Rohrleitner brings the collection to a close by tracing Danticat's engagement with resilience and survival across several of her fiction and nonfiction texts. Although her work addresses tragedies such as death, environmental catastrophe, genocidal racism, abject poverty, and an inhumane US immigration system, Danticat highlights the survivors' resilience, focusing on their turn to writing and social activism. For Danticat's characters, home is often collectively created in sharing stories of survival in the diaspora.

Danticat's literature, public intellectualism, and ceaseless witnessing and *testimonio* are a model for us all as we work to usher in a more just world. In an interview with Maxine Lavon Montgomery, Danticat says, "There is no separation between the work I do as a writer and my personal commitment as a citizen. We write about the things we are passionate about and I am passionate about Haiti. I think all politics affect human beings, and as a writer, I am writing about people, so the personal is always political and the political is always personal."[9] Her engagement with such concepts as history, home, and nation, which inform all of our identities and experiences in myriad ways, attends to the specificity of too-often marginalized Haitian people and experiences, centering and validating their existence within the hemispheric Americas and the broader Haitian dyaspora.

NOTES

1. Edwidge Danticat, *Create Dangerously: The Immigrant Artist at Work* (Princeton, NJ: Princeton University Press, 2010), 49.

2. Danticat, *Create Dangerously*, 50.

3. Danticat, *Create Dangerously*, 51.

4. Nadège T. Clitandre, *Edwidge Danticat: The Haitian Diasporic Imaginary* (Charlottesville: University of Virginia Press, 2018), 14.

5. Edwidge Danticat and Michael S. Collins, "An Interview with Edwidge Danticat," *Callaloo* 30, no. 2 (Spring 2007): 471.

6. Danticat, *Create Dangerously*, 17.

7. Danticat, *Create Dangerously*, 51.

8. Danticat, *Create Dangerously*, 6.

9. Maxine Lavon Montgomery, "Putting Together the Fragments: A Conversation with Edwidge Danticat," in *Conversations with Edwidge Danticat*, ed. Maxine Lavon Montgomery (Jackson: University Press of Mississippi, 2017), 205.

Part I

Another Country: Nation and Dyaspora

Chapter One

FROM HER "LITTLE MIDDLE PLACE"

Edwidge Danticat's Diasporic Identity and Poetics

MARIA RICE BELLAMY

In her award-winning 2007 memoir *Brother, I'm Dying*, Edwidge Danticat writes her way through both the loss of her biological and surrogate fathers and her conflicted relationships with her two homelands, Haiti and the United States. While Haiti, the land of her birth, is her cultural home, it is also the nation from which both of her fathers felt forced to flee. The United States, Danticat's adopted homeland, is the place where she became the writer and advocate she is today, but it is also the nation that indirectly or directly caused the deaths of both of her fathers and many other troubles. Through the stories of her father and uncle, Danticat renders a model immigrant to the United States and a heroic son of Haiti while revealing the ugly consequences that accrue from each identity position, and the constant pushes and pulls that make neither nation a place of true rest or a place she can truly leave behind. In *Brother, I'm Dying*, Danticat positions herself both between her Uncle Joseph (who raised her in Haiti until the age of twelve) and her father Mira (who emigrated to the United States when the author was just two), and between the two countries they come to represent. During her uncle's first visit to the United States after her reunion with her parents, Edwidge, now a teenager, finds herself "walking between Uncle Joseph and [her] father, with both their arms around [her] as if it were the most natural thing in the world."[1] The mutual embrace of her fathers suggests the identity position Danticat will seek throughout her life and writing career. Inhabiting the liminal space[2] between homelands, however, Danticat experiences distance from and accusations of inauthenticity in both cultural contexts, rather than the hoped-for embrace. From this locus, she establishes her authorial voice and renders in narrative her conflicted bonds with her two homelands.

13

While Danticat chronicles the history of her relationships with Haiti
and the United States through the stories of her uncle and father in *Brother,
I'm Dying*, she reflects more directly on the complexities of her cultural
identity and the development of her authorial voice in *After the Dance: A
Walk through Carnival in Jacmel, Haiti* (2002), and *Create Dangerously: The
Immigrant Artist at Work* (2010). In her travelogue/memoir *After the Dance*,
Danticat returns to Haiti as an adult to chronicle her first experience as a
reveler in carnival. There, she masks herself as an observer while anticipating
the festivities, and unmasks to immerse herself in the carnival as a cultural
rite of passage. In *Create Dangerously*, Danticat reflects on her life as an
immigrant writer and her efforts to establish her authorial voice and stance.
In an interview with Elvira Pulitano, she characterizes "the immigrant's reality" as being "inauthentic here [. . .] [and] inauthentic there" but proclaims
that "inauthenticity is my life and it's a perfect place for me to do the kind of
writing I want to do. [. . .] You don't have to follow anybody's playbook for
authenticity. You can create your own rules from your little middle place."[3]
Realizing that as an immigrant artist she represents millions of persons of
Haitian descent who live in the "middle place" between nations, Danticat
claims the power of this liminal position to create her own diasporic identity
and poetics.

ENTERING THE LIMINAL SPACE BETWEEN NATIONS

Exploring her father's decision to emigrate to the United States and her
uncle's decision to remain in Haiti in *Brother, I'm Dying*, Danticat represents
the former as a model immigrant and the latter as a heroic son of Haiti
without privileging either choice. Through their experiences, she reveals
the societal forces that undergird their choices and begins to theorize the
ambivalent, in-between position that characterizes her cultural experience.
Danticat's father, André Miracen Danticat (called Mira), technically enters
the United States illegally by overstaying a one-month tourist visa; however,
Mira's determination to succeed and build a better future for his children
renders him a model immigrant.[4] At the time of his death, he is a homeowner
and entrepreneur and, with his wife, has raised and educated four successful children. As he faces a terminal illness, his eldest son asks him whether
he has enjoyed his life. Mira's halting and layered response reveals his deep
ambivalence about the decision that changed all of their lives. He eventually
concludes, "I've had a good life"—not because of the places he's seen or the
things he's done but because "[y]ou, my children, have not shamed me. [. . .]

It could have been so different. [. . .] You all could have turned bad, but you didn't. I thank God for that. [. . .] Yes, you can say I have enjoyed my life."[5] Mira's response is essentially a negative affirmation. He is thankful because he has not been shamed by the audacious decision to build a life in the United States and has survived to position his children for success. Personal pleasure and accomplishment are not relevant in this model immigrant's measure of success.

Danticat's recounting of the forces that push Mira from Haiti toward the hope of a better life abroad reveals the United States' direct and indirect intrusions into Haitian affairs. Her father, a trained tailor, is run out of business by the influx of "Kennedys"—cheap, used clothing donated from the United States that begin arriving during the John F. Kennedy administration. He later becomes a shoe salesman only to find himself risking his life daily to protect the storeowner's inventory from being pillaged by Tonton Macoutes, the henchmen of François "Papa Doc" Duvalier: "In the end, it was this experience of bending shoes all day and worrying about being shot that started him thinking about leaving Haiti."[6] Although Mira (unlike his brother) never involves himself in politics, his difficulties providing for his family are the personal consequences of larger political forces. The destruction of the cottage industry of tailoring represents an unexpected consequence of US charity toward Haiti, while the US aid money Duvalier misappropriates to fund the training of Tonton Macoutes directly strengthens his increasingly oppressive hold on his nation.[7]

By embracing his liminal status in the United States, Mira eventually finds a measure of a success; however, as Danticat narrates his experiences, she reveals the inescapable perils of immigrant life. Mira's difficulty finding and keeping steady work delays Edwidge and her brother Bob's entrance into the United States for several years. The day of their arrival, Mira loses the last of a series of factory and menial jobs and decides to start his own business, using his personal vehicle as a taxicab. A teenage Edwidge muses: "*My father's cab is named for wanderers, drifters, nomads. It's called a gypsy cab.*"[8] The name fits the transitional, nationless status of this recent immigrant. Exploiting this position, Mira builds a business that establishes the family's economic foundation in the United States. This success is tarnished, however, by the daily threats of violence Mira faces, as he allows strangers into his vehicle, and by the consequences to his health. Mira tries to shield his family from full knowledge of the perils he faces as a cabdriver, but the "street adventures" he recounts at church prayer meetings reveal him being shot at, held at gunpoint, robbed, stiffed, and berated by angry customers.[9] These daily humiliations and dangerous confrontations represent the ugly

underside of the immigrant success story. When Mira is diagnosed with
terminal pulmonary fibrosis early in *Brother, I'm Dying*, Danticat blames his
illness on "the persistent car fumes [he inhaled during] the twenty-five-plus
years [he] had worked as a cabdriver."[10] Mira's greatest success is also the
greatest representation of his precarity as an immigrant. Wendy Knepper
argues that in *Brother, I'm Dying*, Danticat "highlights conditions of precarity for Haitians at home and in the diaspora, whether experienced as street
crime in the USA or state-sponsored crime in Haiti."[11] This precarity originated at Haiti's founding when the United States and other Western nations
refused to recognize its legitimacy as a sovereign state and subjected Haiti
to centuries of destabilizing interventions into its political and economic
systems. The United States' xenophobia only exacerbates the precarity and
liminal position of Haitian immigrants.

Mira's hesitation in answering his son's question about whether he enjoyed
his life reveals the struggles undergirding his success and lingering ambivalence about his choice. After his brother Joseph's death, he laments, "If our
country were ever given a chance and allowed to be a country like any other,
none of us would live or die here [in the United States]."[12] Mira recognizes
the instability that pushed him from his homeland to be the consequence
of Haiti's long history of underdevelopment and destabilizing interventions
by other nations. In the end, Mira finally is remembered as a model immigrant who dies in the embrace of his family and under the protection of law
enforcement officers.[13] Joseph, by contrast, lives his life determined not to
be pushed from his homeland, but dies alone in a hospital prison ward after
seeking temporary asylum in the United States, a nation he'd visited dozens
of times during his career. Danticat demonstrates throughout *Brother, I'm
Dying* that both brothers' lives and deaths are intricately bound to their
national and personal relations with the United States.

Danticat's uncle, Joseph Nosius Dantica, represents the best of the Haitian
spirit but experiences during his life the best and worst of the United States'
interactions with Haiti. This loyal son of Haiti follows the path set for him
by his father and devotes his life to serving his community. As a young adult,
Joseph builds his home in the Bel Air section of Port-au-Prince, the site of
a famous battle during the Haitian Revolution and the location from which
"Haitian guerilla fighters, called Cacos, organized attacks against U.S. Forces"
during their occupation of Haiti.[14] The son of a Caco, Joseph becomes an
outspoken community leader for Daniel Fignolé, believing that his Mouve-
ment Ouvriers-Paysans (Laborers and Peasants Party) will best serve the
needs of the people. Joseph rejoices when his candidate wins the national
election and is sworn into office in 1957, but discovers the precariousness

of Haitian politics when Fignolé is ousted nineteen days later by the now infamous François "Papa Doc" Duvalier. Accepting the church's "promise of a peaceful and stable life," Joseph joins the Baptist Church and soon begins training to become a pastor. During his ministerial training, he forms relationships with American missionaries who help him establish his base for services in Bel Air by funding the construction of his church and school, as well as a free lunch program for his students. Although he remains "wary of Americans from his memories of the U.S. occupation," Joseph's desire to serve his community overwhelms his fear and enables him to accept help offered.[15] Years later, when American doctors diagnose his sudden loss of voice as a life-threatening malignant tumor on his larynx, his American missionary friends negotiate and pay the cost of life-saving surgery in a New York hospital. Danticat positions her uncle as an inheritor of the spirit of Haitian independence who leverages the resources available to him to uplift and support his local community.

Joseph's determination to serve the people of Bel Air represents the essence of his heroism and the source of his downfall. In the face of growing instability within Haiti, political violence in Bel Air, and relatives abroad inviting and later imploring him to leave, Joseph remains adamant in his determination to stay.[16] When Danticat asks her uncle why he never left Haiti to join his brothers in New York, he explains: "Exile is not for everyone. Someone has to stay behind, to receive the letters and greet family members when they come back."[17] As the eldest son, he may have felt the responsibility to maintain a homestead and be the one to whom relatives return. Responsibility and sense of mission cause Joseph to end each trip abroad with a hasty return to Haiti because "he had more work to do, more souls to save, more children to teach."[18] His loyalty to Bel Air eventually extends beyond what many would consider reasonable. While Joseph manages, for a time, to "stay out of harm's way by avoiding [all] overtly political activity," on Sunday, October 24, 2004, the violence comes to him when his church is overrun by Haitian riot police and UN peacekeeping forces, who shoot suspected gang members from his roof.[19] When the smoke clears, gang leaders charge Joseph with allowing military forces access to his roof in hopes of collecting the advertised reward for capturing local gang leaders. They then demand an impossible sum of money to cover the cost of funerals for the deceased and medical care for those injured during the shooting. Once accused, Joseph stays too long, believing his long history in the community will resolve the situation: "Before [his accusers] were called dreads or even chimères [local gangs], they were young men, boys, many of whom had spent their entire lives in the neighborhood. [. . .] Surely one of them would have a fond memory that could override what they wrongly believed he'd done."[20] Believing that his loyalty will be reciprocated by the people of his community, Joseph stays to see his home and church compound overrun by looters who carry off, burn, and destroy all of his and his family's possessions. While some envious and greedy neighbors use Joseph's fall from grace as an opportunity for gain, other loyal friends and relatives facilitate his escape.

Even after being forced into exile and losing his home and church to looters, Joseph remains resolute in his loyalty to his community and his desire to rebuild his life there. Before and after the crisis, Joseph attempts to create narratives that bear witness to the lives and struggles of the people of Bel Air and testify to the injustices he suffers. Having lost his ability to speak decades before, Joseph develops what Danticat calls "an obsession" with jotting things down.[21] In the face of rising violence in his community, Joseph serves his neighbors by chronicling the dead, devoting notebooks and endless scraps of paper to remembering each precious life. Joseph's notebooks and personal papers, which he'd hoped to turn into a book about the people of Bel Air, are among the things burned by looters. After leaving Bel Air, Joseph redirects his narrative energies to filing reports with the Haitian police antigang unit, the United Nations Civilian Police Unit, and, upon arrival in the United States, US immigration officials. Each attempt to narrate his story represents Joseph's desire to give testimony to the injustices he has suffered, be recognized for the service he has given, and have a person with authority act on his behalf. He hopes that these agencies will do for him what he has tried to do for the people of Bel Air. Unfortunately, after decades of actively taking responsibility for the care and well-being of others, Joseph Dantica faces the complete abdication of responsibility for his well-being by both the Haitian and international authorities tasked with keeping the peace and protecting civilians from harm. Mary Jo Caruso suggests that "Danticat uses *Brother, I'm Dying* to charge the Haitian government with negligence. She depicts how Uncle Joseph was able to escape from being gang murdered [. . .] [but] once he made it out of his own neighborhood, there was nowhere else in Haiti for him to go."[22] Each agency Joseph visits is less interested in his testimony than the one before, and the last, rather than providing sanctuary until he can return to his life in Haiti, refuses to hear him altogether.

Facing the loss of his home and base of operations, Joseph sets aside a lifetime of wariness of American authority and places his fate in the hands of US immigration officials by requesting temporary asylum upon arrival in the United States. In spite of advanced age (eighty-one) and having a valid tourist visa, Joseph is imprisoned and stripped of his medicine. During his asylum interview, he experiences a medical emergency and is unable to tell his story after his mechanical voice box is damaged. Within five days of entering the United States, Joseph Dantica dies alone in the prison ward of a Miami hospital after receiving what Danticat and medical practitioners "agree [. . .] was deplorable care."[23] Reflecting on Joseph's final hours, Danticat wonders, "When did he realize he was dying? [. . .] Did he think it ironic that he would soon be the dead prisoner of the same government that had been occupying his country when he was born? In essence he was entering and exiting the world under the same flag. Never really sovereign [. . .] never really free." After clinging to his home, determined not to be pushed out, Joseph "would be exiled finally in death."[24] Danticat's model of Haitian fealty becomes the victim of both his loyalty to Haiti and the barbarity of the United States. Danticat's narrative reconstruction of his ordeal presents the unspeakable cruelty suffered by her heroic uncle, a man her readers have come to love and admire while reading *Brother, I'm Dying*.

Telling the stories of her two fathers and their interactions with her two nations, Danticat completes for her father and uncle what Joseph had wanted to complete for the people of Bel Air. Beginning her memoir with her father's spoken words about the life he lived as an immigrant in the United States, Danticat later chronicles the systematic silencing of her uncle, who, in Knepper's words, is transformed "from a sacred figure, a minister, to *homo sacer*, a man who might be killed without impunity" by the forces of US bureaucracy, racism, and xenophobia.[25] In the aftermath of such loss, her relationships with both nations are notably shaken: "I live in a country from which my uncle was catastrophically rejected, and come from one which he had to flee."[26] Refusing to be silenced by her grief, Danticat writes *Brother I'm Dying* to narrativize her process of working through her disappointment and grief. Her personal mission becomes communal when she uses her memoir to give narrative voice to "all these people who can't tell their stories—and not just my father and my uncle, but the people they leave behind, who have this heavy weight of silence."[27] After witnessing the triumph and tragedy of immigration to the United States through her father's life and the heroic Haitian spirit in her uncle's, Danticat is left in the space between nations with only her writing to help her navigate the distance.

Adding to the complexities of her national identity and her work as a writer is the second liminal space Danticat inhabits in *Brother, I'm Dying*. Anticipating the birth of her daughter Mira as she witnesses her father's decline and suffers the shock of her uncle's sudden death, Danticat straddles birth and death. In her interview with Pulitano, Danticat remembers the passage from Gabriel García Márquez's *One Hundred Years of Solitude* in which Colonel Buendía states, "We have still had not a death." This passage suggests that having buried someone creates a connection to a new place. Uncle Joseph's death has the opposite effect on Danticat and her family by alienating them from their new home, but the births of her daughters cause her to feel that she has "a lineage" in the United States.[28] This confluence of events creates what Danticat calls "a new definition of Americanness in this age of immigration controversies" as she simultaneously experiences "one foot that's digging in deeper and another one that's being yanked out."[29] Danticat's movement between her nation homes models this new type of Americanness. While Joseph Dantica finds himself "in a kind of 'social death' in the no man's land between two countries," Edwidge Danticat, a Haitian American writer armed with the privileges of US citizenship and education, inhabits the space between countries as a place of "privileged cosmopolitan mobility," which facilitates her writing even if it muddies her allegiances and raises questions of cultural authenticity in both Haiti and the United States.[30]

UNMASKING IN *AFTER THE DANCE*

In *After the Dance*, her travelogue about carnival in Jacmel, Danticat peels back layers of distance to explore, redeem, and renew her Haitian self. As she meets with Jacmel carnival expert Michelet Divers early in her journey, she is hesitant to admit that she has never been "an active reveler at carnival in Haiti."[31] Recognizing carnival as a quintessentially Haitian cultural experience, Danticat feels a level of inauthenticity at not having experienced it and longs for this opportunity to confirm the Haitian part of her identity. The most notable characteristic of *After the Dance*, however, is how little time Danticat actually spends discussing her revels in the carnival. Only one short chapter of the travelogue is devoted to the carnival.[32] Before joining the festivities, Danticat works through many levels of distance from carnival, beginning with biases she learned during childhood. Uncle Joseph had not allowed her to participate in carnival when she was in his care because of the licentious behavior he observed among revelers—people hurting themselves by "gyrating with so much abandon that they would dislocate their hips and shoulders and lose their voices while singing too loudly," and "young girls [being] fondled, squeezed like sponges by dirty old, and not so old, men."[33] As an adult, Danticat continues to avoid carnival: "Even after I thought I had forgotten my uncle's tales, I developed a mild fear of being buried alive in too large a crowd. [. . .] So I avoided carnival, except as a distant observer." Being asked to write a travelogue on carnival in Jacmel appeals to Danticat because it allows her both to remain a "distant observer" and to experience "a baptism by crowd [. . .] among [her] own people."[34] Danticat fulfills her distant observer role by devoting the chapters between her initial meeting with Divers and her actual experience of the carnival to numerous vignettes on the pageantry and artistry surrounding the carnival and the history of important sites in and near Jacmel. During the brief time Danticat allows herself to participate in the carnival, she describes herself as "part of a group possession, a massive stream of joy."[35] Before releasing herself fully, however, Danticat filters through layers of her intellectual training, remembering, from Mikhail Bakhtin's writing, an early description of carnival as "a priest's mystic vision of hell [. . .] [where] marchers were souls of dead sinners[,] [. . .] migrants from purgatory expatiating their sins." She then characterizes herself as returning "from the purgatory of exile, expatiating sins of coldness and distance."[36] Elizabeth Walcott-Hackshaw suggests that by giving herself over to the revels, Danticat "exorcises her carnival demons," releases the limits placed on her by her upbringing and education, and experiences "movement from the purgatory of exile to baptism and renewal."[37] Danticat realigns with her Haitian self during the carnival and atones for her sin of cultural distance, but emerges from the water or flames of her baptism to resume her role as observer.

Danticat renders her experience as an observer through masking, a common and important trope of carnival. Ultimately, masks enable her to maintain her position of observer and strengthen her cultural and authorial positions. The day after the carnival, Danticat sees herself in video footage of the festivities and experiences "a strange feeling of detachment." She asks, "Was that really me? So unencumbered, so lively, so free?"[38] During her revels, Danticat experiences the true purpose of carnival: the opportunity to set aside the cares of life and experience joy in communion with other Haitians. Her experience of communion is facilitated by the removal of her distancing mask: "Even as others had been putting on their masks, just for one moment, I had allowed myself to remove my own."[39] Later, with her reflective mask restored, she realizes that even when she was prohibited from participating in carnival as a child and when she prohibited herself from participating as an adult, she "was already part of the carnival." Although she first experiences carnival as a reveler in Jacmel, she recalls, "I'd had days like this before, even if in fragments and pieces. The carnivals I had spent in the mountains [as a child] were not all that different from the one I had seen today. [. . .] Those too were celebrations of life, community, and belonging, explosions of rapture and beauty in a country that is not supposed to have any joy."[40] Carnival is so integral a part of the Haitian culture and cultural imagination that even when actively avoiding it, Haitians participate in variations of it.

Danticat's mask-wearing functions similarly to the masks worn during carnival. She explains to David Barsamian that "there are masks that shield us
from others, but there are masks that embolden us. [. . .] So sometimes we
mask ourselves to further reveal ourselves, and it's always been connected
to me with being a writer: We tell lies to tell a greater truth. The story is a
mask: the characters you create are masks."[41] Behind her authorial mask,
Danticat feels emboldened to reveal herself, communicate the challenges of
her cultural position, and chronicle personal and collective tragedies. In *After
the Dance*, she considers her position inside and outside of Haitian culture
and, in the process, reaffirms her cultural identity and further develops her
writerly authority.

DEFINING DIASPORIC POETICS
IN *CREATE DANGEROUSLY*

In *Create Dangerously*, Danticat interrogates and situates the cosmopolitan
mobility that enables her to participate in carnival in Jacmel and advocate
abroad for the victims of Haiti's natural and unnatural disasters. That mobility is often tested in transitional spaces, particularly in airports. In *Brother,
I'm Dying*, she writes of feeling "a bit traitorous" traveling to Haiti with her
American passport.[42] In her essay "Our Guernica" in *Create Dangerously*,
Danticat writes of encounters with US Customs and Border Protection officers at Toussaint L'Ouverture Airport as she returns to the United States
after visiting relatives following the devastating earthquake of 2010. The first
officer carefully scrutinizes her US passport. Once she is cleared, two Haitian
American officers, speaking Kreyòl, wish her "a good return trip 'home.'"[43]
Although she feels "embarrassed and slightly humiliated" by the first officer's
efforts to ensure the authenticity of her passport, she feels both comforted
and discomfited by the other's wishes for her return *home*. In many ways,
she is leaving her home. Her last stop before returning to the United States
is Uncle Joseph's church compound where his son Maxo and his family were
killed when their home collapsed on them.[44] Earlier, she had visited relatives
living in temporary shelters after being left homeless by the earthquake.
Returning to the order and comfort of her Miami home, Danticat is left to
negotiate these conflicting images of home. In this border crossing, Danticat
experiences the conflicts her cosmopolitan mobility engenders, the difficulty
of locating home, and the strain of doubled national allegiance.

   In "I Am Not a Journalist," another essay in *Create Dangerously*, Danticat
recalls a conversation with Jean Dominique, the Haitian radio journalist,

activist, and agronomist who was later assassinated, regarding her status as *dyaspora*, or a person of Haitian descent living abroad. She explains, "My country [. . .] is one of uncertainty. When I say 'my country' to some Haitians, they think I mean the United States. When I say 'my country' to some Americans, they think of Haiti."[45] In spite of her continuous engagement with Haiti,[46] Danticat is only perceived as Haitian among Americans, while Haitians see her as less than fully Haitian. Dominique challenges her to rethink her status by encouraging her to see herself and "the *Dyaspora* [as] people with their feet planted in both worlds. [. . .] There's no need to be ashamed of that. There are more than a million of you. You all are not alone."[47] Just as her father built his career on his liminal status, Danticat accepts her position between nations and centers her writing on the "notion of nation as *imagi*-nation" because it allows a writer "to create [her] nation both in [her] imagination and on paper."[48] As a writer with feet planted in and continuously moving between two worlds and who wears masks both to distance and embolden herself, Danticat creates her own nation in her diasporic writing. There, she reflects on the trials of leaving and staying, the intricacies of Haiti's simultaneously paternalistic and hegemonic relationship with the United States, and the casualties that litter the space between nations.

Ultimately, Danticat's authorial ethos may best be defined, in J. Michael Dash's words, as the practice of a "new ungrounded poetics [. . .] in which national and ethnic difference gives way to a collective, borderless identity that is increasingly hybrid and unstable [. . .] [which] permits each individual to be here and elsewhere, rooted and open."[49] In her nonfictional work, Danticat establishes her authorial voice and poetics by embracing her position in the liminal space between nations and imagining her own borderless homeland peopled by those rooted in and uprooted from her Haitian and American homelands.

NOTES

1. Edwidge Danticat, *Brother, I'm Dying* (New York: Vintage Books, 2007), 128.

2. By *liminal space* I refer to the threshold space between two entities or states of being. In some ways, this is a no-man's land, but it is also a state of possibility where one can be two things at once, both/and. In the liminal space between homelands, Danticat is both Haitian *and* American, and her cultural authenticity results from the blending of, rather than distinction between, two identity positions.

3. Elvira Pulitano, "An Immigrant Artist at Work: A Conversation with Edwidge Danticat," *Small Axe* 15, no. 3 (November 2011): 48.

4. I mention Mira's immigration status only to highlight the contrast between contemporary fears of illegal immigration and the reality of immigrants establishing themselves in the United States through hard work and determination.

5. Danticat, *Brother, I'm Dying*, 21.

6. Danticat, *Brother, I'm Dying*, 52.

7. Danticat implicates the United States in the militarization of Haiti during the 1915–1934 US occupation, for leaving behind a brutal army capable of propping up and deposing presidents at will, and for providing aid to Haiti during the Duvalier regime (in spite of its human rights violations) in the hope of reducing the spread of communism in the Caribbean. Danticat references some of these issues in *Brother, I'm Dying*, 171.

8. Danticat, *Brother, I'm Dying*, 120 (emphasis in original).

9. Danticat, *Brother, I'm Dying*, 121–22.

10. Danticat, *Brother, I'm Dying*, 11.

11. Wendy Knepper, "In/justice and Necro-Natality in Edwidge Danticat's *Brother, I'm Dying*," *Journal of Commonwealth Literature* 47, no. 2 (2012): 200.

12. Danticat, *Brother, I'm Dying*, 251.

13. Mira dies at home from pulmonary fibrosis. Police officers come after his death to ensure that no foul play or euthanasia was involved.

14. Danticat, *Brother, I'm Dying*, 29.

15. Danticat, *Brother, I'm Dying*, 33.

16. Joseph's heroism is communal and personal. He and his wife, Denise, foster the children of many relatives and friends, including a friend's daughter, Marie Micheline, whom they raise from infancy. When she is a young adult, Joseph risks his life to rescue her and her infant daughter from her brutal Tonton Macoute husband. Joseph provides for Marie (and her children) until her untimely death. Edwidge Danticat recounts her story in "Marie Micheline: A Life in Haiti," *New Yorker*, June 11 & 18, 2007, 96–103.

17. Danticat, *Brother, I'm Dying*, 140.

18. Danticat, *Brother, I'm Dying*, 140.

19. Danticat, *Brother, I'm Dying*, 139. For more detailed discussion of the failure of military and political entities in Haiti to restore peace and protect the Haitian people, see Knepper, "In/justice and Necro-Natality"; and Mary Jo Caruso, "The Diaspora Writes Back," in *Critical Perspectives on Caribbean Literature and Culture*, ed. Dorsía Smith, Tatiana Tagirova, and Suzanna Engman (Newcastle upon Tyne: Cambridge Scholars Publishing, 2010), 215–28.

20. Danticat, *Brother, I'm Dying*, 182–83.

21. Danticat, *Brother, I'm Dying*, 176.

22. Caruso, "The Diaspora Writes Back," 221.

23. Danticat, *Brother, I'm Dying*, 248.

24. Danticat, *Brother, I'm Dying*, 250–51.

25. Knepper, "In/justice and Necro-Natality," 196.

26. Quoted in Maya Jaggi, "Island Memories," *Guardian*, November 20, 2004, http://guardian.co.uk/books/2004/nov/20/featuresreviews.guardianreview9.

27. Quoted in Caruso, "The Diaspora Writes Back," 223.

28. Pulitano, "An Immigrant Artist at Work," 47.

29. Pulitano, "An Immigrant Artist at Work," 47.

30. Jo Collins, "Bricolage and History: Edwidge Danticat's Diasporic Life Writing in *After the Dance*," *Life Writing* 10, no. 1 (2013), 21.

31. Edwidge Danticat, *After the Dance: A Walk through Carnival in Jacmel, Haiti* (New York: Vintage Books, 2002), 12.

32. See Collins, "Bricolage and History," for a lengthier discussion of Danticat's decentered authorial voice and insider-outsider status in *After the Dance*.

33. Danticat, *After the Dance*, 13.

34. Danticat, *After the Dance*, 14–15.

35. Danticat, *After the Dance*, 147.

36. Danticat, *After the Dance*, 146–47. Danticat provides a paraphrase of an uncited passage from Bakhtin.

37. Elizabeth Walcott-Hackshaw, "Dancing at the Border: Cultural Translations and the Writer's Return," in *Echoes of the Haitian Revolution, 1804–2004*, ed. Martin Munro and Elizabeth Walcott-Hackshaw (Mona, Jamaica: University of the West Indies Press, 2009), 154, 158.

38. Danticat, *After the Dance*, 158.

39. Danticat, *After the Dance*, 158.

40. Danticat, *After the Dance*, 151–52.

41. David Barsamian, "Edwidge Danticat, October 2003," in *Louder Than Bombs: Interviews from "The Progressive" Magazine* (Cambridge, MA: South End Press, 2004), 9.

42. Danticat, *Brother, I'm Dying*, 146.

43. Edwidge Danticat, *Create Dangerously: The Immigrant Artist at Work* (Princeton, NJ: Princeton University Press, 2010), 172.

44. Only Maxo's body was recovered from the rubble and buried in a makeshift grave inside the church. Although Maxo's family had escaped the violence of 2004 and recovered the church compound, they could not escape the earthquake.

45. Danticat, *Create Dangerously*, 49.

46. Danticat completed more than twenty-five trips to Haiti in the decade between 1994 and 2003.

47. Danticat, *Create Dangerously*, 51.

48. Pulitano, "An Immigrant Artist at Work," 47.

49. Quoted in Alicia E. Ellis, review of *Create Dangerously: The Immigrant Artist at Work*, by Edwidge Danticat, *Journal of French and Francophone Philosophy* 19, no. 2 (2011): 205.

Chapter Two

LÒT BÒ DLO, THE OTHER SIDE OF THE WATER

Examining the Kongo Cosmogram in Edwidge Danticat's *The Farming of Bones*

JOYCE WHITE

The Farming of Bones is a novel that explores the brutal 1937 massacre of Haitians living and working in the border towns between Haiti and the Dominican Republic. Orchestrated by Generalissimo Rafael Trujillo and executed by his soldiers, these massacres—often referred to as "the Parsley Massacres," "El Corte," "the Cutting," "Kout Kouto," and "the Stabbing"— form the textual landscape and backdrop the novel uses to navigate the interior lives of the massacre victims ("Dominicans, Haitians" 2012). Narrated by the main protagonist, Amabelle Désir, *The Farming of Bones* functions as a testimonial that bears witness to the untold stories and history of the massacre.[1] Paralleled with the death of Joël, an itinerant sugarcane cutter, the novel begins and ends at the site of the narrative's trauma, on the banks of the Dajabón River, where Amabelle must confront the life-altering tragedy of her parent's death and later traverse to save her own life.

Her parents' death leads to a traumatic exile from her home, Haiti, and her bloodline. Forced to build a new life or die, Amabelle creates a home and a family with other Haitian workers in a liminal space and place where belonging is always in question. Joël's death, which foreshadows the advent of the great massacre, is the catalyst that begins to reveal the answer to the fundamental question, for the Haitian domestic workers living and working on the Dominican Republic side of Hispaniola, of whether to stay or go back home. Each of the novel's main characters—Amabelle, Sebastien, Joël, Kongo, Yves, and Father Romain—must negotiate the line between life and death. The crossroads for Amabelle and Sebastien is love, for Kongo and Joël it is a place to call home, for Yves it is the freedom to live life, and for Father Romain it is cultural and spiritual continuity. Ultimately, *The Farming of*

Bones is a novel about endurance through pain, struggle, and trauma. And, like all souls at the crossroads, each of these characters must return to the site of new beginnings—the Kalaunga, the primordial waters, via Amabelle—to heal and transform life.

Robert Farris Thompson deems Haiti "Africa in the West Indies" (1984, 164). Additionally, enslaved West Africans, namely Dahomean and Yoruba peoples forcibly transported to Haiti, carried with them cosmological and ontological frameworks to rebuild and re-create themselves in the "New World." Perhaps the most important and influential religious concept, the symbol of the crossroads, has maintained its relevance in traditional West African religion and been transfigured in "New World" syncretic religions such as Haitian Vodun. A symbol imbued with a cosmological and onto-logical framework, the crossroads provides an essential function as a major structural component in religious occurrences, in particular ritual.[2] Every time the crossroads, symbolized by the cross, is manifested, the merging of two worlds, two realms, is replete. Hence, the import of the crossroads from a cosmological perspective remains paramount in religious philoso-phy and actions like ritual. In fact, in order for ritual to occur, the physi-cal and the spiritual realms must intersect or meet at the crossroads. The center of the roads, represented by the peristyle[3] in Vodun, is where great change, decisions, and destiny occur. Thus, everyone must negotiate this divine intersection.[4]

As a central perspective of this chapter, I argue that the paralleling of the spiritual and physical realms is an imperative structural element of Danticat's *The Farming of Bones*. The novel employs water as a conduit and utilizes its ebb and flow to bridge the narrative passageways that allow char-acters to move through realms of the cosmogram. In particular, Amabelle moves through realms defining major points in her life along the way. The novel's epigraph points to water as the essential motif and theme, as Amabelle submits the story, and ultimately herself, to the "Mother of the River" (Danticat 1998, 1). Replicating the primordial waters of the other side, Amabelle is the novel's physical midwife who ushers in life and death, like her earthly parents and her spiritual mother, Yemoja.

The oscillating font in various chapters separates the spiritual realm from the physical realm within the narrative space; however, the paralleling of realms functions through the unifying voice of Amabelle and the cyclical movement of her narrative. In fact, it is the interchanging font that indicates Amabelle's movement through realms. The bolded font corresponds to Ama-belle's spiritual and memorial movement, while the standard font represents her life's physical movement and the novel's plot. The doubling of the font also permits the doubling of voice. As such, Amabelle is the agent in the reconstruction and retelling of her narrative, history, and trauma both in oral and written form. Ultimately, because Amabelle functions within two realms, she is also bequeathed the duty to speak into existence the truth of her people.[5]

Historically, Amabelle's character plays an integral role in the reconstruction of this particular period in Haiti's history and the narration of the great trauma and tragedy of this massacre. *The Farming of Bones* operates in the shadows of empty monuments dedicated to the great heroes and history of Haiti's venerated past, but also exposes the narrative of Haiti's hidden trauma. The doubling of visible historical realms and invisible historical traumas creates a narrative space able to dispel preconceived notions of Haiti and Haitians by exposing truths. In his forward to Gina Ulysse's *Why Haiti Needs New Narratives*, Robin D. G. Kelley argues that "both narratives treat Haiti as a symbol, a metaphor, rather than see Haitians as subjects and agents, as complex human beings with desires, imaginations, fears, frustrations, and ideas about justice, democracy, family, community, the land, and what it means to live a good life" (Ulysse 2015, xiii). These intersecting identities and narratives, not bound to heroic nationalistic identity or victimology, create space for a revision of Haitian iconography. Although a creative endeavor, *The Farming of Bones* constructs a realistic narrative of Haiti and Haitians by piecing together a history that functions not as a still-life snapshot stuck in time, but as a moving and ever dynamic narrative that represents and communicates the interior lives of the people—an ideograph.

Thus, this chapter argues that Danticat's *The Farming of Bones* textualizes the symbolic ideograph and principles of the Kongo cosmogram through the conceptual framework of the crossroads.[6] Expanding the notion of twinning and doubling by doubling the double, Danticat creates mirror images of the physical and spiritual realms; in this way, the novel constructs a quadruple graphic that textually follows the cosmogram's directional force and form and reflects the four stages that lead anyone at the crossroads to the highest point or full consciousness on the cosmogram.[7] The four points of the cosmogram are Tukula (supreme consciousness, or high noon); LuVempa (death, or the setting sun); Musoni (rebirth, or midnight); and Kala (birth, or the sunrise). These evolving and emergent realities and realms develop a textual ideograph of the cosmogram whereby the written word is inscribed with the principles of the cosmogram. As the words are so imbued, meaning is able to transcend mere pagination. The textual inscription creates a mimesis of the path and passageways through the quadrants of the cosmogram. Beginning with death, the textual cosmographic movement and form shape the trajectory of Danticat's novel and follow the patterns of the cosmogram spanning textual ideograph, textual inscription, and textual apotheosis.[8]

LUVEMPA

A textual ideograph refers to the transmission of what an emblem represents and communicates. Much like the water in the novel is emblematic of the crossroads, Danticat's structural choice of Amabelle's double-voiced narrative works in a similar way as Grey Gundaker's description of the cosmogram's graphic system in "The Kongo Cosmogram in Historical Archaeology and the Moral Compass of Dave the Potter":

> Like African and diasporic twinning, doubling graphic systems implies the existence of a third presence, an implicit "and" born from and reframing the two stated "boths," obviating their duality. . . . Such doubling expands the communicative range of a message, ensures wider readership, capitalizes on how two systems never quite say the same thing, shows mastery of both schooled and ancestral codes, and foregrounds the inscriber's command of practical (alphabetic) and deep (dikenga/old-time) knowledge. (Gundaker 2011, 179)

Gundaker's theory of graphic systems expands the notion of doubling by exposing the implied third space produced by the combination of the double. The space for a third presence exposes a potential spatial augmentation that the novel form provides. This combination of the spiritual, physical, and novel space creates a fourth space—ritual. Indeed, the meeting of the spiritual and the physical realms in a diasporic context signifies the necessity and potentiality for ritual. Ritual functions as the interconnector between realms and also creates, like the common ritualistic element of water, a passageway to transcend spatial reality. Moreover, ritual as a fourth space re-creates a complete replicated image of the cosmogram in ideographic form. Death, and the rituals that occur as a result, provide a poignant example.

Death alters the course of life and necessitates ritual to restore balance in the universe. Death requires life as sunset requires sunrise. Between the two is rebirth, the liminal womb where life is re-created after death. It dictates and transmits the ancient methods of cosmology to a modern people. It passes tradition, belief, and knowledge from one generation to the next. Through the practice of ritual, people learn how the mythical and mundane coexist and interact. For example, Gundaker, in discussing diasporic burial rituals, posits that "community members incorporated cosmographic motion into burial ritual . . . also reminding us that cosmograms are performed and that gestures are thresholds to understanding. [Cosmograms] commemorate the dead, instruct the living, assert rights in place, and proclaim stature in the community in the face of oppressors" (2011, 177–78). Joël's death functions as the catalyst that changes the directional course for all the characters and sets in motion the natural movement and balance of the cosmogram. Joël is the crossroads. His death inscribes on his flesh the cruciform, which functions as a cultural road map leading to the other side of the water where departed souls go, the road that leads the soul from the physical into the spiritual. Kongo says that Don Ignacio "wanted to make a cross and write my boy's name on it . . . to put the cross on my son's grave. I told him no more crosses on my boy's back" (Danticat 1998, 144). Kongo makes an important distinction. Although the cosmogram in form makes a cross, it is not the cross Don Ignacio is referring to. Kongo is unwilling to allow Joël, even in death, to bear the burden of his demise like a sacrificial lamb. Instead, Kongo buries Joël on the road where he died. Joël's body, then, physically becomes embedded in the organic composition of the road and land. Because his body is an indelible part of the landscape, his flesh functions as a crossroads and opens communication between the realms.

As such, the character Kongo functions as the locator of his people's history, traditions, and origins. Emblematic of the concept of the other side of the water, and as his name suggests, Kongo symbolizes the cultural and physical origin of this particular group of diasporic people, and holistically the origin of all of humankind. A textual and symbolic father, Kongo bears a name that gestures to the land from which the waterways carried the enslaved from their homeland to the newfoundland, which became for Haitians an extension of Africa through their gained independence and cultural retentions. The character Kongo represents the spiritual realm lingering beyond the horizon and the physical realm, where he is a constant reality. Clearly, in *The Farming of Bones*, Kongo personifies Babaluaiye, the "Father, Lord of the World. . . . He is depicted as a human being . . . forced to endure the earth's anger and is the symbol of what happens when the earth turns against you." Representative of the textual crossroads, Kongo's spiritual symbolism is woven into the physical occurrences of the plot. "Babalú, like Elégbá, is an orisa of the road" (Edwards and Mason 1998, 72).

Kongo, alone, buries his son. Physically carrying Joël on his back, Kongo returns his son's body to the earth. Kongo bears the weight of Joël's physical body with the spiritual burden of being unable to return him home. He recounts to Amabelle: "I wanted to bury him in our own land where he was born . . . but he was too heavy to carry so far. . . . It wasn't ceremonious the way I buried him, I know. No clothes, no coffin, nothing between him and the dry ground" (Danticat 1998, 108). Kongo, unable to physically return Joël, and symbolically his people, to the "other side of the water," inters him in the earth the way he came into the world. Kongo's mention of the burial not being ceremonious gestures toward ritual, a symbolic gesture operating in a state of limbo, transnationally and diasporically, while also exposing the constraints and limitations of returning "home." For it is Joël's death that precipitates the meeting of the physical and the spiritual realms necessary for ritual to occur, and thus moves the text, characters, and audience through another dimension of the cosmogram.

MUSONI

Textual inscription relates to the form and function of interweaving a people's cosmological perspective, through myths, fables, and folktales, into their everyday physical lives and narratives. The mythical and the mundane create two narrative spheres interdependent in the creation of the textual life narrative of a people. The combinatory relationship between mythical and mundane, and spiritual and physical realms of existence, again, etches the quadruple graphic of the cosmogram and reflects the philosophical and cosmological underpinnings of an ancient and modern community of people by retelling and reinscribing the ancient into the modern. While the ideograph of the cosmogram is symbolic, its function nevertheless remains visible through the concept of the crossroads inherent in the social order and ritual practices. The implicit nature of the cosmogram is explicitly inscribed into the textual form of *Farming*. As the directionality of the cosmogram moves the text through the four points—death, rebirth, birth, and consciousness— it reproduces the symbolic meaning of and a people's relationship to the points. Ultimately, the movement provides a method to "read" communal and spiritual consciousness in *Farming*.

Myths, fables, and folktales prepare the consciousness of a people by establishing a matrix for communal being. Community exists through the interconnection between the spiritual realm and the physical realm, between people and ancestors. Amabelle's movement through the plot creates cosmographic direction for the characters in the novel, while her subconscious movement and doubling of inner and outer voice re-members and reconnects the narrative of the characters, including her own, to the cultural consciousness and fabric of the community.[9] Amabelle recalls:

> Father Romain always made much of our being from the same place. . . .
> Most people here did. . . . It was their way of returning home, with you
> as a witness or as someone to bring them back to the present, either
> with a yawn, a plea to be excused, or the skillful intrusion of your own
> tale. (Danticat 1998, 73)

Through the communal consciousness of the people, one can travel through realms and exist in both the present state of reality and the spiritual space and memory of home. The ability to double the self and exist within two realms simultaneously is imperative to the preservation of a people's identity, collectivity, and ideology. Amabelle recalls, "This was how people left imprints of themselves in each other's memory so that if you left first and went back to the common village, you could carry, if not a letter, a piece of treasured clothing, some message to their loved ones that their place was still among the living" (Danticat 1998, 73). The connective tissue of the narrative inscription of the cosmogram ensures the survival of individuals and the community immemorial. If one is intertwined into the narrative fabric of the community, then one can never be extracted from it. Or, as Amabelle recounts: "In his sermons to the Haitian congregants of the valley[,] [Father Romain] often reminded everyone of common ties: language, foods, history, carnival, songs, tales, and prayers. His creed was one of memory, how remembering—though sometimes painful—can make you strong" (Danticat 1998, 73). The cosmographic inscription of memory is, as Father Romain comports, the strength of a people. The conscious act of memory as a ritualistic component reinforces the philosophical and cosmological underpinnings of a community.

Central to any ritual is the presence of ancestors and the orishas, whose existence in the same space intertwines the past and the present, the spiritual and the physical, and the mythical and the mundane. *Farming* illustrates the role of the orishas in the everyday life and routine of the community. The textual inscription of the orishas doubling the characters' movement through the plot creates intertextuality between the people's narrative and the myth and lore of the divine.

Amabelle recalls that, in a stream with "women . . . who were ancient enough to be our great-grandmothers . . . helping a few of the orphaned girls to wash themselves," the community gathers to usher, communally and ritually, Joël into the next realm (Danticat 1998, 62). In this moment, the significance and meaning of the water is not to be lost: "For the BaKongo, the ocean Kalunga separates the land of the living from Mpemda, and in crossing Kalunga's waters, one travels to the other world. Kalunga not only separates the worlds but also subsequently links the two" (Gundaker 2011, 159). Through the cleansing of the communal and corporeal body, the scene in the river signifies and prepares the members of the community, and by extension Joël, to commune with the spiritual realm. The elders help the younger ones with the ritual practices and imprint them by way of demonstrative and performative acts. The acts both teach and ensure continuity among the community. Here again, water functions as a conduit for the crossroads and exemplifies the two realms, or contrasting sides of the water. Kongo's solitary act of burying his son negates the role of ceremony, often embedded in funeral practices, and confirms the requirement of ritual. Accordingly, Amabelle recalls: "Void of ceremony, this was a silent farewell to Joël, a quiet wake at dawn." Ironically the novel juxtaposes this with the mass "Doña Eva's . . . having . . . for the anniversary of her birth" (Danticat 1998, 60–63). The contrasting scenes of life and death demonstrate the directional movement of the cosmogram and foreshadow the impending massacre of many of the same people in the river.

Furthering the irony is the symbolic doubling of the ritual burying of Joël and what can be read as divine warning of the massacre. Ominously, Kongo notes that "the most respected elder" cleanses his body with parsley, which becomes the agent of death and ethnic cleansing. The Spanish word for parsley, *perejil*, was used as an indicator of whether one was Dominican or Haitian, and its mispronunciation warranted death, often by machete. Amabelle observes that

> he moved slowly to . . . allow the parsley to brush over the map of scars on his muscular back, all the while staring at the water's surface, as though he could see more than his reflection there. Kongo dropped the used parsley in the stream and raised his machete from the water. Holding his work tool up to the sun, he stroked the edge of his blade as though it were made of flesh. (Danticat 1998, 62–63)

Amid realms, Kongo is the receptor of the vision and knowledge of the fate of his people.

Amabelle witnesses the response to Joël's death on multiple levels, which also recalls the textual inscription of the cosmogram. For example, her association with both the murderer and his family, and the victim and his family, tempers Amabelle's personal response to the tragedy. Amabelle attempts to mediate between the two sides in order to quell the growing conflict and tension. However, Joël's death signifies the apex of this tension and the novel's resolution. Amabelle mirrors both sides in this tension through her re-membering of not only Joël's death but also the tragedy of losing her parents at the river and being saved by Don Ignacio. Joël's death also signals the beginning of Amabelle's movement through the cosmogram. She begins to conceptualize the idea of returning to a home and "a life that would be fully mine . . . hoping for a voice to call to me from across the river, someone to arrive saying 'I have come for you to bring you back'" (Danticat 1998, 80). As the novel progresses and the details of Joël's death unfold, the idea of home becomes more evident and essential to her survival and her people's survival. Amabelle must return to the river and cross it back home.

Joël's death prompts Amabelle to re-member the death of her parents, a moment when life and death converge, and Amabelle's path permanently alters. Shortly after the death of Joël, Amabelle recalls the story of her parents at the river: "It is a Friday, market day. My mother, my father, and me, we cross into Dajabón, the first Dominican town across the river. My mother wants to buy cooking pots" (Danticat 1998, 50). The threat of rain hurries their crossing back onto Haitian soil, and Amabelle's father's attempts to gauge the safety of crossing the swelling river. The textual inscription of the family's crossing draws a cruciform and symbolically connotes the crossroads and the presence of Papa Légbá. Her mother professes, "Hold the pots . . . Papa will come back for you soon," and Amabelle observes "a few river rats, young boys . . . afraid to cross" (Danticat 1998, 51). Rats commonly symbolize the presence of Papa Légbá and, like the rat, Légbá "is a homeless wandering spirit who inhabits the marketplace, the crossroads" (Edwards and Mason 1998, 18). Amabelle's parents do not pay particular attention to the physical manifestations of Elégbá as the river rats and, instead, give homage and reverence to other orishas and other religions. Amabelle recounts: "My father . . . sprinkles his face with water, as if to salute the spirit of the river and request her permission to enter. My mother crosses herself three times and looks up at the sky" (Danticat 1998, 51). However, West African reverence to Elégbá as the purveyor of crossings retains its continuity.[10] As a result, the river swallows Amabelle's parents, and she is left holding the pots. She says, "I walk to the sands to throw the pots into the water and then myself. . . . Two of the river boys grab me and drag me by the armpits away from the river. . . . Unless you want to die, one of them says, you will never see those people again" (Danticat 1998, 52). At the crossroads, Papa Légbá gives Amabelle a choice between life and death; her mother's omen proves true. The river rats representing Papa Légbá come back for her. The pots that Amabelle throws back into the river return to the spiritual "mother of the rivers" she submits her narrative to in the beginning. This also fulfills her father's request to enter the river. Accordingly, Yemoja symbolizes "a pot of river water . . . [and is] the matriarch who resides over the bloodstreams of the world" (Edwards and Mason 1998, 87). Joël's death prompts the retelling of her parents' tragic end and reinscribes Amabelle's own obligation to bear witness and carry forth ancestral, communal, and spiritual lines of her people. In order to do so, Amabelle must negotiate the intersections of life and death, the crossroads.

At the center of the crossroads, Amabelle pays heed to Papa Légbá's warning by choosing life and ritualizes her parents' transition from the physical to the spiritual by throwing the pots to the other side of the water. Inevitably, Amabelle must return to the crossroads to complete her journey home. As the initial site of trauma and death, the river functions as a mirror reflecting and doubling what she has and must endure to survive the journey home. The contrast between this attempt to return home and the death of her parents in the first attempt is the use of ritual and her understanding her fated role. Emily Clark contends that "the cosmogram suggests that the bowls possessed [pots in *Farming*] religious and ritual properties. . . . [T]heir presence in rivers connects directly to the symbolism of the cosmogram itself" (Clark 2011, 160). And while the pots are not marked with the cosmogram as the quotation indicates, because the characters are at a literal crossing and the crossroads is textually inscribed, the cosmogram is implied. Given the intermingling of the divine and mundane worlds, Amabelle's parents' death requires ritual, like Joël's death mandates: "The cosmogram would properly consecrate the space and prepare it for religious ritual by establishing a connection between the space . . . and the world of the spirits" (Clark 2011, 160).

Kongo prepares the way by invoking Elégbá to ensure safe passage. He creates a *vévé*, or "a large letter V on the floor" (Thompson 1984, 146). Thompson explains a *vévé* as "ritual ground paintings . . . traced by a priest or priestesses in powdered substances (usually cornmeal) on the earth about the central column of the Vodun dancing court" (1984, 188). Just as a cosmogram is a visual inscription that communicates and functions as a representation of the connection between the spiritual and the physical realm, "the vévé represent[s] the physical crossroads connection between the worlds" (Clark 2011, 160). In a Vodun ritual, openings and closings are traditionally performed by a priest or priestess, a person highly trained in proper practices to ensure the success of a ritual and the transformation of adherents. Suggesting that he belongs to a long line of priests, Kongo explains to Amabelle, Yves, and Sebastien that "this is something my old grandfather used to do before I went on a journey" (Danticat 1998, 146). A further indication of his role as a priest is the clothes he wears, ironically Joël's burial clothes: "He was wearing a yellow shirt and black pants that Sebastien had given him to dress his son for burial" (Danticat 1998, 119). As the color black traditionally

symbolizes death, "in Yorubaland members of [Elégbá's] priesthood wear
yellow to commemorate his close association with Orunmila (deity of divina-
tion)" (Edwards and Mason 1998, 19). Therefore, Kongo prepares them, and
in particular Amabelle, for the journey back to Haiti. Kongo tells them, "I
make this mark for you. . . . Your trail of rivers and mountains, and on your
journey you will require protection" (Danticat 1998, 146). At the conclusion
of the ritual, as Amabelle, Sebastien, and Yves prepare to leave, Kongo's eyes
are fixed on the *vévé* etched into the ground, seemingly reading the inscription and interpreting the events to come for the trio.

Significant to the textual inscription of the cosmogram is Kongo's reference to Saint Christophe, whose African counterpart is Aganju: "Aganju is
also said to be the ferryman and the custodian of the river. . . . Aganju carries
people across great obstacles" (Edwards and Mason 1998, 50). The reference
is particularly important in the ritual space created by the *vévé* because, as
the text suggests, this would likely be the last time any of the three would see
Kongo alive. Amabelle laments: "I would never hear about it when Kongo
dies" (Danticat 1998, 147). Kongo knows that he must pass on the traditions
and customs of his people to someone. But with his son dead, Kongo ordains
Amabelle, the holder of Joël's death mask, to become the priestess who will
carry with her the memory of her people back to their land. Gary Edwards
and John Mason posit that "Aganju is important to the growth of civilization
because he . . . opens uncharted geographic and psychological frontiers, and
stimulates cosmopolitanism" (1998, 51). Without someone to carry the memory
of the community, the community would cease to exist. Who better to navigate
the river than one who can ferry the community back to existence?

KALA

At the heart of this novel is the all-encompassing love story of Amabelle
and Sebastien. After the massacre, Amabelle returns to the other side of the
Dajabón and attempts to find Sebastien at the site representative of their
love, the waterfall leading to a cave. The waterfall and cave function as yet
another intersection between the physical and spiritual planes, and Amabelle
and Sebastien cross from their physical reality into the spiritual womb of
the cave. However, she fails to find him or the cave, and their love remains
in the spiritual womb-like space the cave represents. Similar to the way Oya
deifies Sango after his death, Amabelle narratively speaks the stories of the
dead and effectively, as Teresa Washington proclaims, "unleashed the winds
of change and propelled . . . [them] to immediate ancestral transmigration

and Orisa status" (2005, 48). After bestowing her narrative to "Metrès Dlo, Mother of the Rivers," Amabelle begins her account with a memory of Sebastien. Written in the bold font that indicates Amabelle's dialogue within the spiritual realm, she submits: "His name is Sebastien Onius" (Danticat 1998, 1). Although Sebastien does not cross the river physically, spiritually his narrative is inscribed within Amabelle's memory and on her flesh. Amabelle, as the narrative witness to and keeper of communal knowledge and history, especially of the dead, proclaims: "Now my flesh was simply . . . a marred testament" (Danticat 1998, 227). By telling the story of the massacre and those lost to this tragedy, *The Farming of Bones* becomes the material site for the monuments that, historically, were not erected in honor of those who perished. Amabelle's words build shrines to honor the dead, and the survivors of the massacre birth a narrative replete with what was hidden.

Once she completes her life's work of carrying the stories of the dead back home, Amabelle's purpose and role in the novel become less imperative. She searches for meaning and purpose in mundane tasks such as sewing, but finds no life for herself among the living. In the greatest act of the novel, Amabelle does for herself what no one else can: she submits her life to the "Mother of the Rivers." As Aganju "allows . . . new realities and is associated with the rising sun and the dawn of a new day," Amabelle ends the novel with the words, "He, like me, was looking for the dawn" (Danticat 1998, 310). Her words, just like the words of the dead, point to the motion of Amabelle moving toward the highest point of consciousness. Amabelle experiences everything she needs in the physical realm, and now her journey will continue in the spiritual realm. The continuation of her journey indicates the rebirth of a divine being whose story of love through trauma serves as a witness and testimony to all those at a crossroads.

TUKULA

The brilliance of Danticat and, in essence, of *The Farming of Bones*, is that all along the reader believes that it is Amabelle's, and the novel's, burden alone to carry the stories of her people back home. However, by the end of the novel the reader realizes that they have become a witness, participant, and receptor, too. The material manifestation of the cosmogram—the reader—must journey through the trauma with the characters and, thus, participate in the narrative movement through the cosmogram and ritual practices. As ritual transforms all who participate, it heals as the collective speak or read the words of trauma that open the crossroads and ask the divine for healing balm. Danticat's text is a living narrative, an embodied text, a breathing text that functions within the liminal spaces of the physical and the spiritual realm waiting for a willing participant take on the journey.

Although the characters' stories are tragic, there is triumph in the possibility of a "new dawn," a new day, a new life the novel's end gestures toward—the creation of "Quisenya," an idyllic place where diasporic people can exist without any preconceived notion of self and being, or, as Danticat opines, our "Precolumbian selves" (Candelario 2004, 72). A place where the Black body is not a site of exploration and discovery at the hands of an oppressor, but is rather a site of agency that engenders self-definition and personhood. *The Farming of Bones* creates a spiritual text and guide for this deliverance and insistently gestures to the crossroads.

NOTES

1. For further explanation of the concept of testimonial, see Yúdice 1991, 18–19.
2. The crossroads is symbolic of its cosmological container, the cosmogram, and reflects the intersection of the four moments of the sun.
3. "Peristyle" refers to the center post of a ritual structure and demarcates the center of the crossroads and the convergence of the physical and spiritual realm. For a more complete explanation and discussion of the concept, see Thompson 1984.
4. For further discussion, see Gates 1988.
5. For an example of the differing fonts, see the beginning of chapter 1 and chapter 2 of *Farming*.
6. The cosmogram represents the philosophical and ontological idea of the soul's journey through life constructed and demarcated through the four moments of the sun.
7. For further discussion of the Marassa as it relates to twinning and doubling, see Deren 1970.
8. See Thompson 1984 for a cosmogram graphic.
9. For further explanation of the concept of "rememory," see Morrison 1988, 35–36.
10. Elégbá is used to refer to the West African iteration of the orisha, while Papa Légbá refers to the Haitian iteration.

BIBLIOGRAPHY

Brown, Karen McCarthy. 2001. *Mama Lola: A Vodou Priestess in Brooklyn*. 3rd ed. Berkeley: University of California Press.
Candelario, Ginetta E. B. 2004. "Voices from Hispaniola: A Meridians Roundtable with Edwidge Danticat, Loida Maritza Pérez, Myriam J. A. Chancy, and Nelly Rosario." *Meridians: Feminism, Race, Transnationalism* 5, no. 1: 68–91.

Clark, Emily. 2011. "Cosmogram." In *World of a Slave: Encyclopedia of the Material Life of Slaves in the United States*, edited by Martha B. Katz-Hyman and Kym S. Rice. Vol. 1. Santa Barbara, CA: Greenwood.

Danticat, Edwidge. 1998. *The Farming of Bones*. New York: Soho Press.

Danticat, Edwidge. 2010. *Create Dangerously: The Immigrant Artist at Work*. Princeton, NJ: Princeton University Press.

Deren, Maya. 1970. *Divine Horsemen: The Voodoo Gods of Haiti*. New York: Chelsea House.

"Dominicans, Haitians Remember Parsley Massacre." 2012. *Tell Me More*. National Public Radio, October 1. https://www.npr.org/2012/10/01/162088692/Dominicans -haitians-remember-parsley-massacre.

Edwards, Gary, and John Mason. 1998. *Black Gods: Òrìṣà Studies in the New World*. 4th ed. Brooklyn: Yorùbá Theological Archministry.

Gates, Henry Louis, Jr. 1988. *The Signifying Monkey: A Theory of African-American Literary Criticism*. New York: Oxford University Press.

Gundaker, Grey. 2011. "The Kongo Cosmogram in Historical Archaeology and the Moral Compass of Dave the Potter." *Historical Archaeology* 45, no. 2 (June): 176–83.

Janzen, John M. 1982. *Lemba, 1650–1930: A Drum of Affliction in Africa and the New World*. New York: Garland Publishing.

Kolawole, Mary E. Modupe. 1997. *Womanism and African Consciousness*. Trenton: Africa World Press.

Morrison, Toni. 2004. *Beloved*. New York: Vintage Books.

Thompson, Robert Farris. 1984. *Flash of the Spirit: African and Afro-American Art and Philosophy*. New York: Vintage Books.

Ulysse, Gina Athena. 2015. *Why Haiti Needs New Narratives: A Post-Quake Chronicle*. Middletown, CT: Wesleyan University Press.

Washington, Teresa N. 2005. *Our Mothers, Our Powers, Our Texts: Manifestations of Àjé in Africana Literature*. Bloomington: Indiana University Press.

Washington, Teresa N. 2012. "Nickels in the Nation Sack: Continuity in Africana Spiritual Technologies." *Journal of Pan African Studies* 3, no. 5: 5–25.

Yúdice, George. 1991. "*Testimonio* and Postmodernism." *Latin American Perspectives* 18, no. 3 (Summer): 15–31.

Chapter Three

"CAST *LÒT BÒ DLO*, ACROSS THE SEAS"

Re/Writing Home and Nation in Edwidge Danticat's *Create Dangerously: The Immigrant Artist at Work*

OLGA BLOMGREN

What does it mean to come home as a writer, an immigrant artist? Does this question have a different inflection today, when immigrant writers have multiple places they may call home? Weaving together a different way to understand history, nation, and home, Edwidge Danticat encourages archipelagic thinking in the essay collection *Create Dangerously: The Immigrant Artist at Work*. Archipelagic thinking is steeped in continuous movement, and in this text immigrant artists are at home with mobilities and transit. In addition, physical and transnational human movements stimulate and create opportunities for the movement of ideas, languages, art, and more. The mobilities of the immigrant artist in this text describe a more fluid relationship with a country, suggesting spatial configurations more closely tied to seas and oceans. Danticat offers waterways that join and transport people as a counter to territorial connections, as well as a space of potential and hope. This hope encompasses the unifying work produced by artists who, for various reasons, travel or find themselves beyond the shores and stories nations tell about themselves. And, instead of singularity, Danticat writes about and for a unified multiplicity. Danticat's text considers the way art unites people beyond borders, a community that includes the diasporas. Ultimately, literature and art are unifying forces that exceed the power and bounds of any one nation or geographical space.

INTRODUCTION: COMPLICATING HOMELANDS

Globalization has shifted the significance of territory and political borders in the conception of home and nation. Today, even when weakened or in decline, nations thrive and rely on the myths they create and perpetuate about themselves. In his research on globalization, anthropologist Arjun Appadurai explains that these narratives are a global phenomenon: "It has been widely noted that the idea of a singular national ethnos, far from being a natural outgrowth of this or that soil, has been produced and naturalized at great cost, through rhetorics of war and sacrifice, through punishing disciplines of educational and linguistic uniformity, and through the subordination of myriad local and regional traditions."[1] In effect, these national narratives normalize systems of exclusion while they claim to define an ethnos and so must be produced, taught, and enforced indefinitely. Yet significant economic and political turmoil, such as globalization, war, and natural disaster, disrupts the power and efficacy of the master narrative. Appadurai claims that the "essential principles and procedures of the modern nation-state—the idea of a sovereign and stable territory, the idea of a containable and countable population, the idea of a reliable census, and the idea of stable and transparent categories—have come unglued in the era of globalization."[2] This lack of certainty about the nation-state diminishes a nation's authority and makes it difficult to control national narratives, particularly of citizenship.[3] Circumstances resulting in transnational human movements, for example, have persistently destabilized national narratives "of purity, authenticity, borders, and security."[4] Transnational mobilities signify the crossing of established borders, immediately placing notions of citizenship and belonging into question. Furthermore, these movements indicate that both nations and humans are changeable, contradicting national narratives that naturalize singularity and sameness. In *Create Dangerously*, Danticat reflects on how literature helps her question ideas connecting humans to a national territory. The unifying capability and humanistic enterprise of the art Danticat describes both in Haiti and elsewhere brings people, literature, and languages together. This chapter will observe the significance of water in the text and explain how it reflects archipelagic thinking and decoloniality. I will also analyze how literature that relies on personal and public histories brings people into relations beyond borders and national narratives.

A LITERARY HOME AT SEA:
LETTING GO OF LAND, CONNECTING WITH WATER

As in the case of Danticat, immigrant artists often find themselves outside the narratives nations tell about themselves, and sometimes beyond the nation itself. In the essay "I Am Not a Journalist," Danticat introduces one of these artists, "one of Haiti's most famous journalists, the radio commentator Jean Dominique."[5] Dominique suffered many exiles from, and returns to, Haiti; nonetheless, he continued working until his assassination in April 2000.[6] His untimely death reminded Danticat of a conversation they had shared about the words "my country."[7] Whereas Dominique spoke the words affirmatively, Danticat said: "My country, Jean, [. . .] is one of uncertainty. When I say 'my country' to some Haitians, they think I mean the United States. When I say 'my country' to some Americans, they think of Haiti."[8] Her frequent transit between the two nations connects her to both places, yet master narratives joining people with a national territory exclude a mobile person like Danticat. Furthermore, her presence and interest in both places contributes to how those around her imagine her connection to both nations. Dominique, until his death, remained "one of Haiti's most famous journalists,"[9] and this may mark a difference between the two friends. Is Danticat a writer from Haiti or from the United States, or do these questions no longer answer to contemporary transnational mobilities?[10] Danticat continues: "My country, I felt, both as an immigrant and as an artist, was something that was then being called the tenth department. Haiti then had nine geographical departments and the tenth was the floating homeland, the ideological one, which joined all Haitians living outside of Haiti, in the *dyaspora*."[11] The past tense indicates that this conversation took place before Nippes became the tenth department created by the Haitian government in 2003. Nonetheless, the word "floating" suggests a homeland that is unanchored and perpetually moving. This metaphor, the tenth department, is neither a nation nor even territory but a "floating homeland" that unites a large population of Haitians, including those of second-generation Haitian ancestry and beyond. She explains that "in the Haitian context [diaspora] is used 'to identify the hundreds of thousands of Haitians living in many countries of the world.'"[12] Yet no longer is the highly mobile diaspora conceived of as singular, or as a solitary individual; instead, it recognizes belonging to a multiplicity. To this realization, Danticat adds Dominique's statement: "The *Dyaspora* are people with their feet planted in both worlds. [. . .] There's no need to be ashamed of that. There are more than a million of you. You all are not alone."[13] Dominique also locates the diaspora outside of a nation, invoking the inclusive plural term "worlds" to describe the global spaces the population inhabits. He again affirms the multiplicity of the diaspora, underscoring the influence and power it has as a collective.

This discussion suggests the ways archipelagic scholars seek to reorganize thinking about relations between water and land by instead concentrating on associations in relation to waterways. Reframing interdisciplinary fields of study around oceans, sea basins, and maritime interactions requires "a new kind of mapping in social scientific terms [which] also points to the need for a new kind of cognitive mapping in more humanistic terms, that is, the interrogation of the continental logic and discourse."[14] Unsettling this mode of thought is one of the aims of archipelagic studies. Archipelagic perspectives respond to this urgency to rethink theoretical frames, ontologies, and epistemologies established and perpetuated by European colonial projects. Scholars include archipelagic studies in what has been described as the spatial turn, a recent organization of studies that can be understood as "above all, an attack upon grand narratives of modernity, colonialism, and development."[15] Grounded in what Peruvian sociologist Aníbal Quijano identifies as the coloniality of power, Walter Mignolo explains that "Quijano's proposal was that coloniality is a necessary component of modernity and therefore it cannot be ended if global imperial designs in the name of modernity continue. Coloniality, in other words, is the darker side of Western modernity."[16] Even after colonizers have been ousted, their institutions and epistemologies remain: "Decoloniality means first to delink (to detach) from that overall structure of knowledge in order to engage in an epistemic reconstitution. Reconstitution of [. . .] ways of thinking, languages, ways of life and being in the world that the rhetoric of modernity disavowed and the logic of coloniality implement [*sic*]."[17] A "new kind of cognitive mapping" is offered by archipelagic studies, one that Danticat adopts within her discussion of the diaspora and tenth department. Archipelagic thinking questions rather than perpetuates the ideas of modernity and coloniality, including the constructed ideas of the nation-state. Identifying with a "floating homeland," unanchoring the terrestrially bound nation, and returning attention to water encompass the multiplicities and relations understood within archipelagic thinking.

Having invoked the tenth department, a metaphor rooted/routed in mobility, Danticat's identity as an artist raises another question. Does mobility cultivate a certain type of artist? In other words, what does it mean to join the word "immigrant" with "artist"? In the essay "The Other Side of the Water," written about her cousin's passing and his body's return to Haiti, Danticat combines the tropes of death and transit to offer a response to this question and demonstrate how writing from a floating, nonterrestrial homeland is unifying. The essay introduces the adage *lòt bò dlo*, which she echoes throughout the book. This phrase uses the metaphor of water to signify mobility, and in doing so emphasizes movement and water beyond any ties to land: "In Haiti the same expression, *lòt bò dlo*, the other side of the water, can be used to denote the eternal afterlife as well as an émigré's eventual destination."[18] Departing from an island, *lòt bò dlo* is a literal description of a traveler's journey, no matter where the voyage ends. This expression also moves with the speaker/migrant, carrying equal force and meaning whether uttered in Haiti proper, in the tenth department, or elsewhere. Danticat and her deceased cousin Marius fly from the United States across the sea to Haiti, so the trip resonates with the literal and figurative meanings of the adage. Upon death, Marius is *lòt bò dlo*, fulfilling the second meaning of the expression. He returns from *lòt bò dlo* to his final resting place. In the essay, Danticat features a mobilized literary community; Sophocles and Gabriel García Márquez help Danticat question how the laws and rituals around death dis/connect humans from a national territory.

Before Danticat references Sophocles directly, she poses a question his protagonist Antigone could have asked following the deaths of her only brothers, Eteocles and Polynices. Danticat interrogates the relation between death and belonging with her question: "Were we still aliens in death, I asked, our corpses unwanted visitors still?"[19] Can a body rest, despite the relation it may have had with, or to, the land? Can loved ones bury that body in alien territory? Sophocles is invoked in the essay when Danticat observes that there was "nothing *Antigone* about" her efforts to return her cousin's body to Haiti.[20] Antigone refutes the king's edict against burying Polynices and is condemned to death for breaking the law. Polynices's war against his own city of Thebes leaves him a deterritorialized stranger. Marius had entered the United States without documentation. Can one make sense of whether a final resting place is determined by a person's choices, or legal status and documentation? Although this allusion is meant to illustrate how business-like and "sanitized"[21] Danticat's efforts for her cousin had been, Marius's mother, Tante Zi, introduces another direction to the classical allusion. She asks her niece about those who return: "Some people come back from the other side of the water, don't they? [. . .] You're proof of that, *non*?"[22] Like the expression, Tante Zi's question can be understood in two ways. First, her son never returned from the other side of the water alive, so her niece's presence is evidence that some émigrés do return. However, this question can also mean that some people return from death back to life. According to Greek myths, the river Styx unites the land of the living with the underworld, and so the other side of this water is literally the realm of the dead, similar to the eternal afterlife understood by the Haitian expression. The second inflection of this poignant query made by a mother who has recently lost a son calls to mind the heroic efforts of Odysseus, Herakles, and Orpheus, men known to have returned from the land of the shades, the other side of the water. In this conversation, she includes her niece among those who return, and Danticat responds to her aunt's question: "They do."[23] In this mythic company, the other sense of Tante Zi's question sees Danticat's return as heroic and aided by gods. Navigating waterways is a literary experience shared by the living, the dead, and the mythical. Danticat remains in transit; water connects the places she chooses to travel. As an artist, literature provides her with a way to synthesize these experiences in her own writing.

García Márquez is likewise included in this essay as a literary figure whose writing unites terrestrial belonging and death. The essay cites the Colonel's words from *One Hundred Years of Solitude*: "A person does not belong to a place until someone is dead under the ground." In response, Danticat asks, "Does that person still belong if someone died there, but is not buried under that ground?"[24] García Márquez's novel affirms that people tie one another to the land, and not national myths or political narratives. In either case, the earth holds the dead, and not the living. In Danticat's essay, she and Tante Zi engage in an unspoken question in the presence of the sea:

> "Why didn't Marius come back?" She seemed to be asking both me and the sea.
> "I don't know," I said.
> "It's stupid to even ask," she said, scratching the short gray hair under the white kerchief that covered her head. "How could any of us know the answer to something like that? Only the sea and God know. Right?"[25]

Although no response is required, Danticat voices her agreement. The sea carries people away and sometimes brings them back from their journey. In acknowledgment of the awesome power of the sea, Tante Zi "walked toward the ocean for an afternoon swim."[26] The essay concludes with this apotheosis of the sea; she has abilities and knowledge unknown to humans. Yet the sea also connects those who migrate, the living and the dead; the sea, more than any territory, in/forms the geographical dynamics of the artist in Danticat's essay collection.

Although the expression *lòt bò dlo* appears at various points throughout the book, the final essay, a postscript titled "A Year and a Day," reprises images of water and death, with a difference. It begins by explaining that "in the Haitian Vodou tradition, it is believed by some that the souls of the newly dead slip into rivers and streams and remain there, under the water, for a year and a day."[27] After this period of time, the souls leave the water and are reborn. In this view, "more than two hundred thousand souls went *anba dlo*—under the water—after the earthquake on January 12, 2010."[28] Danticat associates these deaths with words she heard from a quake survivor:

"[D]uring the earthquake it was as if the earth had become liquid, like water."[29] This transformation, of the earth to liquid, generates Danticat's optimism: "My hope came not only from the possibility of their and our communal rebirth but from the extra day that would follow the close of a most terrible year."[30] After the tragedies of a natural disaster, and the book's earlier associations of water and death, the postscript uses these images to invoke a rebirth, a rebirth of a people temporarily leveled by an earthquake and subsequent outbreak of cholera. These images also suggest the beginning and anticipation of a new year. This is evidenced by the extra day that "will lead us into the following year, and the one after that, and the one after that."[31] This renewal is an ongoing process, and it is continuous in a sense similar to the processes of archipelagic thinking. When studying the diverse concepts of this interdisciplinary field, archipelagic scholars often analyze them in terms of mobility. In "Envisioning the Archipelago," authors Elaine Stratford, Godfrey Baldacchino, Elizabeth McMahon, Carol Farbotko, and Andrew Harwood describe the organizing principles of an island grouping: "Perhaps, at least as conceptual manifestations, archipelagos are fluid cultural processes, sites of abstract and material relations of movement and rest, dependent on changing conditions of articulation or connection."[32] The island groupings themselves are in flux, and changeability is understood as a foundational element. An emphasis on process is a key feature of the field along with an understanding that dynamism is constant. In my own understanding of archipelagic thinking and scholarship, the attention to movement emphasizes not just its significance to the archipelagic grouping, but also the idea of movement as *sustained and ongoing*. This point is underscored in the work of Édouard Glissant. Being "in Relation" is not an end but rather a process, or as Glissant describes it, an "always becoming."[33] Archipelagic thinking is likewise multiple, open, and not fixed. More so than territorial connections, waterways unite and transport people and additionally provide immigrant artists a space of potential and hope.

ART AS A UNIFYING FORCE

The title essay of Danticat's collection focuses on a group of artists telling a counternarrative of resistance to oppression. "Create Dangerously: The Immigrant Artist at Work" explicitly refers to poets, playwrights, and authors who have inspired Danticat by focusing on the public and social power of performance. She recalls the public execution in Haiti of guerrilla fighters Marcel Numa and Louis Drouin by François "Papa Doc" Duvalier in 1964 as a "creation myth,"[34] a fatal act that gave life to myriad forms of artistic disobedience. As a creation myth, this is a story that explains an origin, births a new people who are neither constrained nor defined by a national narrative. The myth is also tied in with the relational flows referenced in the essay. The two men whose execution she calls a creation myth had both traveled to the United States to attend school and work before returning to Haiti. Danticat emphasizes their connection to fellow Haitians: "Marcel Numa and Louis Drouin were patriots who died so that other Haitians could live. They were also immigrants, like me,"[35] and she specifically relates to their transnational movements. This creation myth also introduces the unifying possibility of art in a time when Haiti was forcibly divided by the dictatorship. Eliding what Danticat considers "the mythic elements" of Numa's and Drouin's stories, Duvalier attempted to control the narrative of these events: "In the propaganda preceding their execution, he labeled them not Haitian, but foreign rebels, good-for-nothing *blans* [whites]."[36] This sanctioned narrative was promptly rejected by the public. In her essay collection, Danticat illustrates how Numa and Drouin's execution was a historical watershed that created and impacted artists, as well as how this historical moment engenders multiple narratives. In her neighborhood, a community book group responded to these executions by stealthily staging Albert Camus's *Caligula*, and the cathartic performance birthed a legacy that outlived the elder Duvalier. While the dictatorship's violence continued, literary art was called on to respond: "The legend of the underground staging of this and other plays, clandestine readings of pieces of literature, was so strong that [. . .] every time there was a political murder in Bel Air, one of the young aspiring intellectuals in the neighborhood [. . .] might inevitably say that someone should put on a play."[37] In this manner, Greek classics were rewritten in Kreyòl and set in Haitian neighborhoods by the dramatist Franck Fouché and the poet Félix Morisseau-Leroy.[38] The classics were creolized in keeping with the demands of the historical moment and audience. These theatrical performances responded to the social and political context, uniting the community of artists and audience in resistance. Via these readings and performances, Danticat describes Haiti as an opening to Algeria, Greece, Russia, Martinique, and many more places, as well as the freedom this provided Haitians living under dictatorship. The literature and culture they already possessed, written by Haitians or brought by the historical flows of the archipelago, was taken up and creolized to create new narratives and construct their own art.

Although the essay begins by observing writers and artists, the communities they create with readers and audiences are also vital to this creation process. Writers are readers, and textual creolization, as in the process of translation,[39] requires close, even intimate reading.[40] Danticat explains that the impetus toward creation is "what I've always seen as the unifying principle among all writers."[41] This is an act of disobedience: "Create dangerously, for people who read dangerously. This is what I've always thought it meant to be a writer. Writing, knowing in part that no matter how trivial your words may seem, someday, somewhere someone may risk his or her life to read them."[42] Danticat creolizes Camus's essay, making it specific to her social and political context, adding what she believes it means to write and create in the twenty-first century. These sentences emphasize the power of the executions as creation myth. It is the life and times of the reader that inject vitality and relevance to the text. The artist's courage is matched by that of the reader in circumstances unforeseen or unknown to the writer. As in the example of the community-generated theatrical performances, the artistic resistance forges a collective. This relationship cannot be controlled or disrupted by a dictator or nation; it will continue to evolve. Invoking another origin myth by comparing the reader to Eve eating the apple in the Garden of Eden, Danticat asks: "How does that reader find the courage to take this bite, open that book?"[43] One response is in "the writer's courage in having stepped forward, in having written, or rewritten, in the first place."[44] In a sense, the author's creation is the foundation of a community; the reader understands that she is not alone. Writer and reader are unified, beyond any national border, narrative, or language.

"Create Dangerously: The Immigrant Artist at Work" emphasizes the reader's role in a text's mobility, further developing a community unifying writer and reader. The relationship between art, artist, and reader refers to and unites the multiple narratives on the island. Danticat cites Camus's order to "create dangerously," which is "creating as a revolt against silence, creating when both the creation and the reception, the writing and reading, are dangerous undertakings, disobedience to a directive."[45] Sometimes art captures the danger, or even allows one to move past fear, in a way not yet encountered or understood in life. In another essay, Danticat adds the perspective photojournalist Daniel Morel had of this moment. He spoke of his fear after Numa and Drouin's execution, yet this fear also leads him to take up his camera.[46] Following her conversations with Morel, Danticat is "even more certain that to create dangerously is also to create fearlessly, boldly embracing the public and private terrors that would silence us."[47] An immigrant artist works with fear, out loud and as part of a collective. Excluded from or resisting the sanctioned narrative, she determines her own space from which to create and tell her own stories. This process works within mobilities; it involves "[c]reating fearlessly even when cast *lòt bò dlo*, across the seas."[48] Creation is not confined to any one location and does not stop at the shore. It involves "[c]reating fearlessly for people who see/watch/listen/read fearlessly."[49] Reiterating the association between artist and audience, the creative work is for the equally undaunted reader. This relationship is one of potential: "Somewhere, if not now, then maybe years in the future, we may also save someone's life (or mind) because they have given us a passport, making us honorary citizens of their culture."[50] In multiple ways, readers invigorate a text, making the writer and literature at home, in any place. Dany Laferrière agrees with Roland Barthes that "a text's unity lies not in its origin but in its destination."[51] A confirmation of this is Laferrière's response to the question of his identity in *Je suis un écrivain japonais* (I am a Japanese writer): "I took the nationality of my reader."[52] Notably, it is *readers* who grant passage to writers and their texts, not a border agent or national government, and so this relation is uncontrollable and unpredictable. Danticat wonders, "Is there such a thing as an immigrant reader?"[53] Here, she proposes that readers are also a multiplicity of places and that the nature of their mobilities is unforeseeable.

CONCLUSION: THE TWENTY-FIRST-CENTURY STATE OF NATIONS

As evidenced by the essay collection *Create Dangerously: The Immigrant Artist at Work*, Danticat reflects on how lived experiences together with literature engender processes that interrogate and oppose state narratives, underscoring relational flows and in turn troubling conceptions that confine people and literature to fixed categories and national territories. The title essay also features counternarratives of the ways Haitian artists and audiences opposed the dictatorship by creolizing art and creating stories about Haitian people and experiences. This underscores the new mobilities of people and languages since the rise of globalization. Arjun Appadurai explains that the period since the 1970s has been characterized not only by the movement of culture, which he terms "global cultural flows," but also by the mobility of cultural forms, including those of a literary and artistic nature.[54] In many ways, art and literary texts are in movement, across seas, frontiers, and languages. This literature in transit, written by mobile authors like Edwidge Danticat, subverts narratives of stasis, national narratives that seek to divide and exclude, like those of dictators and authoritarians. Mobile literatures do not necessarily have a national allegiance or any one homeland;

their project encompasses global humanization. Artists may focus their creativity on narratives that are ignored or remain unresolved by regional governments. Their texts may provide social critiques rather than nationalistic themes, and can be composed in a myriad of languages or in no language at all. In these ways, literature and art mobilize against and weaken the narratives of the nation-state. As a multilingual author, Danticat troubles the historical links between languages, home, and nations. Ultimately, she describes how creolization brings literature and languages together, underscoring the unifying power of literature and art.

Although dominant and continental ways of thinking and knowing privilege the boundaries drawn on political maps, Camus asserts that "the sea, rains, necessity, desire, the struggle against death—these are the things that unite us all."[55] Waterways that join and transport people form an alternative to connections to soil, as well as a space of potential and hope. And in place of nations and their narratives that exclude by attempting to define who belongs, Danticat's writing communicates that "art . . . unites whereas tyranny separates."[56] In different ways, she is rewriting the ideas of what it means to be American and Haitian, creolizing both and offering a counternarrative to national myths rejected by the public. For many of the same reasons I have discussed, Danticat's art along with global literatures written in French may also be destabilizing French state narratives and corresponding discourses. As in other nations, Françoise Lionnet writes that "the traditional model of democratic belonging and the exceptionalism of French cultural and linguistic universalism continue to be in crisis, as indeed they have been for more than twenty-five years."[57] Perhaps these crises indicate a time for major shifts in thinking and acting. These times speak to transformation, a time when so many people around the world see no other option but migration, to take their loved ones and whatever belongings they can carry, and walk, sail, or swim to safety and opportunity. Nongovernmental organizations (NGOs), more than nation-states, have taken the lead in aiding the untold multiplicity on the move today. Adopting the term "cellular" to describe the nimble and dynamic operations of NGOs, Appadurai strikes an optimistic note: "The coming crisis of the nation-state may lie not in the dark cellularities of terror but in the utopian cellularities of these other new transnational organizational forms."[58] And, perhaps, in the cellularities produced by artists, literatures, and their various forms. Although Appadurai is describing NGOs, in many ways art and literary texts, including those of Edwidge Danticat, may also be understood by the qualities of cellularity. As Danticat states: "The immigrant artist shares with all other artists the desire to interpret and possibly remake his or her own world."[59] This was Camus's call in 1957 after accepting the Nobel Prize in Literature. Camus found hope not in nations or borders but rather in the "solitary individuals whose deeds and works every day negate frontiers and the crudest implications of history."[60] Aware of their realities and shaping the eternally unfinished, these individuals continuously impel the artist in her work.

NOTES

1. Arjun Appadurai, *Fear of Small Numbers: An Essay on the Geography of Anger* (Durham, NC: Duke University Press, 2006), 6.

2. Appadurai, *Fear of Small Numbers*, 6.

3. Appadurai's research posits that these changes are associated with an increase in "large-scale, culturally motivated violence" (*Fear of Small Numbers*, 1).

4. Appadurai, *Fear of Small Numbers*, 22–23.

5. Edwidge Danticat, *Create Dangerously: The Immigrant Artist at Work* (New York: Vintage Books, 2011), 41.

6. Danticat, *Create Dangerously*, 42.

7. Danticat, *Create Dangerously*, 49.

8. Danticat, *Create Dangerously*, 49.

9. Danticat, *Create Dangerously*, 41.

10. Mimi Sheller and John Urry, "The New Mobilities Paradigm," *Environment and Planning* 38, no. 2 (2006): 207–26.

11. Danticat, *Create Dangerously*, 49.

12. Danticat, *Create Dangerously*, 49.

13. Danticat, *Create Dangerously*, 51.

14. Brian Russell Roberts and Michelle Stephens, "Archipelagic American Studies and the Caribbean," *Journal of Transnational American Studies* 5, no. 1 (2013): 8.

15. Jonathan Pugh, "Island Movements: Thinking with the Archipelago," *Island Studies Journal* 8, no. 1 (2013): 12.

16. Walter Mignolo, interview by Alvina Hoffmann, *E-International Relations*, January 21, 2017, https://www.e-ir.info/2017/01/21/interview-walter-mignolopart-2-key-concepts/.

17. Mignolo, interview by Alvina Hoffmann.

18. Danticat, *Create Dangerously*, 94.

19. Danticat, *Create Dangerously*, 91.

20. Danticat, *Create Dangerously*, 94.

21. Danticat, *Create Dangerously*, 94.

22. Danticat, *Create Dangerously*, 95.

23. Danticat, *Create Dangerously*, 95.

24. Danticat, *Create Dangerously*, 94.

25. Danticat, *Create Dangerously*, 95.

26. Danticat, *Create Dangerously*, 96.

27. Danticat, *Create Dangerously*, 175.

28. Danticat, *Create Dangerously*, 175.

29. Danticat, *Create Dangerously*, 177.

30. Danticat, *Create Dangerously*, 177.

31. Danticat, *Create Dangerously*, 177.

32. Elaine Stratford, Godfrey Baldacchino, Elizabeth McMahon, Carol Farbotko, and Andrew Harwood, "Envisioning the Archipelago," *Island Studies Journal* 6, no. 2 (2011): 122.

33. Édouard Glissant, "The Poetics of the World: Global Thinking and Unforeseeable Events," trans. Kate Cooper Leupin, Chancellor's Distinguished Lectureship Series, April 19, 2002, Louisiana State University, Baton Rouge, https://sites01.lsu.edu/wp/the glissanttranslationproject/2017/10/20/the-poetics-of-the-world-global-thinking-and -unforeseeable-events/.

34. Danticat, *Create Dangerously*, 5.

35. Danticat, *Create Dangerously*, 7.

36. Danticat, *Create Dangerously*, 7.

37. Danticat, *Create Dangerously*, 8.

38. Danticat, *Create Dangerously*, 9–10.

39. Édouard Glissant writes: "The language of the translator operates like Creolization and like Relation in the world. That is, its language produces the unforeseeable. Translation is a veritable operation of Creolization." Translated by and quoted in Sandra L. Bermann, "Édouard Glissant and the Imagination of World Literature: Relation, Creolization, and Translation," in *Writing and Translating Francophone Discourse: Africa, the Caribbean, Diaspora*, ed. Paul F. Bandia (Amsterdam: Rodopi, 2014), 80. The passage originally appeared in Édouard Glissant, *Introduction à une poétique du divers* (Paris: Éditions Gallimard, 1998), 45–46.

40. In the preface to her translations of Bengali poetry, Gayatri Chakravorty Spivak claims: "Translation is the most intimate act of reading." Gayatri Chakravorty Spivak, "The Politics of Translation," in *The Translation Studies Reader*, ed. Lawrence Venuti (London: Routledge, 2004), 398.

41. Danticat, *Create Dangerously*, 10.

42. Danticat, *Create Dangerously*, 10.

43. Danticat, *Create Dangerously*, 10.

44. Danticat, *Create Dangerously*, 10.

45. Danticat, *Create Dangerously*, 11.

46. Danticat, *Create Dangerously*, 148. This is from the essay "Acheiropoietos."

47. Danticat, *Create Dangerously*, 148.

48. Danticat, *Create Dangerously*, 148–49.

49. Danticat, *Create Dangerously*, 149.

50. Danticat, *Create Dangerously*, 10.

51. Danticat, *Create Dangerously*, 15.

52. Danticat, *Create Dangerously*, 15.

53. Danticat, *Create Dangerously*, 16.

54. Arjun Appadurai, "How Histories Make Geographies: Circulation and Context in a Global Perspective," *Journal of Transcultural Studies* 1, no. 1 (2010): 4–13, https://doi.org/10.11588/ts.2010.1.6129.

55. Albert Camus, *Create Dangerously*, trans. Justin O'Brien (London: Penguin Books, 2018), 13.

56. Camus, *Create Dangerously*, 28–29.

57. Françoise Lionnet, "Continents and Archipelagoes: From *E Pluribus Unum* to Creolized Solidarities," *PMLA* 123, no. 5 (October 2008): 1504.

58. Appadurai, *Fear of Small Numbers*, 137.

59. Danticat, *Create Dangerously*, 18.

60. Camus, *Create Dangerously*, 33.

Chapter Four

LÒT BÒ DLO AND THE SPATIAL RELATIONS OF DYASPORA

GWEN BERGNER

In *Create Dangerously*, Edwidge Danticat attests that writing and reading have been dangerous practices for Haitians living under the Duvalier dictatorships and subsequent authoritarian regimes. If you can be tortured, exiled, or even killed for reading and writing in "disobedience to a directive," then artistic practices have material effects.[1] That materiality drives the urgency of Danticat's own literary project to create dangerously for those who have sacrificed to give her voice—victims of Haitian political violence, migrants exiled from the homeland, relatives left behind in Haiti, and ancestors who paved the way. But what difference does her art make? How does it mediate Haiti's diasporic possibilities? Danticat suggests that in representing the voiceless, she more than memorializes the dead and exiled; she resurrects them. In this way, her aesthetic practice follows Haitian traditions such as the one performed by some families to call the spirits of the dead from *anba dlo*, under the water, so they may be reborn to occupy the trees, mountains, and grottoes of the Haitian landscape. This commemorative practice, she writes, "assures a transcendental continuity . . . that has kept us Haitians, no matter where we live, linked to our ancestors for generations" (175). By implication, Danticat also animates the ancestors and the exiles to ensure a transcendental continuity not only among the generations but also between Haitians in the homeland and those in the diaspora.

That Danticat simultaneously mediates across the time of the ancestors and the space of the diaspora makes sense, because the dead and the exiled are in the same boat. As she explains, the Kreyòl phrase *lòt bò dlo*, on the other side of the water, "can be used to denote the eternal afterlife as well as an émigré's eventual destination" (94). That is, the phrase *lòt bò dlo* refers to the ancestors' location in Ginen, or Africa, where Haitian tradition dating from the time of colonial slavery says they will return. It refers also to

Haitian migrants' location across the sliver of Caribbean Sea in the United States and Canada. Thus, *lòt bò dlo* takes Haiti as the point of reference and locates the dead and the exiled in relation to Haiti's island geography, Vodou epistemology, and the Atlantic history of slavery, revolution, and migration. *Lòt bò dlo* also locates Danticat's position as an immigrant artist "[c]reating fearlessly even when cast *lòt bò dlo*, across the seas" (148–49). Thus her aesthetic project aims to connect Haitians across the water, even as she herself must occupy one shore. In this sense, she experiences the paradoxical dynamic of simultaneous separation and connection that characterizes Haiti's diaspora. Taking direction from *Create Dangerously*, I use *lòt bò dlo* as a portal to explore Danticat's mediation of the Haitian diaspora in her migration short-story cycle *The Dew Breaker*.[2] In its collection of loosely linked stories of Haitian migrants to the United States, their US-born children, relatives left behind in Haiti, and returnees to the homeland, *The Dew Breaker* enacts the movement of bodies in the diaspora and explores the time-lag effects of memory and history.

In exploring Danticat's mediations among history, home, and dyaspora through the portal of *lòt bò dlo*, I heed recent calls from postcolonial critics to pay greater attention to environment and geography.[3] First, *lòt bò dlo* infuses what has become an overgeneralized notion of diaspora with meaningful historical, geographic, and cultural specificity.[4] Originating in the cross-cultural contact occasioned by Atlantic slavery and repurposed for contemporary patterns of migration, *lòt bò dlo* encapsulates transnational history in the vernacular. Second, *lòt bò dlo* counterbalances the critical tendency to celebrate the mobility, hybridity, and cosmopolitanism of the global migrant at the expense of the emplaced resident.[5] *Lòt bò dlo* locates the migrant from the resident Haitian's viewpoint, thereby defining diasporic identity in relation to the homeland rather than as deracinated cosmopolitanism. Third, *lòt bò dlo*, the other side of the water, simultaneously evokes (is)land and ocean, two geographic features that Atlantic studies scholars consider crucial to the ongoing project of worlding American studies. Following Caribbean writers such as Édouard Glissant, Kamau Brathwaite, and Antonio Benítez-Rojo, environmental postcolonialists reorient our global perspective to map the world as a series of culturally interlinked islands joined by ocean waters, a "terraqueous" globe.[6] This "repeating island" or "archipelagic" worldview decenters continental landmasses and equalizes the islands of the Global South conventionally seen as peripheral to modernity.[7] Locating the ancestors in Ginen and the migrants in North America, *lòt bò dlo* recognizes these archipelagic circuits of time and place to yield a specifically Haitian transnationalism.

Lòt bò dlo also resonates with the Caribbean concept of tidalectics. A term coined by Brathwaite, "tidalectics" refers to the repeating and mutually informing dynamic between land and sea, waves and shore.[8] This dynamic contests Western ideas of linearity and progress, instead emphasizing time as ebb and flow, place as flux and motion, and history as repetition rather than teleology.[9] Thus, *lòt bò dlo* references the tidalectic relationships between the living and the ancestors, the emplaced and the dyasporas,[10] and the histories of colonialism, revolution, and neoimperialism that underlie Haitians' return to Ginen and sojourns to the United States.

The nonlinear rhythms of tidalectics helps make sense of *The Dew Breaker*'s formal structure, its assemblage of "fragmented, fictionalized testimonies" of state violence under the dictators François "Papa Doc" Duvalier (1957–1971) and his son, Jean-Claude "Baby Doc" Duvalier (1971–1986), its "kaleidoscope" of diasporic subjectivities, and its lack of narrative closure.[11] In this light, the seemingly tangential connections among stories and characters indicate the global forces that shape transnational migration. Considering that Haiti's centuries of "slow violence"—in the forms of genocide, slavery, economic exploitation and embargo, occupation, dictatorships, environmental degradation, and epidemics of AIDS and cholera—erupt into US visibility only during peaks of political unrest or natural disaster, *The Dew Breaker*'s decidedly unspectacular, even detached tone counters this crisis mode and resists the "sentimentality and political moralizing" that is sometimes substituted for narrative drama.[12] Instead, *The Dew Breaker*'s tidalectic rhythms merge Haiti's island environment, Vodou traditions, and (de)colonial history into an epistemic perspective on migration.

Before turning to *The Dew Breaker*'s stories, I must explain further the materiality of history embedded in the archipelagic and tidalectic episteme indicated by the Kreyòl expression *lòt bò dlo*. *Lòt bò dlo* names a paradoxical (dis)connection that arises from the migratory patterns and cross-cultural contact of Haiti's history of Atlantic slavery traced through the Haitian belief that the souls of the dead reverse the Middle Passage and return to Ginen, or Africa. In Vodou tradition, the dead make this voyage to "the waters of the abyss below the earth" that hold the "Island Below the Sea."[13] These waters are the source of all life, the home of the *lwas*, the location of Ginen, and the repository of cosmic memory and wisdom.[14] The living access this spiritual realm through the crossroads, the point of intersection between the horizontal plane of the material earth the vertical plane of the heavenly and watery cosmos. Because of this communication between the intersecting worlds, the ancestors' spirits remain accessible to the living. Thus, Vodou practices are more than "ritual reenactments of Haiti's colonial past"; they mediate between the past and present for purposes of care and healing.[15] For this reason, Danticat writes that "in Haiti people's spirits never really die," despite the fact that "people were always dying" from political violence, curable diseases, and natural and man-made disasters.[16] Although she uses the word "spirits" to reference living Haitians' indomitable persistence in the face of suffering and disaster, she also means that the ancestors' spirits persist.

In referencing the souls of the dead as returned to Ginen, *lòt bò dlo* indicates how Haitian practices mediate the dislocating effects of Atlantic slavery. And in locating Ginen in the waters of the spiritual realm accessed through Vodou rituals, *lòt bò dlo* also mediates the contemporary biopolitics of death Danticat lists. In this way, *lòt bò dlo* folds Atlantic slavery into a Vodou episteme in which history has a materiality that shapes the present. We might extend this episteme from ancestors to émigrés, who also remain linked though physically separate from the homeland. As Danticat explains, "Haiti had nine geographic departments and the tenth was the floating homeland, the ideological one, which joined all Haitians living outside of Haiti, in the *dyaspora*" (49). Like the island below the sea, the imagined floating homeland of the dyaspora extends Haiti's geographic territory.

And, like the ancestors, the exiles require memorial art to sustain them. For this reason, Danticat compares the immigrant artist to the artists of ancient Egypt who memorialized the dead on tomb paintings and sarcophagi, not only to usher them into the next world but also to "keep things alive" (20). Like them, Danticat wants to "save lives," to create "as though each piece of art were a stand-in for a life, a soul, a future" (20). In keeping things alive, even saving lives, Danticat's art exhibits a "vibrant materiality"; it not only *represents* the dead and exiled but also *acts* on them, mediating across time (connecting the ancestors and the living) and space (connecting rooted and routed Haitians), through an aesthetics informed by the Haitian vernacular of Vodou, as well as by the mourning rituals of other cultures and artistic media.[17]

Danticat extends this analogy between immigrant art and ancient Egyptian memorials in *The Dew Breaker*'s first story, "The Book of the Dead." The title announces her book's similarity to the ancient Egyptian funerary text of that name, which is a loose collection of stories, told by many voices, that assists the dead through the underworld and into the afterlife.[18] The comparison suggests that the immigrant artist, ancient Egyptian sculptor, or Haitian who serves the spirits creates an assemblage that, in keeping things alive, sustains the connections between lives and afterlives, thereby mediating memory and history to affect sociopolitical relations on a larger scale. Moreover, "The Book of the Dead" concerns an immigrant artist's struggle to keep alive the spirit of an exile, thereby providing a fictional parallel to the craft essays in *Create Dangerously*.

In this first story, Ka, born in New York to Haitian parents, struggles to memorialize her father, though he is still alive, by sculpting him in wood. In her sculptures, she tries to capture this "quiet and distant man who only came alive" while viewing the ancient Egyptian artifacts of mourning at the Brooklyn Museum.[19] The ancient Egyptians remind him of Haitians because they "worshipped their gods in many forms, fought among themselves, and were often ruled by foreigners. The pharaohs were like the dictators he had fled, and their queens were as beautiful as [fictional Haitian American actress] Gabrielle Fonteneau. But what he admires most about the Ancient Egyptians is the way they mourn their dead" (12). Ka attempts to memorialize her yet-living father by sculpting him "the way [she] had imagined him" as a political prisoner in Haiti (6). As a second-generation immigrant, she approaches her emotionally distant father by re-creating in sculpture his traumatic experience in Haiti, a place she has never been. In this way, her art stands in for the man who died in Haiti, who flickers to life only when he views the Egyptian monuments to death that live on in the Brooklyn Museum. The story figures in Ka's sculpture Danticat's own artistic project of remembering the dead to sustain the living.

But Ka is wrong about her father, and the mistaken identity of the man in Ka's sculpture suggests the pitfalls of this project. The past will be misremembered, the family stories told wrongly, the immigrant's view of Haiti from across the waters askew. Her father, she learns, is the titular Dew Breaker, a renowned former Tonton Macoute torturer now seeking anonymity in the United States. As she and her father travel through South Florida on their way to deliver the sculpture to a buyer, Gabrielle Fonteneau, he sinks it in "a man-made lake, one of those marvels of the modern tropical city, with curved stone benches surrounding a stagnant body of water" (15). In explaining why he dumped the sculpture in the lake, he starts with the origin of his daughter's name: "Ka" is the ancient Egyptian term for "the body's companion through life and after life. It guides the body through the kingdom of the dead" (17). In his second language of English, he says that "ka is like soul. . . . In Haiti is what we call good angel, ti bon anj. When you born, I look at your face, I think, here is my ka, my good angel" (17). In Vodou, the *ti bon anj* is that part of the soul that contains one's higher nature, moral compass, and conscience.[20] As his *ti bon anj* and memorial sculptor, Ka is ushering through the kingdom of the dead not a political hero but the man responsible for others' deaths. This is why he sinks the (mis)representation of himself below the stagnant, man-made waters, not to be recalled ever. The sculpture, the facsimile of her father's soul, is below the waters, *anba dlo*, in a man-made and stagnant facsimile of the abyss—not a source of life or repository of memory and wisdom.

Danticat signals the dislocation between the Haitian homeland and the alien land of the United States by comparing the artifice of South Florida's built environment to Haiti's ancestral environment of flowers, rivers, trees, and earth. As Ka and her father drive the next day to the actress's house to tell her that they do not have the sculpture, Ka "grow[s] tired of the fake lakes, the fenced-in canals, the citrus groves, the fan-shaped travelers' palms, the highway so imposingly neat," but her father "takes in the tropical landscape, as though he will never see it again" (27). Where Ka sees the artificially ordered Florida landscape, her father sees abundant tropical variety. He is happy to tour Gabrielle Fonteneau's[21] garden with its cultivated azaleas, hibiscus, dracaenas, and lemongrass—Haiti's flora reproduced in miniature. When the actress's mother says that they are fortunate to visit Haiti every year because "[t]here's nothing like sinking your hand in sand from the beach in your own country," Ka imagines that maybe her father "dreams of dipping his hands in the sand on a beach in his own country and finding that what he comes up with is a fistful of blood" (30). Though Ka's "bond to the land was sealed in blood through generations," it is not the blood of sacrifice she has imagined.[22] For this reason, she realizes, he finds the unfamiliar and artificial Florida landscape "comforting, rather than distressing" (34).

Ka's father tells her that he does not deserve to be memorialized in art, yet he has turned his daughter and wife into living memorials, "his kas, his good angels, his masks against his own face" (34). Ka must now bear the weight of her father's atrocities even as he credits her and her mother with redeeming him. This claim of redemption discomfits some critics, who have asked why Danticat lets the character voice it. I would suggest that the Dew Breaker represents the paradox of Haiti itself, the beloved homeland that generates courage and creativity but has failed to sustain so many of its people. The immigrant lives this contradiction of nostalgic love for the untenable homeland and guilty afterlife in exile. From this ambivalent side of the water, Danticat creates dangerously, recognizing, as does Ka, that we are "offered more choices than being either hunter or prey" (24).

If "The Book of the Dead" addresses the difficulty of reconstructing the intimate history of Haiti's political violence from the temporal and spatial remove of *lòt bò dlo*, the next story in the book, "Seven," explores how *lòt bò dlo*'s space-time (dis)continuum affects intimacy between those on both sides of the water. The story centers on the reunion of a husband and wife, separated for seven years while the husband sought an economic foothold in New York and the wife remained in Haiti. The wife finally traverses the geographic space of the Caribbean to arrive on the other side of the water, but the couple cannot close the temporal gap of seven years. Danticat explores the effect of this tidalectic disjunction between husband and wife, contrasting the proximity of their bodies in the Brooklyn cityscape with the sea of silence that separates them.

In New York's material geography, migrants' identities shift under the pressures of dislocation, the necessity of work, and the continuity of political violence. The circuits of the husband's New York life present a Caribbean immigrant's community map.[23] His daily travel is restricted to narrow routes of work, rest, and leisure and set against the backdrop of racism past and present. He shares a basement apartment with two other Haitian immigrants in a house owned by the Dew Breaker, now a mild-mannered barber (the tenants are unaware of his past as a Macoute). From there he travels between two jobs as a janitor, a day job at King's County Hospital and a night job at Medgar Evers College. Before his wife's arrival, he sometimes went to a local club frequented by other immigrants, but "they hadn't gone much since . . . a Haitian man named Abner Louima was arrested there, then beaten and sodomized at a nearby police station."[24] The husband tells his roommates never to mention the club or "those women who'd occasionally come home with him . . . most of whom had husbands, boyfriends, fiancés, and lovers in other parts of the world" (38). The points of interest on this map connect histories of violence against Black people in the United States—Medgar Evers, the civil rights activist slain in 1963, and Abner Louima, the Haitian immigrant victim of police brutality in 1997. And the immigrants suspend their intimate relationships from home—fiancé, husband, wife—as they seek provisional connection in the multinational diaspora.

"Seven" shifts point of view between husband and wife, and the disorientation occasioned by traveling *lòt bò dlo* becomes apparent when the wife arrives on a flight bringing gifts from the soil and kitchens of Haiti that reflect a still largely agrarian, subsistence farming and cottage labor economy—which a US Customs agent cursorily discards. The agent "unwrapped all her gifts—the mangoes, sugarcane, avocados, the grapefruit-peel preserves, the peanut, cashew, and coconut confections, the coffee beans, which he threw into a green bin" (40). Stripped of her gifts, the wife walks through the airport until "suddenly she found herself before a door that slid open by itself, parting like a glass sea" (40). She may not have traveled by boat, but the sea-like sliding glass door signals that she has arrived on the other side of the water.

When they arrive at the apartment, the husband responds to the wife's obvious disorientation with words of reassurance, but she replies only that she is thirsty. She gulps down the water he brings "as though she hadn't drunk anything since the morning he had gotten on the plane and left her behind" (43). The next day, when he leaves her to go to work, she listens to a radio station broadcasting in Haitian Kreyòl and writes to a neighbor back in Haiti, a man in whose arms she had collapsed in grief when her husband left. He also had brought her a revitalizing glass of water, but she had "swallowed so much water so quickly that she vomited" (48). The neighbor had become her lover even as he assured her that she and her husband must really love each other to have "the courage to abandon the present for a future one could only imagine" (48). The two water-drinking passages join moments of painful separation between the husband and wife, the first when she is in Haiti and he in New York and the second when they are physically together in New York yet still separated by their years apart. On both occasions she drinks as if to consume all the water that separates them, because it "is sometimes impossible even for those of us who are on the same side of *lòt bò dlo* to find one another."[25]

Although the space between husband and wife has closed, the jet lag remains. On the weekend, they visit Prospect Park, an "immense garden" where the husband had earlier gone on his own "to ponder seasons, lost time, and interminable distances."[26] They each, separately, remember how during carnival in Jacmel, a seaside town in Haiti, they had participated in a ritual where couples cross-dress, the man as the bride and the woman as the groom, and go through the streets in disguise asking strangers to marry them. However, they had not cross-dressed when they had played this game; she "had disguised herself as the bride and he as the groom, forgoing the traditional puzzle" (52). Now, thinks the wife, they could walk the streets of Brooklyn "performing their own carnival" because their identities as wife and husband feel like disguises (52). After seven years apart, they are disguised even to themselves and each other.

Just as "Seven" ends with husband and wife unable to bridge their years apart, "Water Child" is also about what cannot be spoken between loved ones across the water. The story's central character, Nadine, is a nurse in Brooklyn who sends the bulk of her paycheck each month to support her elderly parents in Haiti—parents who had "sacrificed everything" to send her to New York for the nursing career she had imagined would allow her independence and the chance to see the world (63). But their sacrifice had only reversed their roles, giving her "the chance to parent them rather than have them parent her" (63). Her parents write letters on fragile airmail paper expressing their need for more money and a wish to hear her voice on the telephone, but Nadine does not call because "her voice might betray all that she could not say" (57). Nadine's silence and despair resist the progressive teleology of the immigrant success story; her minimal financial security in the United States forecloses rather than opens the doors of opportunity, even as it allows her to support family in Haiti.

In New York, Nadine's social relations are mediated through technology. She avoids people generally, leaving her television on as her "way of bring-ing voices into her life that required neither reaction nor response" (56). Her telephone answering machine brings another recorded voice into her apartment, that of Eric, "her former beau, suitor, lover, and the near father of her nearly born child" (56), who now calls once a month to say hello.[27] Just as Nadine carries with her their letters but will not call her parents, she also preserves but does not answer Eric's messages. Rather, she removes the microcassette from the machine and places it on an altar she has created to memorialize the lost relationship with Eric and also their aborted child, whom she represents with a pebble in a glass of water meant to approximate a Japanese shrine to unborn children "where water was poured over altars of stone to honor them" (57). The altar, the airmail paper and microcassettes, the television—all disembodied voices, the proxies for Nadine's dematerial-ized, alienated life.

To underscore the theme of lost voices, Nadine works in an ear, nose, and throat department with patients who have had total laryngectomies. In her inability to speak, Nadine understands the frustration and despair of Ms. Hinds, a now voiceless twenty-five-year-old patient and teacher. Ms. Hinds introduces Nadine to her parents, who have come to take her home, but in this she is unlike Ms. Hinds because she no longer enjoys the care and protection of her parents. Nevertheless, she wishes she could call them "to be reassured now and then that some wounds could heal, and some decisions would not haunt her forever" (63). Yet when she does call, her mother tells her anxiously not to wait too long to find a boyfriend, because "[y]ou don't want to be old alone" (64). Nadine cannot tell her of Eric. Like Ms. Hinds, who will one day forget the sound of her own voice, Nadine no longer knows hers. As the eleva-tor doors close on Ms. Hinds and her parents, Nadine is left thinking "of her parents, of Eric, of the pebble in the water glass in her bedroom at home, all of them belonging to the widened unrecognizable woman staring back at her from the closed elevator doors" (68). As the doors close on her own future, she mourns her parents' lost water child as well as her own.

Like Nadine's collection of second-hand voices, writing from the dias-pora is once-removed from the source, the homeland. In *The Dew Breaker*'s stories, the sterile built environment of the United States contrasts with Haiti's material environment, which serves as an "archive in the absence of written records."[28] The story "Night Talkers," set in Haiti, demonstrates the importance of "the land as ancestral claim," as archive of memory and family history.[29] This story also has a counterpart essay in *Create Dangerously*, in which Danticat explains that her own ancestral land in Haiti anchors a family dispersed through migration. In "Walk Straight," she recounts a pilgrimage to visit her Tante Ilyana, "who is the last close family member still living in Beauséjour," everyone else having migrated to Port-au-Prince or out of Haiti.[30] She climbs the steep and rocky mountain to her aunt's house, remembering similar hikes from her childhood "collecting dandelions as we passed the gardens of people who had known our father and grandfathers when they were our age, people who called us by the names of our aunts and uncles, people of whom there is no longer any trace" (23). The landscape is inseparable from her memories of the people who held the memories of her ancestors, who remain now only in a small cemetery. Sitting at her great-grandparents' mountain grave, she laments the "many separations in our family, constant departures and returns" that cannot be avoided because "they have earned us whatever type of advancement we have made" (35). Within these diasporic tidalectics, Tante Ilyana's "vocation is nothing less than to maintain our family's physical legacy, to guard a very small house in the ancestral village, to sustain a faraway world to which we could return, if we wanted to, and find traces, however remote and faint, of who we are" (38). Danticat provides this material legacy for her character Dany in "Night Talkers," representing Haiti "as a site where the dead are animated and ancestral connections are enabled through the natural world."[31]

In "Night Talkers," Dany makes a similar pilgrimage from the United States to visit his aunt in Haiti. He wants to ask if a man he has seen in New York—the Dew Breaker—is the one who killed his parents twenty-five years earlier, during the dictatorship. Like Danticat, Dany struggles to traverse the mountainous countryside, finally reaching his aunt's house "in a valley between two lime-green mountains and a giant waterfall, which sprayed a fine mist over the banana grove that surrounded her one-room house and the teal ten-place mausoleum that harbored the bones of many of her forebears."[32] The social relations within this detailed landscape are integral to material life in Haiti and "bestow agency and identity on those subjects for whom global mobility is not an option."[33] The whole community knew his aunt and his parents; they welcome Dany with dishes of food brought to his aunt's house. When his aunt dies a few days after his arrival, the community helps Dany with customary funeral arrangements.

The tidalectics of migration impact the rhythms of tradition as the community absorbs the return of several troubled young Haitian American men "sent back" even though they are ignorant of Haiti's land, culture, and language.[34] Dany's aunt had introduced him to one of these men so they could speak "one American to another," but Dany thinks he has little in common with Claude, who killed his own father while high on drugs (96). However, Dany comes to realize that Claude, who is able to voice his regret for having killed his father, can teach him how to grieve the loss of his parents. Whereas Dany is a "palannit," or "night talker," who can speak of his parents' deaths only in his nightmares, Claude is "able to speak his nightmares to himself as well as to others" (120). As an immigrant writer, Danticat also speaks the nightmares aloud—guilty for having left, and able to testify precisely because she did, and returning often to walk the mountains and visit the graves that provide a material environment for the ancestors, a "cartography of history and memory."[35]

Migration dislocates the exile from Haiti's material environment, the repository of family memory and national history. With her writing, Danticat documents that dislocation even as she provides through art the "rivers and streams" that "shelter and return souls" of the ancestors and exiles.[36] We see this restorative literary landscape in The Dew Breaker's tidalectic structure that recounts the (dis)connections of dyaspora through metaphors of water. The Dew Breaker sinks his daughter's commemorative sculpture in a stagnant and man-made Florida lake, a wife gulps glasses of water as if to eliminate the distance between herself and her distant husband, and a solitary woman in Brooklyn makes a memorial to her aborted child and foreclosed future using a drinking glass of tap water. With this aqueous language, Danticat "echoes" the voices on both sides of the water that are usually obscured by "popular discourses of race, immigration, and American mobility."[37] But water here is more than symbolic; it houses the spirits of the ancestors and the exiles, indicating how the material environment shapes the experience of home and migration.

NOTES

Note on the chapter title: Dyaspora *is the Kreyòl for diaspora.* Lòt bò dlo *is a Kreyòl expression denoting the location of those who have left Haiti through death or emigration.*

1. Edwidge Danticat, *Create Dangerously: The Immigrant Artist at Work* (New York: Vintage Books, 2011), 11. Subsequent references are given in the text.
2. Edwidge Danticat, *The Dew Breaker* (New York: Vintage Books, 2005).
3. In addition to the critics cited below in this chapter, see, for example, the call for essays for a new Modern Language Association volume on "the rising field" of postcolonial

environmental literature and media (Cajetan Iheka, "MLA Teaching Postcolonial Environmental Literature and Media," Call for Papers, Modern Language Association, October 21, 2018, https://call-for-papers.sas.upenn.edu/cfp/2018/10/21/cfp-mla-teaching-postcolonial-environmental-literature-and-media).

4. See George B. Handley, "Toward an Environmental Phenomenology of Diaspora," *Modern Fiction Studies* 55, no. 3 (Fall 2009): 649.

5. See Alison Donnell, "What It Means to Stay: Reterritorialising the Black Atlantic in Erna Brodber's Writing of the Local," *Third World Quarterly* 26, no. 3 (2005): 479.

6. See Margaret Cohen, "Literary Studies on the Terraqueous Globe," *PMLA* 125, no. 3 (May 2010): 658.

7. See Brian Russell Roberts, "Archipelagic Diaspora, Geographical Form, and Hurston's *Their Eyes Were Watching God*," *American Literature* 85, no. 1 (March 2013): 123.

8. Kamau Brathwaite, *ConVERsations with Nathaniel Mackey* (New York: We Press, 1999), 34.

9. Elizabeth M. DeLoughrey, *Routes and Roots: Navigating Caribbean and Pacific Island Literatures* (Honolulu: University of Hawai'i Press, 2009), 2.

10. In Kreyòl, *dyaspora* refers to anyone who has emigrated.

11. See Marion Christina Rohrleitner, " 'Breaking the Silence': Testimonio, Revisionary Historiography, and Survivor's Guilt in Edwidge Danticat's *The Farming of Bones* and *The Dew Breaker*," *Interdisciplinary Humanities* 28, no. 1 (2010): 75, 79; and Jo Collins, "Between Worlds: Imagining *Dyaspora* in Danticat's *The Dew Breaker* and Chancy's *The Spirit of Haiti*," *Ariel* 42, nos. 3–4 (2012): 131.

12. Rob Nixon, "Neoliberalism, Slow Violence, and the Environmental Picaresque," *Modern Fiction Studies* 55, no. 3 (Fall 2009): 445, 449.

13. Maya Deren, *Divine Horsemen: The Living Gods of Haiti* (New York: McPherson, 1988), 46.

14. Deren, *Divine Horsemen*, 35.

15. Joan Dayan, *Haiti, History, and the Gods* (Berkeley: University of California Press, 1998), xvii.

16. Danticat, *Create Dangerously*, 176.

17. For a theory of "vibrant materiality," see Jane Bennett, *Vibrant Matter: A Political Ecology of Things* (Durham, NC: Duke University Press, 2010). In *Create Dangerously*, Danticat discusses the influence of "many cultural and geographic traditions" on her and other Haitian and Haitian American artists (133). Thus, she recognizes the fluidity and syncretism of Haitian art and culture, even as she honors and celebrates the traditions of Vodou.

18. "*Book of the Dead*," Wikipedia, https://en.wikipedia.org/wiki/Book_of_the_Dead, accessed June 21, 2018.

19. Danticat, *The Dew Breaker*, 13. Subsequent references are given in the text.

20. Deren, *Divine Horsemen*, 26.

21. Her name means "fountain of water."

22. Bharati Mukherjee, "Immigrant Writing: Changing the Contours of a National Literature," *American Literary History* 23, no. 3 (Fall 2011): 681.

23. See Brenda Parker, "Constructing Community through Maps? Power and Praxis in Community Mapping," *Professional Geographer* 58, no. 4 (November 2006): 470–84.

24. Danticat, *The Dew Breaker*, 38.

25. Danticat, *Create Dangerously*, 94.

26. Danticat, *The Dew Breaker*, 51.

27. Nadine has seven microcassettes with messages from Eric, the same number as years Eric had spent apart from his wife in Haiti and whose arrival in the United States, as described in "Seven," likely occasioned his breakup with Nadine.

28. Donnell, "What It Means to Stay," 482.

29. Donnell, "What It Means to Stay," 482.

30. Danticat, *Create Dangerously*, 23.

31. Anissa Janine Wardi, "The Cartography of Memory: An Ecocritical Reading of Ntozake Shange's *Sassafrass, Cypress & Indigo*," *African American Review* 45, nos. 1–2 (Spring–Summer 2012): 140.

32. Danticat, *The Dew Breaker*, 93.

33. Donnell, "What It Means to Stay," 484.

34. Danticat, *The Dew Breaker*, 100.

35. Wardi, "The Cartography of Memory," 140.

36. Danticat, *Create Dangerously*, 177.

37. Wilson C. Chen, "Narrating Diaspora in Edwidge Danticat's Short-Story Cycle *The Dew Breaker*," *Literature Interpretation Theory* 25, no. 3 (2014): 220. For the political significance of water in "Monkey Tails," see Collins, "Between Worlds," 134.

BIBLIOGRAPHY

Bennett, Jane. *Vibrant Matter: A Political Ecology of Things*. Durham, NC: Duke University Press, 2010.

Brathwaite, Kamau. *ConVERsations with Nathaniel Mackey*. New York: We Press, 1999.

Chen, Wilson C. "Narrating Diaspora in Edwidge Danticat's Short-Story Cycle *The Dew Breaker*." *Literature Interpretation Theory* 25, no. 3 (2014): 220–41.

Cohen, Margaret. "Literary Studies on the Terraqueous Globe." *PMLA* 125, no. 3 (May 2010): 657–62.

Collins, Jo. "Between Worlds: Imagining *Dyaspora* in Danticat's *The Dew Breaker* and Chancy's *The Spirit of Haiti*." *Ariel* 42, nos. 3–4 (2012): 121–41.

Danticat, Edwidge. *Create Dangerously: The Immigrant Artist at Work*. New York: Vintage Books, 2011.

Danticat, Edwidge. *The Dew Breaker*. New York: Vintage Books, 2005.

Dayan, Joan. *Haiti, History, and the Gods*. Berkeley: University of California Press, 1998.

DeLoughrey, Elizabeth M. *Routes and Roots: Navigating Caribbean and Pacific Island Literatures*. Honolulu: University of Hawai'i Press, 2009.

Deren, Maya. *Divine Horsemen: The Living Gods of Haiti*. New York: McPherson, 1988.

Donnell, Alison. "What It Means to Stay: Reterritorialising the Black Atlantic in Erna Brodber's Writing of the Local." *Third World Quarterly* 26, no. 3 (2005): 479–86.

Handley, George B. "Toward an Environmental Phenomenology of Diaspora." *Modern Fiction Studies* 55, no. 3 (Fall 2009): 649–57.

Iheka, Cajetan. "MLA Teaching Postcolonial Environmental Literature and Media." Call for Papers, Modern Language Association, October 21, 2018. https://call-for -papers.sas.upenn.edu/cfp/2018/10/21/cfp-mla-teaching-postcolonial-environmental -literature-and-media.

Mukherjee, Bharati. "Immigrant Writing: Changing the Contours of a National Literature." *American Literary History* 23, no. 3 (Fall 2011): 680–96.

Nixon, Rob. "Neoliberalism, Slow Violence, and the Environmental Picaresque." *Modern Fiction Studies* 55, no. 3 (Fall 2009): 443–67.

Parker, Brenda. "Constructing Community Through Maps? Power and Praxis in Community Mapping." *Professional Geographer* 58, no. 4 (November 2006): 470–84.

Roberts, Brian Russell. "Archipelagic Diaspora, Geographical Form, and Hurston's *Their Eyes Were Watching God.*" *American Literature* 85, no. 1 (March 2013): 121–49.

Rohrleitner, Marion Christina. "'Breaking the Silence': Testimonio, Revisionary Historiography, and Survivor's Guilt in Edwidge Danticat's *The Farming of Bones* and *The Dew Breaker.*" *Interdisciplinary Humanities* 28, no. 1 (2010): 73–85.

Wardi, Anissa Janine. "The Cartography of Memory: An Ecocritical Reading of Ntozake Shange's *Sassafrass, Cypress & Indigo.*" *African American Review* 45, nos. 1–2 (Spring–Summer 2012): 131–42.

Part II

Welcoming Ghosts:
Memory and Historicity

Chapter Five

WRITING AMERINDIAN AYITI

Edwidge Danticat's Reclaimed Memory and Shifting Homes

ERIKA V. SERRATO

In this chapter, I argue that Edwidge Danticat effectively initiates the diaspora into Haiti's national imaginary via a first-person representation of the
Amerindian cacica Anacaona. In *Anacaona: Golden Flower* (2005), Danticat
puts the cacica's life in historical context and relays the historical figure's
subversive message to subsequent generations. I bring to the fore the ways
the author weaves Amerindian origin stories and historical accounts into
larger Haitian histories and experiences. Danticat remains rooted in Haiti,
her native country, and her writings encompass issues regarding life there
and the experiences of the diaspora. *Anacaona: Golden Flower*, as a text
meant for young audiences, inculcates the reader into Haiti's history and
foundational myths regarding Hispaniola's autochthonous populations.

HISTORICAL ANACAONA

The island known today as Hispaniola was once divided into six independent
domains: Marien, Maguana, Magua, Xaraguá, Higuey, and Ciguayo (Tyler
1988, 7).[1] These provinces or *cacicazgos* were led by caciques, or supreme
chiefs or leaders. William F. Keegan writes that the "identification of *caciques*
was crucial for the Spanish conquest" (2013, 73). The anthropologist explains
that focusing on a few individuals allowed the Spaniards to "extract tribute"
in an expeditious manner (73). Keegan details the importance of focusing
their attention: "At the time of the Spanish conquest, two *caciques* (Caonabó
and Behecchio), allied through marriage, are reported to have been paramount *caciques* (*matunherí*) that together ruled most of Hispaniola" (73).
Wedged and invisibilized by Keegan's two commas and the punctuation of

Caonabó's and Behecchio's reigns ("allied through marriage"), Anacaona became the most powerful cacica on the island. Although female leaders were not rare cases in Taíno society (in fact, power was passed on matrilineally),[2] the historical crossroads in which she lived render Anacaona a memorable figure.[3] Anacaona, sister to Behecchio, ruler of Xaraguá, and wife to Caonabó, ruler of Maguana, came to lead half of the island following their deaths.

Edwidge Danticat's *Anacaona: Golden Flower* centers around the eponymous cacica and her coming of age. Her narrative takes place throughout the region of what is now Haiti and tells her life story from before the rite of passage that marked her entrance into womanhood up to the attack on the Spanish fort La Navidad, once she is wife to Caonabó, cacique of Xaraguá, and mother to their child. The narrative unravels the unsettling, inexplicable changes preceding, during, and following the profound break in Anacaona's understanding of the world upon contact with Spanish conquistadores. Danticat's Anacaona articulates her experiences, projects her place in history, and illustrates the major cultural shift in the Caribbean and, by extension, the rest of the so-called New World.

An overview of *Anacaona: Golden Flower*'s compelling paratext sheds light on the elements of the text and its didactic role vis-à-vis its young readers. *Anacaona: Golden Flower* is, after all, a book intended for young readers. Narratives intended for younger audiences impart stories and histories—both fiction and nonfiction—that initiate the young individual into a larger collective identity. In speaking about the history of African American children and young adult literatures, specialist Giselle Liza Anatol writes:

> Biographies allow writers of children's books to imaginatively recreate the past, to teach valuable lessons about bravery, determination, or overcoming fear or anger; to show that brown skin is not solely about the stereotypical media images of rural poverty or urban plight but rather about succeeding against all odds. Biographies can help African American youth to "develop a sense of kinship with their black forebears, letting them know that they do not stand alone," just as they can give the reader a chance "to become deeply involved in the lives of other black people in ways not possible in face-to-face contact." (2011, 624)[4]

I draw a parallel between Francophone Caribbean and African American literatures due to historical similarities including but not limited to shared loss of ancestral land and history, slavery, a history of cultural and economic subjugation, and general marginalization vis-à-vis an institutional power. Danticat provides an example of Anatol's statement regarding biographic narratives. Readers have the opportunity to identify with the characters' fears and be inspired by their bravery.

As I will show, Danticat sets up readers' kinship and attachment not only with "their black forebears," as with Anatol's examples, but *also* with those who inhabited the island long ago. Anacaona's diary entries are followed by "Life in Haiti in 1490," a section that includes a "Historical Note," "Anacaona's Family Tree," "Other Notable Taíno Leaders," five pages of ancient and contemporary renderings of Taíno life, and a "Sample of Taíno Words." The reader's knowledge of Anacaona's life is not only "verified" by official historical information but also supplemented by cultural snippets. Access to extradiegetic information allows the reader to connect a character already carrying her personal investment to historical veracity of Amerindian life. Danticat renders Anacaona as a historical figure whose experiences arrive at the reader via her own physicality. Her inscriptions speak to her reader and bear the weight of their legacy.

WRITING AS ARCHAEOLOGICAL DEVICE

Danticat tackles the dilemma of writing and recording this particular historical character's story before the narrative even begins in an "Author's Note": "Unlike most other young women of the Royal Diary series, Anacaona did not read or write and would not have kept a diary in the traditional sense of written accounts of her daily life. Anacaona's Taíno people, however, had many other ways of recording things crucial to them" (Danticat 2005, 3). Scholastic's Royal Diaries series showcases the stories of major historical figures who held a royal place within their societies and has a geographic and temporal range from the Nile's Cleopatra, France's Eleanor of Aquitaine, Russia's Catherine the Great, Angola's Nzingha, and India's Jahanara Begum to Hawaii's Ka'iulani and beyond. All the books from the Royal Diary series follow the literary device of a diary or epistolary novel. The reader encounters the royal figure's voice as a first-person narrator. The absence of script writing in Amerindian recording practices in the Caribbean poses a unique problem in creating a diary narrative in Danticat's book. Danticat addresses the significance of "areitos"—performances in both danced and spoken form—in a culture that lacked writing in the traditional sense of the word.

Danticat's hints at other, visual possibilities of communication become explicit further down in the "Author's Note": "Even though the Taínos had no written language, they had petroglyphs—rock paintings and pictographs through which they kept records of their lives" (3). Danticat tells the reader about the existence of petroglyphs and other ways of recording indigenous existence onto the natural world. The lack of writing presents yet another layer of unattainability to already obfuscated pre-Columbian history. Creating narratives based on unofficial history and the visual remnants Amerindians left behind allows authors like Danticat to create a story within an imagined reality of a culture that no longer exists, at least not in its past form. Danticat addresses the predicament of writing about those who did not write in the section following the main narrative, entitled "About the Author":

> Even though the Taínos had no written language . . . they had images and symbols through which they told their stories. I see this diary as a series of images and symbols that could have been put away by a storyteller like Anacaona to be interpreted later. Taíno artifacts are being discovered all the time. With each piece found, the story of the Taíno people gets more and more specific, more and more defined. (180)

Danticat imagines the possibility of an Anacaona who inscribes "a series of images and symbols" much like those that have been found throughout the Caribbean. Her vision extends to the optimism Jacques Derrida describes in "Archive Fever in South Africa" (2002), where he articulates the human hope that we might one day attain a more complete story of those no longer with us and whose detailed daily lives may be housed in an as-of-yet inaccessible archive. Danticat forges Anacaona's life story along the same lines. The main character's first entry details how she is able to record her days. Young Anacaona writes that her uncle and preeminent cacique Matunherí's weaver, Cuybio, has created a papyrus-like cloth on which she can record her stories:

> Cuybio has found a way to blend cotton buds into a hard fabric on which I can record my stories, ballads, and some other knowledge that is important to our people. He has seen me many times carving symbols on the plaza walls outside the temple and has remarked that he must find yet another manner for Matunherí's niece, one of Xaraguá's possible future rulers, to record these symbols. (5)

Much like Cuybio's blended cotton-bud creation, Danticat heeds the imperative to "find yet another manner" to convey Anacaona's experience.[5] She entwines the aforementioned "series of images and symbols" into the Western practice of journal writing. Danticat converts petroglyphs—the Caribbean's sole physical remainders of Amerindian existence—into a recording device on which Anacaona can voice her thoughts and from which the reader can access Amerindian life.[6]

Danticat's cognizance of the obfuscation of Haiti's Amerindian past and her receptiveness to its restoration evoke Martinican writer and philosopher Édouard Glissant's pronouncement in *Caribbean Discourse* on the need to explore, meditate, and write about the past:

> The past, to which we were subjected, which has not yet emerged as history for us, is, however, obsessively present. The duty of the writer is to explore this obsession, to show its relevance in a continuous fashion to the immediate present. This exploration is therefore related neither to a schematic chronology nor to a nostalgic lament. It leads to the identification of a painful notion of time and its full projection forward into the future, without the help of those plateaus in time from which the West has benefited, without the help of that collective density that is the primary value of an ancestral cultural heartland. That is what I call *a prophetic vision of the past*. (Glissant 1989, 63–64)

Conquest, genocide, slavery, and assimilation effectively produced a past that is "not-quite-history" throughout the Caribbean. Officially recorded history can be read, reviewed, and analyzed from various perspectives. The loss of atavistic languages, customs, and beliefs suspends in the air those whose ties were cut by the colonial project, be it through conquest, slavery, or both. The void that is nonhistory, suggests Glissant, becomes a space that must necessarily be explored, for it is only what could have been that will give insight into what might be today. It is this "prophetic vision of the past" that compels Caribbean writers. I understand this compulsion to write about the past and ponder its details to be a practice that allows the author to gain a deeper understanding of how history is made and lost, and how we arrive at the present moment. Danticat looks into an even more oblique space of nonhistory, one that relies on a few inscriptions and long-buried artifacts. Creating narratives necessitates conjuring the existence of both concrete lived experiences and individual characters as well as surmising what could have happened.

Writing biographical accounts from the position of historical knowledge and temporal distance creates an inverse phenomenon of Glissant's "prophetic vision of the past" whereby the characters foresee their cultural apocalypse. Authors such as Danticat voice and depict characters who unknowingly confront the beginning of their civilizations' ends. The reader encounters the characters' voices in the ever present. That is, reading animates characters as they remain unaware of what will come to pass. Our authors, however, write from a position and knowledge of *futur antérieur* in which the characters' life-changing adventures and extraordinary accomplishments have expired from the timeline of both author and reader. It is precisely the death of the original, pre-Columbian culture that birthed their characters that opens the space of certain death and vague historicity. I suggest that Danticat, in writing from a position of those who will come to know death, places the objects of her writing into an unsettled, haunting position from which to contemplate the end of their world. Danticat's text manifests this concept, which I call premonitory history, throughout the story. At the same time, conjuring their civilization betrays mourning and the inclination to be a part of their world. In this sense, Danticat refuses to recognize the Caribbean's loss of its autochthonous inhabitants.

Danticat's Anacaona has premonitory visions, dreams, and the eerie sensation that certain things will come to pass throughout her life. These sensations are sometimes aesthetic additions for the sake of the story, as when she sees two pairs of footprints on the sand and later realizes that they announce her uncle's passing and her pregnancy (Danticat 2005, 105). More often than not, however, these sensations are related to the figure's historically accurate death, her husband's, or her people's. The rite of passage that commemorates her womanhood, for example, involves her uncle and tribe leader cutting off her hair with a sharp object:

> For a moment I feared my uncle's hands would tremble and he would let the blade fall on my neck. Then I had one of those sensations that the ancestors might be speaking to me, and what they seemed to be telling me was that I might be in a situation like this again one day, but in that future moment something painful might be done to my neck. (27)

The character expresses the fear of a neck pain reminiscent of the Spaniards' hanging of the historical Anacaona. In a more explicit reference, she has a nightmare of being taken away by the Kalinas, an enemy tribe whose practices are to "pillage and steal" and who also prepare the reader for the Spanish invaders. Anacaona writes in her diary: "None of my dreams has frightened me as much as the one of the Kalinas taking me away, tying a rope around my neck, and hanging me from a tree" (50). Later, in Marién before the attack against the Spanish fort, Anacaona will see local men "hanging from trees near the plaza walls, the bodies dangling above our heads" (142).

These foreshadowing nightmares give the young reader a glimpse of history, for Anacaona does not die within her narrative. Danticat's reader peers at the edge of history but is not thrown over altogether.

Having access to Anacaona's thoughts and emotions humanizes the historical figure in the eyes of the young reader. The reader witnesses Anacaona's formative experiences, including violence and life-threatening events. It is interesting to note that Danticat's characters conform to the tradition of Amerindian self-immolation and suicide, as documented by early chroniclers. Spanish Friar Bartolomé de las Casas, for example, writes that Amerindians, desperate to stop the many abuses they suffered at the hands of the Spaniards, resorted to suicide and taking the life of their loved ones.[7] I suggest, however, that Danticat's text imbues her characters with a complexity unseen in earlier texts such as Las Casas's. This is especially clear in texts where others inflict violence. Las Casas's description of the brutal retaliation on Anacaona and her people displays pathos.[8] He emphasizes that such cruelty could not have been merited by what he considers meek beings.[9] Whether Las Casas's affect constitutes a necessary rhetorical device to appeal to Prince Philip of Spain's graces or a genuine interest in Amerindian well-being, it nonetheless materializes as a subdued representation of voiceless subjects, effectively turning them into objects devoid of agency. By comparison, Danticat's Anacaona wonders to herself about other characters' emotional states, their thought processes, and asks them directly about their own experiences and suffering. Danticat's incorporation of Anacaona's interlocutors makes her diary a plurivocal artifact of Amerindian realities. Anacaona writes of her deceased grandmother and of the enemy Kalinas taking away women, alluding to but not quite putting into words the intimation of their sexual abuse. Her older brother Behechio's first wife Yaruba cannot bear her homesickness, which is compounded by the fact that she has become pregnant.[10] She takes her own life by ingesting "poisonous juices from the yucca roots" (44). Behechio sinks into depression, and Anacaona wonders what he might do: "He does not talk, but simply looks at the sea. I am so afraid for him. I fear that he will throw himself in the sea" (47). Guamayto, her powerful uncle's first wife, wishes to adhere to the custom of being buried with her husband and poisons herself during his wake. Anacaona expresses the difficulty in communicating the loss of her countrymen's limbs and lives: "How do I begin to describe what I have seen on Marién?" (141). Anacaona's writing in her diary despite the suspension of disbelief of writing in a predominantly oral and pictographic culture conveys Danticat's compulsion to impart the stories of autochthonous Haiti and her attempt to concretize the intangible loss.

READING AS WITNESSING

Reminiscent of Glissant's "Mais cela n'est rien encore" in *Poétique de la relation*,[11] Danticat's Anacaona attempts to grapple with the annihilation and plundering before her (Glissant 1990, 17). Glissant contemplates the unfathomable experience of the Middle Passage. Each step of the way—from kidnapping to disembarkation—presents an insurmountable feat and an awesome request of our mind's understanding of the events. Anacaona endures a version of Glissant's speculative "Supposez, si vous le pouvez" (Glissant 1990, 17). Her gradual discovery of a massacre pushes her ability to process the events:

> Caonabó kept saying the word *tuob* [gold] to the pale men. And as we marched up a trail toward the mountains, I felt as though I was suddenly journeying to an uncertain place. All around us, burial plots had been dug up, bones thrown aside, and golden objects removed from sacred soil. Nearby, a pregnant woman lay dead, her still bulging belly leaning slightly away from her body. Corpses were strewn all along our path, heads separated from bodies. The body of one dead child was leaning against a post, as if he had been carefully hooked there. (Danticat 2005, 148)

Anacaona relays seeing bodies dangling from trees as her group heads toward the epicenter of the massacre that catalyzes the Amerindian attack on Fort La Navidad. The images of hanging bodies prepare the young reader for the nearing and increased violence, but they prove to be potent on their own. Danticat's text provides yet another instance of premonitory history. The image conjures "strange fruit hanging from the poplar trees" for a US audience.[12] Danticat fuses the history of hangings and lynchings on US soil with the violence perpetrated against Native peoples of the Caribbean. The image becomes a crystallized memory and takes root on two soils, blending the descendant of the African enslaved person with the Native person of the Americas, who could be one and the same.

While the reader makes multiple historical connections, Anacaona soon finds herself disassociating from the event before her, as if she were "suddenly journeying to an uncertain place." Danticat presents the violent dismemberment displayed in Las Casas's account as a first-person traumatic event. The arrival of the Spaniards and their search for gold brings with it a palpable tear in the order of things: plots dug up, bones out of place, golden objects out of sacred soil, ripped wombs, dismembered heads—the world is unraveled. Anacaona's straightforward account describes the horrid scene without Las Casas's affective fragmentation. The brunt of the event produces a reaction in the reader akin to Anacaona's: another place from which to experience veiled witnessing. Danticat writes from the position of she who sees, processes, remembers, and can speak to a would-be posterior reader. This technique not only humanizes but also imbues Anacaona's tale with a sense of concrete loss. In this sense, Danticat's vocal or, rather, transcribed appropriation of Anacaona becomes a loss from within seeking to correct Las Casas's chronicle from without. Danticat herself reports having a personal stake in writing Anacaona's story: "'My mother was born in Léogâne,' she [Danticat] says, referring to a Haitian town that is generally thought to have been at the center of Xaraguá, where Anacaona ruled. 'Thus in some very primal way, Anacaona has always been in my blood and I remain, in the deepest part of my soul, one of her most faithful subjects'" (Danticat 2005, 180–81). Danticat communicates an elemental attachment to Anacaona, one that surpasses an acknowledgment of the Amerindian cacica's role in history: bloodline and lineage via the inheritance of land.

Danticat's "prophetic vision of the past" interpolates contemporary Haitians into Anacaona's life. Her death, however, remains a distant fact, as the reader does not witness her demise. I suggest that Danticat purposefully ends her tale in an encouraging sense. Following their attack on Fort La Navidad—a place whose colonizers' name for it is never employed—Anacaona and her fellow group leaders retell the story and rejoice in their victory. Anacaona, already known for her areitos, takes particular delight in telling an extended story. She explains:

> I told such a lengthy tale because I did not want our battle with the pale men to become the only story our people would ever recite from now on. For we had other stories, too, happy as well as sad ones. Our encounter with the pale men was only a small piece of that story. Surely an important piece, but not the most important. (155)

Anacaona justifies her insistence on including details both big and small to those listening, because they should have access to the events that took place. In particular, her telling "such a lengthy tale" forces the listener—and reader—to take in a longer narrative that includes the characters' daily existence and formative experiences beyond the attack they have perpetrated against the Spaniards. She makes this explicit later on, when remarking on the magnitude of this particular achievement:

> Yes, I want our victory over the pale men to be a tale that will inspire
> us when we have other battles to fight, one that reminds us that, like
> the Kalinas, we are a strong and powerful people. I do want it to be
> a story whose veracity the young ones will ask me to confirm when
> I am an old woman, a story that my Higuamota [her daughter] will
> tell and retell to her own children. But I do not want it to become the
> only story we ever have to share with one another. It cannot be. It
> must not be. (155–56)

Anacaona wishes their triumph over "the pale men" to be a source of inspiration for future generations. Her wanting to remind her people about their
would-be ancestors' winning qualities ("we are a strong and powerful people") carries the marks of history. The contemporary reader—particularly
one of Haitian descent, like the author herself—would hear the thunderous
echo of such a statement, for it evokes Haiti's eventual fight for independence
from the French beginning in 1791 and the US invasion in 1915.[13]

Anacaona's tragic yet uplifting words resonate: "It cannot be. It must not
be," writes Danticat about the possibility of this tale being "the only story
we ever have to share with one another." Anacaona's minute recording of
this protracted areito—a performance that necessarily requires both voice
and body—compounds the magnitude of this message. The character ges-
ticulates and vocalizes the story of her people and their fateful encounter
with the invaders. Anacaona's words and body join a series of events that
will indeed come to pass and become inscribed in history. The veracity of
her statement proves to be a double-edged sword that cuts across history
and arrives before the reader. It is thanks to this tale that knowledge of her
existence survives. The attack on Fort La Navidad and the ensuing acts of
resistance undertaken by Anacaona and the other leaders become determi-
nant for the history of the island and the succeeding generations. Danticat's
Anacaona: Golden Flower takes part in the resistance of forgetting ("It cannot
be. It must not be"), and yet the cacica's fears foreshadow the foundational
and rallying role of her story.

CONCLUSION

Danticat writes about Anacaona while she herself is removed from Haiti.
Her uprooting compels her to arrive at the most primordial of origins.
The paradigm that is Anacaona puts her in a synecdoche-like position in

which Anacaona means a history of violence and resistance. In *Anacaona: Golden Flower*, Danticat attempts to unearth Amerindian life via Anacaona's writing. The author hopes that we may know more details about Hispaniola's Native inhabitants. Until then, she colors in the silhouette of individuals' lives with thoughts and emotions that succeed in humanizing history for the text's young readers. The scriptural voice Danticat lends to Anacaona is particularly edifying. The author notes the unique experience of the female ruler—a fact either underexplored or ignored by most male authors. Danticat fashions a curious, fearful, yet brave Anacaona. The character cares about her child and her people's future but is defined by neither qualities reminiscent of Mother Nature nor her attractiveness and fertility.

Writing Amerindian stories for children and young adults allows Danticat to initiate young readers into an exploration of pre-Columbian and unofficial history. She renders visible and lends a voice to the cultural remains of Amerindian peoples in the Caribbean. History necessarily leads to the present. *Anacaona: Golden Flower* illustrates the ways in which Danticat muddles and binds the Caribbean's Amerindian past with that of African descendants, as Danticat declares feeling connected to Anacaona thanks to her being born in the place the leader once ruled.

Danticat does not exhaust her interest in exploring Haiti's past and the construction of its present in *Anacaona: Golden Flower* or any other single text. I would like to use this space as a coda to advocate for the fertile ground of Amerindian history and influence within Danticat's oeuvre, Haitian studies, and the literature of the Caribbean diaspora. Danticat scaffolds her oeuvre with references and allusions to Haiti's first inhabitants. The travel narrative *After the Dance* (2002a), for example, focuses on Jacmel's carnival celebrations, and yet Danticat pauses and includes Taíno and Arawak histories and past celebrations into today's cultural landscape, effectively relaying a palimpsestic view of Haiti's cultural narrative. Her early essay "We Are Ugly, but We Are Here" (1996) epitomizes her most pressing questions and compulsions. The piece is brief but powerful. She sets raw yet elegant and seamless parameters of thought, touching a range of topics from history and politics to family myths and national events. Danticat writes of an "endless circle" whereby "the daughters of Anacaona" remember each other's having been there (141). Their existence, contributions, joy, and suffering are acknowledged and kept alive by remembrance. Distance, a shifting "here," is not a negative or even an important element. This is evidenced by Danticat's inclusion of her grandmother—who incidentally first told her the story of

Anacaona—and her belief that "if a life is lost, then another one springs up replanted somewhere else." Replanting somewhere else, then, is part of the circle itself.

NOTES

1. The spelling of Amerindian names and places may change from author to author. I reproduce the spelling of the author whose writing or argument I examine at any given moment.

2. For more information concerning inheritance and succession, see José R. Oliver's "Believers of Cemíism" (Oliver 2009, 6–42).

3. "Despite this traditional division of labor among the sexes, many scholars believe that Taíno society was quite egalitarian and that women chiefs were not uncommon" (Figueredo and Argote-Freyre 2008, 3).

4. Anatol quotes Carol Jones Collins, "African-American Young Adult Biography: In Search of the Self" (1994, 1).

5. Françoise de Graffigny's 1752 *Lettres d'une Péruvienne* (original publication in 1747) seems to be a clear subtext of Danticat's *Anacaona: Golden Flower*. Graffigny's epistolary novel follows Zilia's journey from Peru to France and, more importantly, her desire and attainment of knowledge, namely writing. The young woman "writes" to her would-be future husband Aza via "quipos," weaved knots, a traditional form of communication. Like Danticat's Anacaona, Zilia leaves the actual transmission for a later date and focuses instead on recording her impressions of both daily life and momentous events.

6. As the word's Greek origin indicates, a petroglyph is a carving or inscription (*glyph*) on a rock (*petro*).

7. "Once all the inhabitants of this island found themselves in the same hopeless predicament as had those on Hispaniola—that is, they were either enslaved or foully murdered—some began to flee into the hills while others were in such despair that they took their own lives. Men and women hung themselves and even strung up their own children. As a direct result of the barbarity of one Spaniard (a man I knew personally) more than two hundred locals committed suicide, countless thousands in all dying this way" (Las Casas 1992, 29–30).

8. "All the others were massacred, either run through by lances or put to the sword. As a mark of respect and out of deference to her rank, Queen Anacaona was hanged. When one or two Spaniards tried to save some of the children, either because they pitied them or perhaps because they wanted them for themselves, and swung them up behind them on to their horses, one of their compatriots rode up behind and ran them through with his lance. Yet another member of the governor's party galloped about cutting the legs off all the children as they lay sprawling on the ground. The governor even decreed that those who made their way to a small island some eight leagues distant in order to escape this bestial cruelty should be condemned to slavery because they had fled the carnage" (Las Casas 1992, 22).

9. "I would go further. It is my firm belief that not a single native of the island committed a capital offence, as defined in law, against the Spanish while all this time the natives themselves were being savaged and murdered" (Las Casas 1992, 23).

10. The character's name immediately brings to mind both the Nigerian ethnic group Yoruba as well as the religious beliefs that became part of the Caribbean landscape following the arrival of enslaved peoples. Anacaona's diary entries tell us that her sister-in-law Yaruba is from a relatively distant but long-standing and familiar tribe, and not part of any African group (who do not arrive for the duration of the diary). I have not come across texts that refer to Behechio's individual wives, much less the story of one named Yaruba. Danticat's inclusion of the character suggests not only creative license but also a nod to the Yoruba people, religion, and language group.

11. "*Imagine, if you can*, the swirling red of mounting to the deck, the ramp they climbed, the black sun on the horizon, vertigo, this dizzying sky plastered to the waves. Over the course of more than two centuries, twenty, thirty million people deported. Worn down, in a debasement more eternal than apocalypse. *But that is nothing yet*" (Glissant 1997, 5–6, my emphasis).

12. "Strange Fruit," lyrics by Abel Meeropol under the pseudonym Lewis Allan, performed by Billie Holiday.

13. For more information regarding Haiti's history, see Dubois 2012.

BIBLIOGRAPHY

Anatol, Giselle Liza. 2011. "Children's and Young Adult Literatures." In *The Cambridge History of African American Literature*, edited by Maryemma Graham and Jerry W. Ward Jr., 621–54. Cambridge: Cambridge University Press.

Collins, Carol Jones. 1994. "African-American Young Adult Biography: In Search of the Self." In *African-American Voices in Young Adult Literature: Tradition, Transition, Transformation*, edited by Karen Patricia Smith, 1–29. Metuchen, NJ: Scarecrow Press.

Danticat, Edwidge. 1996. "We Are Ugly, but We Are Here." *Caribbean Writer* 10: 137–41.

Danticat, Edwidge. 2002a. *After the Dance: A Walk through Carnival in Jacmel, Haiti*. New York: Vintage Books.

Danticat, Edwidge. 2002b. *Behind the Mountains*. New York: Orchard Books.

Danticat, Edwidge. 2005. *Anacaona: Golden Flower*. New York: Scholastic.

Derrida, Jacques. 2002. "Archive Fever in South Africa." In *Refiguring the Archive*, edited by Carolyn Hamilton, Verne Harris, Jane Taylor, Michele Pickover, Graeme Reid, and Razia Saleh, 38–80. Dordrecht: Kluwer Academic Publishers.

Dubois, Laurent. 2012. *Haiti: The Aftershocks of History*. New York: Picador.

Figueredo, D. H., and Frank Argote-Freyre. 2008. *A Brief History of the Caribbean*. New York: Facts on File.

Glissant, Édouard. 1989. *Caribbean Discourse: Selected Essays*. Translated by J. Michael Dash. Charlottesville: University Press of Virginia.

Glissant, Édouard. 1990. *Poétique de la relation*. Paris: Éditions Gallimard.

Glissant, Édouard. 1997. *Poetics of Relation*. Translated by Betsy Wing. Ann Arbor: University of Michigan Press.

Keegan, William F. 2013. "The 'Classic' Taíno." In *The Oxford Handbook of Caribbean Archaeology*, edited by William F. Keegan, Corinne L. Hofman, and Reniel Rodríguez Ramos, 70–83. Oxford: Oxford University Press.

Las Casas, Bartolomé de. 1992. *A Short Account of the Destruction of the Indies*. Translated by Nigel Griffin. London: Penguin Books.

Oliver, José R. 2009. *Caciques and Cemí Idols: The Web Spun by Taíno Rulers between Hispaniola and Puerto Rico*. Tuscaloosa: University of Alabama Press.

Tyler, S. Lyman. 1988. *Two Worlds: The Indian Encounter with the European, 1492–1509*. Salt Lake City: University of Utah Press.

Chapter Six

INTERTEXTUALLY WEAVING A HOME-PLACE

Viewing the Past as Present in *Breath, Eyes, Memory* and *Untwine*

TAMMIE JENKINS

For centuries, Black writers have been searching for ways to document the lived experiences of their ancestors. They have engaged a variety of academic forums such as diasporic studies, genealogy, cultural studies, and analytical narrative inquiry in order to create alternative interpretations for past events using a present-day lens. Through these concerted endeavors, a group of authors laid a foundation for a literary tradition that mixes historical facts with fictionalized accounts in order to foster a style of storytelling. Authors such as Phillis Wheatley, Harriet Wilson, and Harriet Jacobs were among the first female writers to integrate historical facts, communal memories, and discourses of identity in their texts through first-person narrations, testimonials, and oral storytelling. They included a variety of mediums such as myths, legends, and folklore in an effort to open new spaces connecting past events to the present. These talented writers developed their works in order to bear witness to the lived experiences of their ancestors as well as those of other diasporic Black people. By passing on their knowledge of Black culture, social narratives, and family traditions to future generations, Wheatley, Wilson, and Jacobs adapted their storytelling to convey their familial and communal pasts as new discourses situated in their present.

In this tradition, Edwidge Danticat writes stories syncretized with her understanding of her ancestral and acquired narratives. A prolific writer and intellectual, Danticat draws on situated knowledge and factual evidence as sources of inspiration in her novels. Speaking textually with the embedded voice of her family and community, Danticat's texts portray the diasporic experiences of Black people, particularly women, in the New World. This is significant, because Black women's voices and experiences have often been ostracized in mainstream literary offerings. Following the conventions established by her historical and literary forbearers, in *Breath, Eyes, Memory* (1994) and *Untwine* (2015) Danticat writes stories that are intermingled with her understanding of Haitian culture, social narratives, and family traditions. These novels include Danticat's blending of situated knowledge, factual events, and Haitian folklore alongside fictionalized interpretations from her female characters. This chapter utilizes *Breath, Eyes, Memory* and *Untwine* to investigate how Danticat syncretizes Haitian culture, social narratives, and family traditions with Black diasporic discourses. Employing Robert E. Stake's explanation of case study "as the study of the particularity and complexity of a single case, coming to understand its activity within important circumstances," I examine *Breath, Eyes, Memory* and *Untwine* as fictional narratives written irrespective of fact.[1] By retelling stories from the past using a present-day lens, Danticat illustrates the role of intertextuality in the construction of identity.

I analyze the Caco family, specifically Grandmè Ifé and Martine, and the Boyer family, explicitly Giselle and Isabelle, in order to interpret how Black diasporic discourses are represented through these characters' lived experiences and social realities. Viewing *Breath, Eyes, Memory* and *Untwine* as storied texts containing factual occurrences, I consider Danticat's language use, word choices, accepted meanings, and reappropriated meanings through these characters. For that reason, I draw on James Porter's definition of intertextuality as "the bits and pieces of text a writer or speaker sews together to create new discourses," which provides me with an in-depth interpretation of how Danticat encodes these discourses in the novels.[2] The selection of intertextuality as my conceptual framework enables me to trace the underpinning narratives contained in *Breath, Eyes, Memory* and *Untwine*. Additionally, I deploy narrative analysis as my qualitative research methodology in order to evaluate how Danticat uses intertextuality in each novel to construct identity. I examine Grandmè Ifé, Martine, Giselle, and Isabelle as Danticat's literary elucidations of Black people's desire to learn their history, share memories, and construct a self-defined identity. I utilize relevant excerpts and references from these novels to consider how Danticat connects her characters to their ancestral past, while rewriting their present in ways that create their identity. In this chapter, I use the following guiding questions: In what ways does intertextuality establish a relationship between the past and the present through the characters of Grandmè Ifé, Martine, Giselle, and Isabelle? What are the overlapping (e.g., fictional and factional) stories that

Danticat presents in *Breath, Eyes, Memory* and *Untwine*? How are discourses of identity constructed in these novels?

PAST, PRESENT, INTERTEXTUALITY

The act of rewriting the past as a present-day discourse is an approach to literature for which intertextuality provides a foundation. The inclusion of fictionalized narratives and techniques derived from oral storytelling by Black authors is not a new phenomenon but has been a vehicle for passing on generational knowledge and preserving their culture and social narratives. Writers such as Zora Neale Hurston and Margaret Walker integrated these strategies with documented accounts in their novels in order to relay their lived experiences or those of other people in their texts. Books such as *Jonah's Gourd Vine* (1934) and *Jubilee* (1966) provide glimpses into the social realities faced by slaves and their descendants in the United States by reconceptualizing their experiences in the present. In *Breath, Eyes, Memory*, Danticat builds intertextuality by using storytelling to establish relationships between characters, their past, and current experiences. In analyzing the role of storytelling in Haitian culture among women, Nancy F. Gerber finds that such texts provide wisdom by passing on knowledge from one generation to the next.[3] This enables Danticat to employ intertextuality to reimagine her ancestral, familial, and communal stories through her characters' reiteration of the same narrative from multiple points of view.

The mixing of historical events or figures with fictionalized interpretations is a technique Danticat exerts in *Breath, Eyes, Memory* to enable her "characters to express and negotiate a different set of cultural expectations, while trying to reconcile the differences" between the two, as illustrated by Grandmè Ifé's and Martine's narratives of the Tonton Macoutes.[4] Using myths and Haitian history, Danticat re-creates stories of the Tonton Macoutes and Uncle Gunnysack, a bogeyman whose legend is exploited as a cautionary tale to frighten disobedient or unruly children. In the fictionalized version, the Tonton Macoute is described as "a scarecrow with human flesh" who brutally murders and devours the flesh of children.[5] However, this tale became reality during the presidencies of François "Papa Doc" Duvalier and later his son, Jean-Claude "Baby Doc" Duvalier, when their private militia, the Tonton Macoutes, were assembled to maintain law and order throughout the island nation.[6] The Tonton Macoutes under the Duvaliers were an all-male battalion who wore overalls, dark sunglasses, and straw hats as a representation of their fabled namesake. In reality, the Duvaliers' Tonton Macoutes were glorified criminals who murdered, tortured, robbed, physically abused, and sexually assaulted residents of Haiti, specifically those residing in rural areas. After a nearly thirty-year reign, the Tonton Macoutes were disbanded, but their existence and horrifying lore remain part of the history, culture, and narratives of the island's inhabitants.

The tale of the Tonton Macoutes is resurrected multiple times in *Breath, Eyes, Memory* as both a true and a fictionalized narration, depending on which character is telling the story. The first account of the violation of women by Tonton Macoutes is provided by Martine as she explains to her twelve-year-old daughter the circumstances of her conception and father-less birth. Martine states, "It happened like this. A man grabbed me from the side of the road, pulled me into a cane field, and put you in my body."[7] Martine appropriates the phrase "put you in my body" to replace the actual sexual assault trauma she endured at the hand of her rapist.[8] This narrative was oversimplified by Martine, possibly due to her daughter's age. However, the violence is stressed in the words "grabbed" and "pulled," indicating that a level of force was required by the perpetrator to ensure Martine's compliance.[9] Later, the history of the Tonton Macoute is revisited by Grandmè Ifé, who employs symbolism to retell Martine's sexual assault as a cautionary tale featuring a lark and a little girl to a group of young boys. Grandmè Ifé states that "a lark saw a little girl, who he thought was the most beautiful little girl he had ever seen, from the top of his pomegranate tree."[10] The lark introduces himself to the little girl and offers her a pomegranate, which she graciously accepts. The lark then asks her to leave her village with him, to which she initially consents before having second thoughts. The little girl is able to escape from the lark and return safely home, never to see him again. When Martine returns home following her ordeal, however, she is ostracized by her family and community. The unplanned pregnancy that results only furthers Martine's estrangement from her homeland, and she emigrates to the United States for a fresh start.

In Grandmè Ifé's narration, the Tonton Macoute who sexually assaulted Martine is the lark and Martine is the little girl. Although Martine was six-teen years old at the time of her rape, she embodied a naïve little girl persona, as she walked along the side of the road oblivious to her surroundings and its hidden dangers. Martine's brief lapse in judgment transformed her physi-cally and emotionally, at that moment, which enabled her to temporarily become her own Marassa. Like the lark, a Tonton Macoute saw a pretty girl that he wanted to possess even if only for a moment, and like Martine, the little girl initially resists. But the little girl briefly relents; Martine continues to struggle until she is physically bullied into compliance. The stories and realities of the Tonton Macoute are contrasted by Danticat with fictionalized accounts. This enables Danticat to situate the narratives of Grandmè Ifé and Martine as a present-day reality through encoded language and symbolic representations. Yet, vestiges of the Tonton Macoute remain embedded in both narratives for future generations.

In *Untwine*, Danticat presents the Boyer family, specifically the identical twins Giselle and Isabelle, in order to explore Haitian culture and social narratives. The Boyers are en route to an after-school event when another vehicle strikes their car, causing it to flip several times before hitting an embankment. The accident kills Isabelle. Awakening alone in a hospital room, Giselle is unable to speak or move, but she is able to share her memories as internal monologues through Danticat's narrative while drifting in and out of consciousness. Unable to express herself orally, Giselle mentally travels back to the accident and recalls that at the moment of impact, she and Isabelle were holding hands "the tightest [they had] ever held hands in [their] entire lives," just as they had done the day that they were born.[11] The words "tightest" and "held hands" demonstrate the lifelong interconnectivity that has existed between Giselle and Isabelle. Additionally, Giselle's realization that they were holding hands at the time of their birth as well as at the moment of impact during the accident reestablishes their relationship with the Marassa. Excavating the ways that Danticat ingrains narratives of yearning in her texts, Susana Vega-González finds that Danticat dislocates her characters' lived experiences by recentering them as longing remembrances embedded in their dialogical exchanges.[12] This enables Danticat's characters to convey overlapping multiplicitous narratives to the reader simultaneously as one continuous retelling of a single event or story. Featuring nostalgia as a form of intertextuality in *Untwine*, Danticat incorporates the Haitian Vodou *lwas*, specifically the Marassa, to represent the shared history of experience that exists between Giselle and Isabelle.[13]

During one of her streams of consciousness, Giselle describes how twins are viewed in Haitian culture. She states that "in some parts of Haiti, for example, twins were thought to have special powers, and if you didn't give them what they wanted, they could put a spell on you."[14] The belief that twins possess supernatural attributes is derived from Haitian Vodou mythology, specifically the Marassa. These deities are family-oriented spirits who are represented as identical children who are considered wise beyond their years. Although the Marassa number is perceived as two, there are actually three gods in the narrative of the Marassa, with one being the "*dosa* or the untwined one."[15] The Marassa in *Untwine* represent life, death, and rebirth. These are innate traits that Giselle experiences as she overcomes the loss of

her twin and heals herself. By examining Danticat's ability to rewrite familial and communal stories in her novels, Elvira Pulitano finds that Danticat
manipulates her characters' memories to develop their stories.[16] Employing
first-person narrations and internal dialogues, Danticat integrates Haitian
cultural scripts such as the Marassa in *Untwine*. These stories appear in
Giselle's testimonials documenting her past with Isabelle resituated into
her present-day context. Like *Breath, Eyes, Memory*, *Untwine* is filled with
spiritual narratives, yearning, and sentimental retellings.

Mythological narratives and symbolism in *Breath, Eyes, Memory* and
Untwine create counternarratives in which intertextuality breathes new life
into older Haitian cultural and social narratives. This enables Danticat to
merge recorded events with sacred wisdom in ways that strategically rein-
scribe the paradoxical relationship between past and present. Grandmè Ifé,
Martine, and Giselle each recite familiar stories from multiple points of view.
The use of intercharacter storytelling of the same narrative enables Danticat
to create spaces where discourses of yearning rupture history in ways that
situate their experiences between Haiti and the United States. This approach
to character development is present in the stories of the Tonton Macoutes
as well as that of the lark and the little girl. These cultural memories appear
in these texts in order to develop a contemporary world view.

COLLECTING MEMORIES . . . FINDING HIDDEN MEANINGS

The merging of different stories into a single narrative is an approach that
writers such as Myriam J. A. Chancy and Junot Díaz use to bridge past and
present discourses. Each draws on an aspect of the Marassa mythology to
articulate the lived experiences of their characters. For instance, Chancy's
The Loneliness of Angels traces the spiritual practices of her Caribbean-born
characters as they travel to other parts of the world. In Chancy's novel, the
Marassa appears in the hyphenated ethnicities adopted by her characters,
such as Ruth's designation as "Haitian-Syrian." This hyphenation demonstrates Ruth's duality while maintaining her ancestral markers of identity.
Conversely, Díaz's *The Brief Wondrous Life of Oscar Wao* details the life and
struggles of its protagonist, Oscar de León. Díaz incorporates the Marassa
in this story as an alter-ego of himself, which enables him to engage with his
readers as one or more of his characters. These authors reinvent the Marassa
as a consciousness allowing them to create stories and characters with dual-
istic underpinnings through overlapping, multivocal narratives. In *Breath,
Eyes, Memory* and *Untwine*, Danticat employs the Marassa to demonstrate

the "twinned nature" that exists in humankind.[17] This permits Danticat to parallel the lived experiences of her characters across these novels. Like her literary counterparts, in *Breath, Eyes, Memory* and *Untwine*, Danticat employs intertextuality to methodically place Haitian culture and social narratives in the stories her characters share with readers. Additionally, Danticat interpolates fragmentation to reappropriate language and accepted meanings in both texts in ways that enable her characters to articulate their narratives of lived experiences, while connecting their stories to their ancestral past, family customs, and spiritual heritage. Vega-González, by investigating Danticat's use of geographical fragmentation, determines that Danticat dislocates her characters' lived experiences in Haiti by resituating them in the United States.[18] In *Breath, Eyes, Memory*, Martine relives her sexual assault and unplanned pregnancy when she is reunited in New York with her daughter, Sophie, and her night terrors intensify when she visits Haiti. During Martine's stay in Haiti, she is plagued by nightmares that render her paranoid and distraught. Martine states, "Whenever I'm here, I feel like I sleep with ghosts."[19] Clearly, Martine is haunted by her past in Haiti, and her night terrors are a constant reminder of the sexual assault and trauma she endured as well as the ostracism she experienced as an unmarried, pregnant, teenage girl. Danticat's use of the words "sleep with ghosts" shows the interconnectivity that exists between Martine, Haiti, and her rapist.[20] The word "ghost" represents the social stigma Martine experiences and the spiritual aspects of Haitian culture and her family traditions. These narratives emerge through Martine's dreams and are reinforced by her memories of her sexual assault when she returns to Haiti.

Unlike Martine, Giselle's memories of Isabelle do not manifest as horrifying dreams but as a combination of fantasy and reality blended together from Giselle's perspective. Readers are never formally introduced to Isabelle but are provided with her narratives through the stories and monologues Giselle shares with them. In her dreams, Giselle situates Isabelle's existence in the past before moving her to the present. For example, Giselle states that "Isabelle would have been popular in the ancient world. Some great artist would have made a statue of her. In ancient Egypt, she would have been Nefertiti's friend. In ancient Greece, she would have been a Muse, a goddess of music."[21] Using the word "ancient," Danticat places Isabelle in the early days of humankind by connecting her to pillars of Western civilization such as Egypt and Greece. Throughout Giselle's monologues, Danticat endows Isabelle with attributes reserved for spiritual figures such as "muses" and "goddesses" as well as royalty such as Queen Nefertiti. From Giselle's description, Isabelle is reimagined as an inspirational person with a charismatic personality who makes those around her feel as if they were in the presence of greatness or the divine.

In her waking hours, Giselle relives her life with Isabelle by focusing on the unknown aspects of Isabelle's future. Giselle wonders "what Isabelle would be doing now if she were sitting in my place. Maybe she'd be vowing to go out and fight a way for me. Maybe she'd be losing it and yelling at everyone, asking them to leave. Her *fou ire* would have probably crushed this numbness I can't shake."[22] Giselle believes that Isabelle was the stronger of the two and desires her strength to "crush the numbness" or feelings of loss that she is experiencing.[23] During her waking hours, Giselle recollects Isabelle and resituates her in the past as a distant ancestor. In her dreams, Giselle juxtaposes Isabelle's narrative by contemplating how Isabelle may react to a given event. Although unspoken in Giselle's inventive realities, the presence of the Marassa remains a constant part of her memories of Isabelle. Giselle's dreams and fantasies reimagine the lived experiences of Isabelle by drawing on Haitian culture and social narratives. Through Martine's and Giselle's dreams and fantasies, Danticat provides readers with her characters' testimonials regarding past events as present-day discourses.

Grandmè Ifé and Martine, as well as Giselle and Isabelle, engage in diasporic conversations in which their intermingled histories create dialogue through revisionist storytelling derived from Haitian culture and social narratives. Investigating how diasporic Black peoples employ narratives of the past as discourses of the present, Paul Gilroy determines that diasporic texts transform cultural spaces in ways that are generational, communal, and political.[24] Gilroy concludes that these locations enable diasporic Black people to share their histories and rewrite their stories of lived experiences.[25] In like fashion, Danticat includes the Marassa in her novels to "reclaim [these] histories" and share them with her readers through the characters of Grandmè Ifé, Martine, Giselle, and Isabelle.[26] This enables Danticat to separate her characters' lived experiences and reposition them in the present while preserving them for future generations as a source of identity construction.

CONSTRUCTING A SELF THROUGH OTHERS

Relationships among Black writers, as well as between Black writers and the larger society, have been anchored in diasporic notions of a common history and similarities across lived experiences. These generational connections provide authors such as Samuel Delany, Toni Morrison, and Randall Kenan with access to their historical past through storytelling situated in the present. These authors have adopted a palimpsest approach to articulating their narratives in ways that "scrape off preconceived, predetermined external expectations, and the reinscription of self-definition" in order to retell their familial or communal stories.[27] Investigating the role of tradition in the construction of a Black diasporic identity, Gilroy finds that Black people draw on layered storytelling to re-create their fragmented history, culture, social narratives, and family traditions in an effort to establish their self-defined identities.[28] These authors, including Danticat, employ hyphenated, nonlinear storytelling, and space (e.g., physical; mental) to give their text a palimpsest world view using a contemporary lens. This is presented in *Breath, Eyes, Memory* and *Untwine* in ways such that Danticat resituates her characters' narratives between Haiti and the United States as discourses of the past revisited in the present as a source of their identity construction.

Using locatedness, Danticat uproots and transplants Haitian culture and social narratives as "deconstructive critiques of the world" in her narratives.[29] Danticat employs the act of naming to create identities in these novels, a technique in which hyphenated, epistemic, and "matrifocal" approaches rewrite the identity of her characters across multiple settings.[30] For example, Grandmè Ifé's name is a reappropriation of the Kingdom of Ife, a Yoruban polity located in present-day Nigeria and the place where humankind is believed to have originated. Meaning "love," Ife serves as a mother-line between Africa, Haiti, and the United States. Grandmè Ifé is "a wise woman, a seer, and a healer" who transmits familial and cultural histories to her descendants and her community through her storytelling.[31] This enables Danticat's characters to maintain their connection of Haitian culture and social narratives in which naming "represent[s] life and permanence in memory."[32]

Martine depicts the contentious nature of living between two worlds while constructing a self-defined identity. Each time Martine relives her rape, she loses her ability to define herself apart from this traumatic experience. Therefore, her identity is forever connected to her body's violation. We see this in her choosing the word "ghost" to describe how she feels when she returns to Haiti to visit; Martine's "ghosts" included the Tonton Macoute who raped her, her unplanned pregnancy, and her ostracism by her Haitian community. Eternally marred by her sexual assault, Martine's identity becomes one in which she is mentally imprisoned in the past, in which she is constantly victimized in her sleep and unable to truly live in her present. The legacy and ramifications of the Tonton Macoutes and their sexual assaults on women in Haiti contribute to the manner in which Grandmè Ifé reconstructs Martine's identity in her familial and communal relationships. Grandmè Ifé thus develops the story of the lark and the little girl who survives the encounter with the lark unharmed. In this context, Grandmè Ifé's identity becomes that of storyteller and transmitter of generational knowledge.

In *Untwine*, Giselle, like Grandmè Ifé, embodies the role of storyteller to construct not only her identity but also that of Isabelle through the sharing of internal and external memories, dreams, and fantasies with readers. Giselle interconnects her existence with Isabelle's; as a result, she experiences difficulty distinguishing herself from her "twindom."[33] Upon realizing that Isabelle is dead, Giselle endeavors to accept this fact while opting to fantasize about her sister's actions in the present. This is corroborated in the scenario in which Giselle wonders what steps Isabelle would take if their situations were reversed. As a result, in *Untwine* identity is a product of the relationship between Giselle and Isabelle, constructed through Giselle's memories and fantasies. Before the accident, their identities were those of twins with separate interests; afterward, however, their physical connection is severed, and Giselle is left to maintain their affiliation through imagination. By emphasizing duality in *Untwine* as a method of identity construction through the characters of Giselle and Isabelle, Danticat re-creates Haitian culture and social narrative through the Marassa. The presence of the divine twins reinforces the significance of creating a self-defined identity across contexts, which tasks Giselle with constructing her *dosa* in her family, community, and other social relationships.

Through first-person accounts and coming-of-age stories, Danticat blends semiautobiographical and imaginative retellings with Haitian culture and social narratives, creating transient boundaries and a subversive hybridity that deconstructs her texts by resisting dichotomous notions of homeland versus adopted land. In these novels, Danticat demonstrates the relationships among her characters, and between them and their communities and the larger society, by enabling Grandmè Ifé's, Martine's, Giselle's, and (by proxy) Isabelle's storytelling to navigate the ways in which their identities are constructed. This permits Danticat to apply her knowledge of Haitian culture and social narratives to interconnect her characters' ancestral past to discourses of identity in the present. In the tradition of Black diasporic authors, Danticat's novels create spaces that enable future generations to access their familial and communal past by deconstructing generational stories that have been handed down to them.

CONCLUSION

Black writers search for ways to document the lived experiences of their ancestors. Their incorporation of fictionalized accounts in their texts, which provide counternarratives for historical events, is an essential component in Black literary works. In some Black literature, authors of African descent retell the diasporic experiences of their ancestors and their descendants in the New World. Danticat shows the significance of remembering the past as present-day discourses. Blending generational narratives together in ways that interact and conflict with "tradition and modernity" in the present, Danticat "set[s] aside" these discourses "with the consequent implications of this process" using intertextuality and identity dynamics in her novels to share her Haitian culture and social memories with her readers.[34]

From *Breath, Eyes, Memory* to *Untwine*, Danticat uses post-memories in the form of dreams, fantasies, and oral storytelling to re-create her characters' narratives in ways that deconstruct and reconstruct their lived experiences from multiple points of view. In both books, Danticat introduces intertextuality as reimagined accounts of actual events resituated as fictionalized interpretations that are passed down as cautionary tales or expository narratives of lived experiences from one generation to the next. These renderings rely on the collective memories of each character through the stories that Danticat chooses for them to share with readers. Those provided by Grandmè Ifé, Martine, and Giselle give unique glimpses into the ways that Danticat constructs her characters' identities while enabling their storytelling to unpack the layers of their experiences across time, space, and retellings. Each character's narrative provides readers with a counternarrative regarding their past that is a retrospective interpretation of older stories situated in the present.

NOTES

1. Robert E. Stake, *The Art of Case Study Research* (Thousand Oaks, CA: Sage Publications, 1995), xi.

2. James E. Porter, "Intertextuality and the Discourse Community," *Rhetoric Review* 5, no. 1 (Autumn 1986): 34.

3. Nancy F. Gerber, "Binding the Narrative Thread: Storytelling and the Mother-Daughter Relationship in Edwidge Danticat's *Breath, Eyes, Memory*," *Journal of the Association for Research on Mothering* 2, no. 2 (November 2000): 188–99.

4. Isabel Valiela, "The Distorted Lens: Immigrant Maladies and Mythical Norms in Edwidge Danticat's *Breath, Eyes, Memory*," *Women, Gender, and Sexuality Studies Faculty Publications* 9 (July 2015): 1, https://cupola.gettysburg.edu/wgsfac/9.

5. Edwidge Danticat, *Breath, Eyes, Memory* (New York: Vintage Books, 1994), 137.

6. Michael J. Stevens, "What Is Terrorism and Can Psychology Do Anything to Prevent It?," *Behavioral Sciences and the Law* 23, no. 4 (July–August 2005); and Susana Vega-González, "Exiled Subjectivities: The Politics of Fragmentation in *The Dew Breaker*," *Revista Canaria de Estudios Ingleses* 54 (April 2007): 183.

7. Danticat, *Breath, Eyes, Memory*, 59.

8. Danticat, *Breath, Eyes, Memory*, 59.

9. Danticat, *Breath, Eyes, Memory*, 59.

10. Danticat, *Breath, Eyes, Memory*, 57.

11. Danticat, *Untwine* (New York: Scholastic, 2015), 7.

12. Vega-González, "Exiled Subjectivities." See also Richard L. Freishtat and Jennifer A. Sandlin, "Shaping Youth Discourse about Technology: Technological Colonization, Manifest Destiny, and the Frontier Myth in Facebook's Public Pedagogy," *Educational Studies* 46, no. 5 (September 2010): 506.

13. Ashley Greenwood, "Floating Roots: Diaspora and Palimpsest Identity in Danticat's *Breath, Eyes, Memory*," *Watermark* 7 (September 2013): 194.

14. Danticat, *Untwine*, 7.

15. Danticat, *Untwine*, 21.

16. Elvira Pulitano, "Landscape, Memory and Survival in the Fiction of Edwidge Danticat," *Anthurium: A Caribbean Studies Journal* 6, no. 2 (December 2008): 1–20.

17. Maya Deren, *Divine Horsemen: The Living Gods of Haiti* (New York: McPherson, 1985), 38.

18. Vega-González, "Exiled Subjectivities."

19. Danticat, *Breath, Eyes, Memory*, 192.

20. Danticat, *Breath, Eyes, Memory*, 25.

21. Danticat, *Untwine*, 25.

22. Danticat, *Untwine*, 25.

23. Danticat, *Untwine*, 265.

24. Paul Gilroy, *The Black Atlantic: Modernity and Double Consciousness* (Cambridge, MA: Harvard University Press, 1993), 192.

25. Gilroy, *The Black Atlantic*.

26. Greenwood, "Floating Roots," 193.

27. Greenwood, "Floating Roots," 193.

28. Gilroy, *The Black Atlantic*.

29. Greenwood, "Floating Roots," 191.

30. Greenwood, "Floating Roots," 191.

31. Gerber, "Binding the Narrative Thread," 191.

32. Vega-González, "Exiled Subjectivities," 63.

33. Danticat, *Untwine*, 4.

34. Gilroy, *The Black Atlantic*, 191.

BIBLIOGRAPHY

Assmann, Jan, and John Czaplicka. "Collective Memory and Cultural Identity." *New German Critique*, no. 65 (Spring–Summer 1995): 125–33.

Bragg, Beauty. "Edwidge Danticat's *Breath, Eyes, Memory*: Historicizing the Colonial Woman." In *Literary Expressions of African Spirituality*, edited by Carol P. Marsh-Lockett and Elizabeth J. West, 163–84. Lanham, MD: Lexington Books, 2013.

Brandon, George. *Santeria from Africa to the New World: The Dead Sell Memories.* Bloomington: Indiana University Press, 1997.

Danticat, Edwidge. *Breath, Eyes, Memory.* New York: Vintage Books, 1994.

Danticat, Edwidge. *Untwine.* New York: Scholastic, 2015.

Deren, Maya. *Divine Horsemen: The Living Gods of Haiti.* New York: McPherson, 1985.

Dunham, Katherine. *Island Possessed.* Chicago: University of Chicago Press, 1969.

Edith, B. Edna. "Rootlessness and Search for Self-Identity in Edwidge Danticat's *Breath, Eyes, Memory*." June 2018. http://www.tjells.com/article/255_EDNA.pdf.

Federmayer, Eva. "Violence and Embodied Subjectivities: Edwidge Danticat's *Breath, Eyes, Memory*." *Scholar Critic* 2, no. 3 (December 2015): 1–17.

Fernández Olmos, Margarite, and Lizabeth Paravisini-Gebert. *Creole Religions of the Caribbean: An Introduction from Vodou and Santería to Obeah and Espiritismo.* 2nd ed. New York: New York University Press, 2011.

Freishtat, Richard L., and Jennifer A. Sandlin. "Shaping Youth Discourse about Technology: Technological Colonization, Manifest Destiny, and the Frontier Myth in Facebook's Public Pedagogy." *Educational Studies* 46, no. 5 (September 2010): 503–23.

Fuchs, Rebecca. "Hiding and Exposing Violence: Euphemisms in Edwidge Danticat's *The Dew Breaker*." *L'Érudit Franco-Espagnol* 7 (Spring 2015): 51–65.

Funkenstein, Amos. "Collective Memory and Historical Consciousness." *History and Memory* 1, no. 1 (Spring–Summer 1989): 5–26.

Gabbin, Joanne V. "A Laying On of Hands: Black Women Writers Exploring the Roots of Their Folk and Cultural Tradition." In *Wild Women in the Whirlwind: Afra-American Culture and the Contemporary Literary Renaissance*, edited by Joanne M. Braxton and Andrée Nicola McLaughlin, 246–63. New Brunswick, NJ: Rutgers University Press, 1989.

Gerber, Nancy F. "Binding the Narrative Thread: Storytelling and the Mother-Daughter Relationship in Edwidge Danticat's *Breath, Eyes, Memory*." *Journal of the Association for Research on Mothering* 2, no. 2 (November 2000): 188–99.

Gilroy, Paul. *The Black Atlantic: Modernity and Double Consciousness.* Cambridge, MA: Harvard University Press, 1993.

Greenwood, Ashley. "Floating Roots: Diaspora and Palimpsest Identity in Danticat's *Breath, Eyes, Memory*." *Watermark* 7 (September 2013): 191–203.

Hewett, Heather. "Mothering across Borders: Narratives of Immigrant Mothers in the United States." *Women's Studies Quarterly* 37, nos. 3–4 (Fall–Winter 2009): 121–39.

hooks, bell. *Ain't I a Woman: Black Women and Feminism.* Boston: South End Press, 1981.

Kissel-Ito, Cindy. "*Currere* as Transformative Story Telling in Religious Education." *Religious Education* 103, no. 3 (June 2008): 339–50.

Matory, J. Lorand. "Surpassing 'Survival': On the Urbanity of 'Traditional Religion' in the Afro-Atlantic World." *Black Scholar* 30, nos. 3–4 (Fall–Winter 2000): 36–43.

McDowell, Deborah E. "'The Changing Same': Generational Connections and Black Women Novelists." *New Literary History* 18, no. 2 (Winter 1987): 281–302.

Morrison, Toni. *Playing in the Dark: Whiteness and the Literary Imagination*. New York: Vintage Books, 1993.

Moyano, Marcela. "Understanding the *Restavèk* Phenomenon in Haiti through Storytelling and Film." *International Relations and Diplomacy* 3, no. 2 (February 2015): 141–50.

Porter, James E. "Intertextuality and the Discourse Community." *Rhetoric Review* 5, no. 1 (Autumn 1986): 34–47.

Pulitano, Elvira. "Landscape, Memory and Survival in the Fiction of Edwidge Danticat." *Anthurium: A Caribbean Studies Journal* 6, no. 2 (December 2008): 1–20.

Ramsey, Kate. "Without One Ritual Note: Folklore Performance and the Haitian State, 1935–1946." *Radical History Review* 84, no. 1 (Fall 2002): 7–42.

Stake, Robert E. *The Art of Case Study Research*. Thousand Oaks, CA: Sage Publications, 1995.

Stanford Friedman, Susan. "Borders, Bodies, and Migration: Narrating Violation in Shauna Singh Baldwin and Edwidge Danticat." *mediAzioni* 6 (2009): 1–9.

Stevens, Michael J. "What Is Terrorism and Can Psychology Do Anything to Prevent It?" *Behavioral Sciences and the Law* 23, no. 4 (July–August 2005): 507–26.

Valiela, Isabel. "The Distorted Lens: Immigrant Maladies and Mythical Norms in Edwidge Danticat's *Breath, Eyes, Memory*." *Women, Gender, and Sexuality Studies Faculty Publications* 9 (July 2015): 1–11. https://cupola.gettysburg.edu/wgsfac/9.

Vega-González, Susana. "Exiled Subjectivities: The Politics of Fragmentation in *The Dew Breaker*." *Revista Canaria de Estudios Ingleses* 54 (April 2007): 181–93.

Willis, Susan. *Specifying: Black Women Writing the American Experience*. Madison: University of Wisconsin Press, 1987.

Wright, Janet. "Lesbian Instructor Comes Out: The Personal Is Pedagogy." *Feminist Teacher* 7, no. 2 (Spring 1993): 26–33.

Chapter Seven

UNTWINE

Navigating Memories through Healing and Self-Definition

SHEWONDA LEGER

> I often feel like I am writing for the teenage girl I once was, the one who
> was looking for herself in all kinds of books. That's why I tend to write
> about people who share my culture and heritage, characters who are like
> myself and family and friends, people who are in my life every day but
> who I don't see enough in literature.
>
> —EDWIDGE DANTICAT[1]

Edwidge Danticat's work as a fiction writer offers a sense of familiarity for
Haitian American girls.[2] Familiarity is a "shared space of dwelling in which
things emerge";[3] it is "shaped by the 'feel' of a space or by how spaces 'impress'
upon bodies."[4] Familiarity is a moment of not feeling alone or out of place.
Like Danticat, I am always searching for characters and scholars like myself.
Growing up, I was not exposed to Haitian American characters in literature
or to writers like Danticat. Reading *Untwine* brought a sense of home for me
because of cultural familiarity with Giselle's character. As I read this story
about a sixteen-year-old girl growing up in South Florida, I was able to revisit
my memories, because even if Giselle may be a fictional character imagined by Danticat, the places Giselle describes are familiar to young Haitian
American girls growing up in South Florida. *Untwine* is a young adult novel
that creates and opens moments of realities for Haitian American girls. The
imagery Giselle shares of sitting in I-95 traffic listening to her parents argue
make me remember sitting with my siblings in the back seat of our mother's
1998 Toyota 4Runner, while she and our dad argued. As Giselle navigates
her memories, I also navigate mine to reflect on my experiences growing up
Haitian American in North Miami.

The novel opens with the words "I remember," and the narrator continually echoes "I remember" throughout the novel, which shows that continuous
reflection is Giselle's way of responding to her recent traumas. When we
persistently reflect, we approach past experiences with fresh perspectives
that come from meditating on memories that then allow us to gain, define,
or make sense of past experiences and how they have or continue to influence our identities in the present. It is during these different moments of
healing and reflection that Giselle comes to learn how much of her identity
connects to Isabelle, her twin sister. Giselle's experience emphasizes how
reflection contributes to conceptions of identity, memory, the process of
recovering memories, and making sense of them. Often before coming to
terms with the identities we recognize and name ourselves, reflection allows
us to consider why, in particular moments, we take an interest in specific
identities. Furthermore, reflection allows us to revisit and make sense of
memories and how those moments have contributed to our self-definition
and who we may become.[5] In *Untwine*, Giselle cannot understand the value
of reflection until she is forced to ruminate while recovering.

Untwine tells the journey of how Giselle Boyer deals with the aftermath
of a fatal car accident. Partially comatose, in a state that allows her to hear
but not respond, Giselle discovers that Isabelle did not survive the crash.
She spends several days "trapped in the prison of her own body," reflecting on her memories in order to find ways of healing and determine what
it will mean for her to continue a life where she will no longer identify as
a twin. In her thoughts, Giselle says: "I know that I am not remembering,
but somehow seeing something that is happening somewhere else, without
me. Maybe this is like that levitating thing people talk about, that moving
towards the light. Except I am moving back towards my old life."[6] Giselle
"moving backward" is her navigating memories to find moments when
self-definition does not revolve around Isabelle. Giselle has experiences
as an individual, but her sister's presence did not allow many moments
when she could question these experiences to recognize identities separate
from Isabelle.

Giselle's trauma forces her to reminisce about past memories. Trauma
"marks the painful aftereffects of a violent history in the body and mind of
the survivor."[7] Giselle's trauma is not defined by the car accident but instead
by how she survives such violence to her body. Giselle's journey to survival
starts in the coma, where she has no choice but to reflect on and analyze her
memories to make sense of her individual identities. Giselle's memories serve
the function of transforming her traumatic experience to self-definition.
By and through reflection, Giselle removes the layers of her identity deeply

connected to identifying as a twin, only to piece these layers back together to make sense of her individual identity.

Giselle explains what it feels like to drift in and out of the coma, expressing that "under is now a dark empty space that I slip into when my mind wants to rest. When things become too difficult to process, I sink under."[8] Although Giselle cannot respond to the people around her when she is awake, those present in the room and their conversations influence which memories come to surface, and those are the memories she navigates when she drifts back into the coma. Giselle further conveys, "[W]hile I am under, I remember some things and not others. Under can be a blank space, like an empty sketch pad or canvas, or an empty room."[9] The voices of family, friends, and medical staff help Giselle to commence sketching on an empty sketch pad. The "empty sketch pad" is a metaphorical space where healing and the (re)construction of identity begin to take place for Giselle. The images that take shape on the canvas allow her to make meaning of past lived experiences that have contributed to her identities. The images that appear or begin to take form on the canvas are determined by how she makes meaning of her memories as she copes with her trauma.

The two defining moments Giselle reenters during her hospitalization are her experiences just before the car accident and during the car accident. By revisiting these two moments, Giselle allows grief to pass through her heart. Aurora Levins Morales depicts grief as a delicate state of existence, since "it is not possible to digest atrocity without tasting it first, without assessing on our tongues the full bitterness of it."[10] Levins Morales further conveys that we live in "a society that does not do grief well or easily, and what is required to face trauma is the ability to mourn, fully and deeply, all that has been taken from us. But mourning is painful and we resist giving way to it, distract ourselves with put-on toughness out of pride."[11] Here, Levins Morales describes what is required to face trauma: the ability to fully mourn what has been taken from us. Giselle cannot avoid addressing what has been taken from her while comatose—she must face her grief. Her moments of reflection force her to taste and mourn the pain of a life without Isabelle, because all her past memories include her twin.

Notions of healing are complex, as it is both an individual and a collaborative practice; there is no one way to define or understand the process of healing. Sitting with grief is one of many steps toward healing. We see this complexity drawn out in *Sisters of the Yam*, in which bell hooks dedicates space toward healing and looks at the ways Black women have attempted to make hurt disappear. She explains that "healing takes place within us as we speak the truth of our lives."[12] Giselle's sense of healing starts from her commitment to grasp what it means to survive in a world without Isabelle. She must find reconciliation in new memories that will not consist of Isabelle, as those of the past have.[13]

Untwine defines trauma, discomfort, reflection, and orientation as steps toward healing. These steps signify the stripping back of layers of our memories in order to emphasize how we make sense of identities we recognize through self-definition. My task in this analysis is to discuss the ways Danticat uses Giselle's story to interrogate the inevitable moments of healing that happen while experiencing trauma. First, I discuss how, when encountering unpredictable and uncontrollable moments in life, we often come to a place where we are forced to orient, disorient, and reorient. To rationalize how cycles of orientation are a repetitive process for living, surviving, and possibly healing, I build on Sara Ahmed's text *Queer Phenomenology: Orientations, Objects, Others*. Ahmed's ideas about how orientation helps readers conceptualize forms of discomfort force us to interrogate and look back at our experiences in order to understand how we interact with the present. I make connections to the ways discomfort can lead to action, such as questioning why at times our bodies may be out of place, which then forces us to take the necessary steps toward adapting and finding new ways to reorient within unfamiliar places. Second, I demonstrate how Danticat works through Giselle's trauma to discuss what happens when trauma leaves us with no choice but to reflect on past memories. Reflection as a process allows us to make our own meaning(s) of past experiences in order to create knowledge that supports identity construction and reconstruction. By piecing together these past memories, we identify and re-create layers that shape our identities on our own terms. Third, I proceed to conceptualize how Danticat's use of individual and historical narratives offers a more comprehensive picture of Haitian cultural identity. Further, I build on Toni Morrison's description of the novel to underline the need for more novels on Haitian American experiences. Haitian American practices, culture, history, and individual experiences survive through novels like *Untwine*. The novel entwines multiple Haitian American lived experiences, and these collections of stories get passed to future generations to help them understand their identities and cultural heritage.

LIVING TO ORIENT, DISORIENT, AND REORIENT

In *Queer Phenomenology*, Ahmed makes the case that "in order to become oriented, you might suppose that we must first experience disorientation.

When we are oriented, we might not even notice that we are oriented: we might not even think 'to think' about this point. When we experience disorientation, we might notice orientation as something we do not have."[14] Ahmed's phenomenological discourse around orientation, disorientation, and reorientation resonate with *Untwine*. Giselle's injuries and the loss of Isabelle put her in an uncomfortable place. Discomfort allows us to identify where our comforts lie, by putting us through "bodily experiences that throw the world up, or throw the body from its ground."[15] Reorientation cannot come about if we do not acknowledge that disorientation has led us to question why we are out of place. Let me be clear: disorientation takes place whether or not the discomfort is recognized. However, confronting discomfort allows us to move toward reorientation. Realizing what may have caused this discomfort or disorientation triggers processes that can be used to reorient. As a Black woman existing in spaces not intended for my body, my processes of surviving consist of continually adapting and finding different ways to navigate in these spaces. At times I am uncomfortable or dissatisfied with the shape my adaptation may take, and I am forced to take action to reorient or temporarily settle.

Giselle's body was physically and psychologically disoriented, as were her family and friends. For example, after the accident, doctors identify Giselle as Isabelle. For a couple days, family and friends are grieving over the loss of Giselle, not Isabelle. When Giselle's aunt discovers that it was Giselle who survived, their grief (re)orients toward the loss of Isabelle. When the things or the people around us whom we trust are also disorienting while we ourselves are disoriented, how do we find that moment of orientation or comfort—especially if it is unavailable or sometimes does not exist? In *Untwine*, various forms of disorientation force characters to reflect and interrogate their trauma toward understanding the present, which leads to the act of trying to reorient the future. I use the phrase "trying to reorient," because the unexpected moments that disorient us continue to influence the future we may have envisioned for ourselves, and at times we cannot disregard the reorientation.

When Giselle returns to consciousness, she faces finding ways to navigate life without her twin and is forced to orient within that shift. Ahmed suggests that "to be oriented is also to be turned toward certain objects, those that help us to find our way."[16] In this moment of isolation, the objects Giselle has to orient herself around are her memories, which she gravitates toward to discover ways of mourning and healing. Levins Morales conceptualizes mourning as a "way to honor what was lost, and only by renouncing all hope of restitution are we free to grieve."[17] Typically, the constant forwardness of living while trying to survive trauma does not allow space to mourn or honor what was lost. But the coma provides space for Giselle to mourn and honor the loss of Isabelle, because she is forced physically to do so. Because Giselle does not have full control of her body, she is positioned toward morning and healing.

Familiarity is conditioned. We do not start in a familiar state; rather, familiarity is shaped by how we interact in space. Giselle's space of familiarity was identifying as a twin. She is now positioned in an unfamiliar direction, working to find ways of accepting this "new life" to move toward healing. Losing her twin disorients Giselle, and she has to work to orient herself back to a space of comfort through her memories. Although her memories offer some comfort, they remain a source of orientation within a new disoriented space brought on by unfamiliarity. According to Ahmed, unfamiliarity can be understood as a moment of being lost, but "getting lost still takes us somewhere," and by being lost we are forced to inhabit what is not familiar to shift into a familiar moment.[18] For a moment, Giselle is lost when she realizes that Isabelle did not survive the accident, and her memories become a space of "wander." Wandering, in Ahmed's formulation, is to "ramble without certain course, to go aimlessly, to take one direction without intention or control, to stray from a path, or even to deviate in conduct or belief."[19] The more control Giselle gains over her memories, the more she orients into a familiar place—a past lived experience centered around living as a twin. Her memories are no longer a space of "wander" but a space for healing through identity construction and reconstruction.

CONSTRUCTING AND RECONSTRUCTING IDENTITY

The construction and reconstruction of identity is an ongoing and inevitable human practice. The stories we remember through reflection explain our present self, but they also force us to acknowledge the past as a powerful resource to explain and justify the present desire to create agendas for the future.[20] Giselle's priority for the future as she heals physically and mentally requires piecing together her past memories. We have to deconstruct in order to construct and reconstruct. This cycle requires us first to acknowledge that identity is "never complete, always in process, and always constituted within, not outside, representation."[21] The notion that identity construction and reconstruction is an ongoing assemblage of interactions from family, friends, and social constructs in our everyday life implies that there are various facets to identity. Avtar Brah explains:

Knowing is not so much about the assemblage of existing knowledge as it is about recognizing our constitution as "ourselves" within
the fragments that we process as knowledge; "hailing" and being
"hailed" within the discourses that produce us and the narratives
we spin; directing our socially, culturally, psychically and spiritually
marked focus of attention upon that which we appropriate as "data"
or "evidence."[22]

Evidence and data may be seen as the things that connect to make up and
define identities. Navigating our memories is similar to piecing together a
puzzle. The things we remember are the pieces in the puzzle box. Because
the production of identity construction and reconstruction is oriented from
different places, our memories give us a box with pieces missing. This phenomenon is evident in *Untwine* when Ron Johnson, Isabelle's friend, stops
by to offer his condolences to the family. At this point in the novel, Giselle is
no longer in a coma and has just attended her twin sister's funeral. Through
her conversation with Ron, Giselle realizes that he has actually come to give
her something rather than take something from her.[23] Giselle reflects on their
conversation and realizes:

> [H]e understands that when you lose someone, it's as if they've been
> smashed into a thousand pieces and what you're doing in the after-
> math is gathering a few of those pieces to put some versions of that
> person back together again. And not all of the pieces are yours. Some
> of them belong to other people. Part of Isabelle now belongs to Ron
> Johnson, too.[24]

Through Giselle's conversation with Ron, she becomes aware that identity
construction and reconstruction are not independent tasks. Friends, families,
loved ones, and others we cross paths with hold the missing pieces from the
puzzle box. At times, we need the memories of others who have interacted
with us to help us reflect and make sense of the pieces of the lived experiences
that have contributed to various aspects of our identities.

Missing pieces of the puzzle can also be retrieved through storytelling.
Emmanuel Obiechina describes a story as a practice "made to supply illus-
trative, authoritative support to an idea, a point of view, a perception, or
perspective in conversation or oral discourse, . . . [which] is thus vested with
much greater significance than is the case in a non-traditional context."[25]
Obiechina's explanation of story connects back to the idea that constructing and reconstructing identity is not an individual process. The content of

stories and how others choose to tell them offer different puzzle pieces—and, at times, some the pieces do not fit into the puzzle.

As Giselle remembers her relationship with Isabelle through reflection, she recollects the story her parents told them about their birth experience. The doctor needed to untwine the twins' fingers to separate them, because they were born holding hands.[26] At birth, the doctor may have untwined their hands, but it was a temporary act of separation because their shared lived experiences entwined a tighter grip. For example, Giselle and Isabelle's grandparents always referred to them as *les filles* (the girls) or *les jumelles* (the twins), which demonstrates that the twins were destined for an entwined relationship. Even Giselle's and Isabelle's names were chosen by their parents to rhyme with the term *jumelles*.[27] It is clear that Isabelle also holds some of the pieces missing from the puzzle box that can help Giselle construct and reconstruct her identity. This raises the questions: what happens when we can never retrieve lost pieces of the puzzle? Are those pieces actually lost?

Giselle grapples with whether she will still identify as a twin. Will she forget about identifying as such? Can she call herself a twin? In finding ways to address these questions, Giselle compares her mixed emotions to Frida Kahlo's painting *Las dos Fridas* (*The Two Fridas*). Even if Kahlo's painting represents her devastating heartbreak, there is a sentimental appropriation connected to Giselle's mixed emotions. Giselle articulates that she is "split in half sometimes, and at other times walking, living, breathing for two. Two hearts are beating in my one chest, but it feels like no heart at all."[28] Giselle and Frida are experiencing grief. In Kahlo's painting, both women have their heart exposed; one Kahlo holds a picture of her ex-husband Diego Rivera, and her exposed heart is whole. This image of Kahlo is similar to Giselle's identity before the accident, before the pain that follows trauma. When Isabelle was alive, Giselle was whole because her identity is connected to Isabelle. In Kahlo's painting, however, the other Kahlo's heart is dissected, and the artery that runs from her heart is cut and bleeding; this is similar to Giselle's tribulation, grief, and feeling of being incomplete. This Kahlo represents Giselle's trauma, brokenness, and pain, while the other Kahlo reflects the moments of Giselle's identities that she cannot forget, a wholeness that is no longer there. Just as in the twins' birth, the two women's hands in Kahlo's painting are entwined, signifying that even if Giselle wants to separate the painful memories from the pleasurable memories, it would be impossible because both the incomplete and the complete moments contribute to her overall identity.

Representative in both Kahlo's painting and *Untwine* are the pieces of the puzzle that prevent us from becoming permanently lost; instead, we find different ways to make sense of pieces that are unclear to us. For example, one of Isabelle's friends approaches Giselle at the funeral and blurts out that she looks just like her sister. A few people gasp, but the friend is telling the truth. And Giselle has to confront an uncomfortable truth—Isabelle will always be part of her identity. Giselle is forced to come to terms with the fact that no one will ever forget Isabelle as long as she is walking around with Isabelle's body and face. Giselle realizes that "her sister is dead and she is her ghost."[29] She cannot erase her lived memories and what they have contributed to their identity as a twin; instead, she can choose how to make meaning of them moving forward.

INDIVIDUAL AND HISTORICAL NARRATIVES

In Haitian culture, writing stories continues to be a form of knowledge making and sharing. Accounts of Haitian lived experiences are told through the practice of writing individual and culturally collective stories. Giselle and Isabelle use the language of the palms to communicate with each other secretly, and from these moments, they control which stories are set free. The language of the palms consists of grabbing someone's hands when having something to say to each other secretly.[30] Out of the secrets Giselle and Isabelle share using the language of the palms, Isabelle would write about those secrets in short stories that often took the form of lyrics:

> On a lovely green block, two identical palm
> trees (Palm A and Palm B) often whispered
> to one another, especially when there was a
> breeze. Sometimes the people on the street
> could hear them whooshing in the wind, but
> since the people didn't speak the language of the
> palms, they didn't understand what they were
> saying. One day, the palms switched places, and
> no one noticed.[31]

Isabelle has become a lyrical storyteller for her and Giselle's lived experiences. The lyrics written by Isabelle describe the secrets and stories she and Giselle share. These stories may be unique to Giselle and Isabelle, but there is value in the way the lyrics indicate how specific moments in their lives contribute to their identities. Isabelle's simple act of writing her and Giselle's stories also creates a space for others with similar experiences to find comfort or familiarity in their stories.

Cheryl Townsend Gilkes reminds us that "sometimes the simple act of writing the culture and its members into existence can be an act subversive of the inhuman consequences of marginalization and domination."[32] Aside from the individual stories of Giselle and Isabelle, Danticat continues to include historical concepts in her writing in order to reclaim Haitian historical narratives that have been misrepresented or underrepresented. Danticat writes Haitian communities into existence through the stories she tells. This practice of including diasporic bodies negates dominant cultures' views and beliefs about Haitian cultural identity. Stuart Hall further explains that the concept of the diaspora can allow for some flexibility around the development of diasporic identity production. To develop this flexibility, Hall describes the imagined "cultural identity" through a sense of oneness and connectedness to an overarching identity as positioned by one's identifying culture. Oneness is a reflection of the collective, "the common historical experiences shared and cultural codes which provide us, as 'one people,' with stable, unchanging and continuous frames of reference and meaning, beneath the shifting divisions and vicissitudes of our actual history."[33] Hall believes in a collective identity connected through history, which has played a significant role in "all the post-colonial struggles which have so profoundly reshaped our world."[34] Hall's collective is represented in Danticat's works as a collective Haitian history.

Readers are introduced to characters whose names are of importance to the collective because they call to mind historical Haitian figures, such as Jean-Jacques Dessalines and Jean-Michel Basquiat. As we see, naming as a rhetorical practice is powerful because it keeps Haitian historical stories alive. Giselle and Isabelle's father suggests that they name their cat Dessalines as an act of teaching Haitian history. Aside from the twins learning about Dessalines and how he contributed to Haitian history, those who inquire about the cat's name will learn that Dessalines, along with Henri Christophe, led an army of slaves during the Haitian Revolution, resulting in Haiti becoming the first Black republic in the world to abolish slavery, in 1804. The name of the boy with whom Giselle is in a growing relationship is also a representation of naming as a way to remember Haitian history. His name is Jean-Michel Basquiat. Basquiat was a Haitian American artist whose art entwined activism and culture to create unique visual metaphors that represent Caribbean and African heritage. The historical facts about Basquiat included in *Untwine* give attribution to his artistic contributions to Haitian cultural identity. By including these historical Haitians in her novels, Danticat shares a piece of history with those who engage with her text. Narrating history is essential for keeping the experiences of a particular culture alive. In my own experience, having conversations with individuals outside of my Haitian community, I find that more often than not they are not knowledgeable about Haitian history, due in part to the lack of conversations and stories about Haitian cultural identity. As readers navigate Giselle's memories with her, those memories bring awareness of Haitian cultural identity and history. Giselle's memories introduce stories of Haitian historical experiences early to children and young adults.

Toni Morrison emphasizes that "the novel is needed by African-Americans now in a way that it was not needed before—and it is following along the lines of the function of novels everywhere."[35] What Morrison expresses here is that at a point in our lives, our parents, family members, and other loved ones will not be around to share individual or historical stories—and that novels will be a source where cultural heritage lives. The novel functions as a space that archives memories, stories, and histories of the individual or community who wrote it; therefore, as a Haitian community, we need to write ourselves, our history, and include the presence of our ancestors. Like Morrison, Danticat continues to create and provide spaces for Haitian and Haitian American readers to participate. As Morrison strongly illustrates: "[I]f anything I do, in the way of writing novels isn't about the village or the community or about you, then it is not about anything."[36] *Untwine* is not about anything; it is about "something," and Giselle's memories help readers to define what that "something" is. For me, it is a sense of familiarity—having a shared space connected to Haitian cultural identity. *Untwine* creates community for Haitian American girls through Giselle's memories.

CONCLUSION

Giselle reflects on her sister's words that "for good things, you think of firsts. For bad things, you think of lasts."[37] Giselle wants to think of "the firsts," "the good things"—but it is hard for her not to think of the lasts. It is difficult for Giselle to ignore the last, because no matter in which direction she navigates her memories, they connect back to her last moment of identifying as a twin. Furthermore, Giselle reflects on how Isabelle would read a book backward. In doing so, Isabelle reads first about how the characters' lives have changed. Readers take a backward journey with Giselle in order to move forward with her on her journey as she constructs and reconstructs aspects of her identities; readers are first introduced to the ways Giselle's life has changed as a result of the car accident. It is through navigating her memories that we come to understand why it is difficult for Giselle to untwine her memories and identities from those of Isabelle.

Untwine is a story in which Giselle examines her life backward in order to find ways of becoming without her sister. The traumas Haitian American girls experience may be different from or similar to Giselle's, but Danticat offers a cohesive way for Haitian American girls to use their traumas and deploy their memories to make sense of their identities so they can move forward on the path to recovery. Using themes such as trauma, discomfort, reflection, and orientation as steps toward healing, Danticat proposes a process to deal with grief and at the same time leaves readers with approaches for becoming and redefining identities, a process that does not involve fast-forwarding—a process that orients differently for each person.

When Giselle conveys that she wants to fast-forward her life and put more distance between that awful night and herself, she realizes that, even as she goes through her process of healing, there will always be fear concerning who she becomes. Giselle will not be able to address her uncertainties until she is comfortable with whom trauma has led her to become. How do we continue to become when the people who have accompanied us in that process no longer exist? How will Giselle become without Isabelle? Who will Giselle become without Isabelle? What will Giselle's stories consist of when they no longer include Isabelle? There is a moment when Giselle realizes that "they're only telling stories about Isabelle and me together. Do they know any stories that are only Giselle stories or only Isabelle stories?"[38] It is not only up to Giselle to reorient; the people around her have to reorient as well. Giselle's family and friends have to orient each other in ways that involve them learning to accept who she will become individually. In the end, Giselle has to reorient to a new way of life because she cannot return to her past life—only to her memories.

NOTES

1. From "A Conversation with Edwidge Danticat," in Edwidge Danticat, *Untwine* (New York: Scholastic, 2015), 308.

2. Jo Collins explains that "Haitian American youth comprise both the 'one-and-a-half generation'—those who migrate to the US in adolescence and who straddle two very different nations—and those born in America." Jo Collins, "Novels of Transformation and Transplantation: The Postcolonial *Bildungsroman* and Haitian American Youth in Danticat's *Behind the Mountains* and *Breath, Eyes, Memory,*" *Wasafiri* 27, no. 4 (December 2012): 28.

3. Sara Ahmed, *Queer Phenomenology: Orientations, Objects, Others* (Durham, NC: Duke University Press, 2006), 124.

4. Ahmed, *Queer Phenomenology,* 7.

5. Patricia Hill Collins defines "self-definition" as "the power to name one's own reality"; Patricia Hill Collins, *Black Feminist Thought: Knowledge, Consciousness, and the Politics of Empowerment* (Boston: Unwin Hyman, 1990), 300.

6. Danticat, *Untwine*, 26.

7. Cassie Premo Steele, *We Heal from Memory: Sexton, Lorde, Anzaldúa, and the Poetry of Witness* (Basingstoke, Hants., England: Palgrave, 2000), 2.

8. Danticat, *Untwine*, 24.

9. Danticat, *Untwine*, 24

10. Aurora Levins Morales, *Medicine Stories: History, Culture, and the Politics of Integrity* (Cambridge, MA: South End Press, 1998), 19.

11. Levins Morales, *Medicine Stories*, 19.

12. bell hooks, *Sisters of the Yam: Black Women and Self-Recovery* (Boston: South End Press, 1993), 29.

13. In *Sisters of the Yam*, hooks defines reconciliation as "evoking our capacity to restore to harmony that which has been broken, severed, and disrupted" (176).

14. Ahmed, *Queer Phenomenology*, 157.

15. Ahmed, *Queer Phenomenology*, 157.

16. Ahmed, *Queer Phenomenology*, 1.

17. Levins Morales, *Medicine Stories*, 19.

18. Ahmed, *Queer Phenomenology*, 7.

19. Ahmed, *Queer Phenomenology*, 29.

20. Levins Morales, *Medicine Stories*, 14.

21. Stuart Hall, "Cultural Identity and Diaspora," in *Identity: Community, Culture, Difference*, ed. Jonathan Rutherford (London: Lawrence and Wishart, 1990), 234.

22. Avtar Brah, "The Scent of Memory: Strangers, Our Own, and Others," *Feminist Review* 61, no. 1 (April 1999): 8

23. Danticat, *Untwine*, 223.

24. Danticat, *Untwine*, 233–34.

25. Emmanuel Obiechina, *Culture, Tradition and Society in the West African Novel* (Cambridge: Cambridge University Press, 1975), 201.

26. Danticat, *Untwine*, 7.

27. Danticat, *Untwine*, 19.

28. Danticat, *Untwine*, 244–45.

29. Danticat, *Untwine*, 169.

30. Danticat, *Untwine*, 20.

31. Danticat, *Untwine*, 35–36.

32. Cheryl Townsend Gilkes, "A Conscious Connection to All That Is: *The Color Purple* as Subversive and Critical Ethnography," in *Personal Knowledge and Beyond: Reshaping the Ethnography of Religion*, edited by James V. Spickard, J. Shawn Landres, and Meredith B. McGuire (New York: New York University Press, 2002), 176.

33. Hall, "Cultural Identity and Diaspora," 223.

34. Hall, "Cultural Identity and Diaspora," 223.

35. Toni Morrison, "Rootedness: The Ancestor as Foundation," in *Black Women Writers (1950–1980): A Critical Evaluation*, ed. Mari Evans (New York: Doubleday, 1984), 494.

36. Morrison, "Rootedness," 497.

37. Danticat, *Untwine*, 274.

38. Danticat, *Untwine*, 293.

BIBLIOGRAPHY

Ahmed, Sara. *Queer Phenomenology: Orientations, Objects, Others.* Durham, NC: Duke
 University Press, 2006.

Brah, Avtar. "The Scent of Memory: Strangers, Our Own, and Others." *Feminist Review*
 61, no. 1 (April 1999): 4–26.

Collins, Jo. "Novels of Transformation and Transplantation: The Postcolonial
 Bildungsroman and Haitian American Youth in Danticat's *Behind the Mountains* and
 Breath, Eyes, Memory." *Wasafiri* 27, no. 4 (December 2012): 27–34.

Collins, Patricia Hill. *Black Feminist Thought: Knowledge, Consciousness, and the Politics of
 Empowerment.* Boston: Unwin Hyman, 1990.

Danticat, Edwidge. *Untwine.* New York: Scholastic, 2015.

Gilkes, Cheryl Townsend. "A Conscious Connection to All That Is: *The Color Purple* as
 Subversive and Critical Ethnography." In *Personal Knowledge and Beyond: Reshaping
 the Ethnography of Religion,* edited by James V. Spickard, J. Shawn Landres, and
 Meredith B. McGuire, 175–94. New York: New York University Press, 2002.

Hall, Stuart. "Cultural Identity and Diaspora." In *Identity: Community, Culture, Difference,*
 edited by Jonathan Rutherford, 222–37. London: Lawrence and Wishart, 1990.

hooks, bell. *Sisters of the Yam: Black Women and Self-Recovery.* Boston: South End
 Press, 1993.

Levins Morales, Aurora. *Medicine Stories: History, Culture, and the Politics of Integrity.*
 Cambridge, MA: South End Press, 1998.

Morrison, Toni. "Rootedness: The Ancestor as Foundation." In *Black Women Writers
 (1950–1980): A Critical Evaluation,* edited by Mari Evans, 339–45. New York:
 Doubleday, 1984.

Obiechina, Emmanuel. *Culture, Tradition and Society in the West African Novel.*
 Cambridge: Cambridge University Press, 1975.

Steele, Cassie Premo. *We Heal from Memory: Sexton, Lorde, Anzaldúa, and the Poetry of
 Witness.* Basingstoke, Hants., England: Palgrave, 2000.

Chapter Eight

COLLECTING AND RELEASING EMBODIED MEMORIES

Redefining Shame in Edwidge Danticat's *Breath, Eyes, Memory*

AKIA JACKSON

Breath, Eyes, Memory (1994) by Edwidge Danticat tells the story of Sophie Caco's struggle with matrilineal generational trauma. Many scholars, such as Simone James Alexander and Masoumeh Mehni, read Danticat's novel primarily through the framework of mother-daughter relationships; however, I will analyze the fragmentation and loss of Sophie's self through her experiences in migration and her relationship to familial shame.[1] The journey of the Caco women focuses on their collective inability to confront and address intergenerational pain in multiple forms, from virginity testing to rape.[2] Danticat's text, set during the late 1970s and 1980s, imaginatively utilizes institutionalized history to show how the violent upheavals that textured Haitian politics impacted the suffering of women on a macro level in the country.[3] For Grandmè Ifé, Atie, Martine, and Sophie, Haiti defines an important part of their subjectivities, but their connection to the nation also exposes their divided desires. In one way, the women pledge allegiance to the country of Haiti because it holds their histories and their memories, and therefore they feel obliged to carry that identity with them. However, in another way, maintaining this bond to Haiti forces each woman to perpetually face and relive painful personal and national past events. This ambivalence, between testifying to the traumas of history and overcoming that history for a healed version of self, emerges as not only Sophie's locus of shame but also Martine's. The disruption of migration places Sophie and Martine between the imperative to remember and the compulsion to forget, negotiating the fine boundary linking history and memory. An important dimension of the Caco women's story is the conception of discontinuity, which I utilize to demonstrate an abrupt rupture between an oppressive past and a new revolutionary future.

The lack of reconciliation of the past and the present for the two women interrupts their path to a coherent resolution by the novel's end.

LEAVING HOME SPACES

Danticat's narrative suggests that what Haiti remembers and what it forgets moves beyond geopolitical borders, and that the act of memorializing the past creates a cycle linking the country to different traumas of its history. During the 1970s, state-mandated language persuaded many Haitians to believe that preserving the memory of the nation meant forgetting government-sanctioned brutality leveled against Haitian women.[4] This paradoxical relationship of praising nationalist protection for men while simultaneously condemning women as second-class citizens emanates throughout the Caco migration journey. Despite Atie's, Martine's, and Sophie's best efforts to remove their physical bodies from locales of pain—literally moving away from spaces of bodily injury—their attempts are useless, because their bodies are burdens of embodied memory.[5] At the beginning of the novel, at age twelve while living in Croix-des-Rosets, Sophie is unaware of the circuit of memories that already taints her young body. The push-and-pull factors between Sophie's Haitian identity and her American one is a conflict that begins very early when Martine sends a cassette recording saying, "I want my daughter."[6] After this moment, Sophie has trouble determining the challenges that will arise when she must part with the only mother figure and home she has known in Haiti to leave for America. Initially, Sophie misunderstands her need to depart and asks her aunt why she must leave alone to go to this new place. Atie responds: "We are each going to our mothers. That is what was supposed to happen. She does not want you to forget who your real mother is."[7] From adolescence, Sophie has objected to social norms about family life that bind her to traditional Haitian mores, but Atie adheres to an unspoken Haitian duty. Danticat illustrates Sophie expressing a strong desire to ignore this duty in asking why she must move. This is Sophie's first act of redefining her young womanhood, because she does not believe that she should blindly follow orders of obligation. In contrast, Atie idealizes her responsibility to take care of her mother, saying, "[T]hat is what was supposed to happen," because she thinks it is a moral commitment that she must uphold as a daughter of Haiti.[8] Atie recognizes that she does not control the narrative of her own life and has accepted it: "Your mother and I, when we were children we had no control over anything. Not even this body."[9] With these words, Atie is passing on a realistic, yet flawed truth to Sophie: that because she will be in America, she will have control over everything in her life including her body. However, this immigrant myth is untrue.

Before Sophie leaves for America, Tante Atie also reveals to her that she shares many traits with Martine, telling Sophie repeatedly: "Promise me that you are not going to fight with your mother when you get there. It would be a shame if the two of you got into battles because you share a lot more than you know."[10] In this passage, Atie identifies any disagreement Sophie has with her mother as a source of shame, which forces Sophie into the same permissiveness as Atie. For Sophie, any dissent would bring shame not only to Martine but also to Atie, because she would be disobeying her wishes. Not realizing the implications of Atie's comment, Sophie passively accepts this instruction from her aunt and vows to honor her request. Unwittingly, because of this promise, Sophie is now moving under the shadow of generational shame that disallows nonconformity. In understanding Sophie's deferential behavior about the blight of shame that forces her acquiescence to Atie, I engage with Melissa Harris-Perry's text *Sister Citizen* on the incommunicable weight of shame on Black women's experience. Even though Harris-Perry does not directly discuss Danticat's novel, she does speak to the complicity that shame creates for Black women in the United States, which Sophie exhibits in this passage because of her relationship to colonialism. Harris-Perry argues:

> In order to understand the politics of shame for Black women, we need to think about fictive kinships and linked fates. [. . .] The emotion of shame is first social. [. . .] We do not feel shame in isolation, only when we transgress a social boundary or break a community expectation. [. . .] Shame comes when we fear exposure and evaluation by others.[11]

Harris-Perry's argument speaks to the continuous, permanent bond Sophie's actions will create with Grandmè Ifé, Atie, and Martine through their familial kinship and linked fates, even after she moves to the United States. This passage by Harris-Perry illustrates Sophie's earliest interaction with shame and warns of the results of breaking the communal expectations of family and country. Sophie's fear of public shaming and evaluation strips her of the ability to act independently because of her emotional proximity to the other Caco women. On Sophie's last trip to La Nouvelle Dame Marie with Tante Atie to say goodbye to her grandmother, she learns of a story about a group of people of creation in Guinea who carry the sky on their head and can bear anything.[12] The mental, emotional, and physical weight of solemnity and shame unconsciously becomes a psychologically destructive part of Sophie's life, even before she arrives in the United States.

In order to fly to America, Sophie must drive through Port-au-Prince and witness the last remnants of her country in chaos. There are buildings burning and many citizens are hurt, while others throw rocks and fight back against the Tonton Macoute soldiers.[13] This scene shows Sophie two sides of Haiti: those who suffer and those who resist the authority of the country. As Sophie boards the plane, she unexpectedly interacts with a small boy who will become a symbol foreshadowing the story of her own existence. He is brought to the flight by the same woman overseeing Sophie's international trip to New York. Danticat's representation of the boy is a microcosm of the trauma and corruption occurring in Haiti as Sophie departs in the early 1980s; the boy is behaving in disorderly fashion because "his father died in that fire out front. His father was some kind of old government official, très corrupt, très guilty of crimes against the people."[14] The figure of the boy in Sophie's narrative is symbolic of the idea of homelessness. Like the small boy, Sophie, as she travels to America, must change her concept of home, and the erratically emotional behavior the child displays signifies her internal distress about the impending changes in her life. Danticat's placement of the violence in the background of Sophie's flight also indirectly alludes to the Jean-Claude Duvalier dictatorship and its aim to subjugate women through political violence, showing Sophie's ability to leave that environment, unlike Atie and Martine.

Duvalier was known as Baby Doc, and he assumed his sudden leadership of Haiti at only nineteen years of age after the death of his father, François Duvalier, who was also guilty of political crimes against the people of Haiti and created chaos among them by instilling fear at the height of his regime.[15] In her novel, Danticat uses the image of a "fatherless country" to signify the disorder such a status creates for a developing nation and its citizens.[16] Likewise, she creates the image of the fatherless boy and a fatherless Sophie on the plane to denote that their initial loss is parallel to the loss of a coherent connection to their nation-state. Both characters must abandon their country to escape to their mothers or maternal figures in their lives—whom Danticat constructs as initial safe spaces for them. However, for Sophie, the movement from Haiti creates disruption from her former life and exemplifies an early loss for her twelve-year-old self. In a close analytical reading of Sophie's mobility from home as disruption and a form of loss, I turn to Saidiya Hartman, who elaborates on the Black diasporic subject's search for belonging and home outside of their birth nation. Hartman's argument about the disruptiveness of mobility foreshadows Sophie's difficulty in leaving

Haiti; "it is [. . .] the scar between native and citizen. It is both an end and a beginning. It announces the disappearance of the known world and the antipathy of the new one. And [there is] longing and loss [. . .] [in that] there is no going back to a former condition. Loss remakes you."[17] Departure from Haiti leaves Sophie with irreparable trauma, and it also erases a portion of who she knew herself to be up to that point. It is my contention that Hartman speaks both to the certainty of a definite separation from Sophie's past self and to the uncertainties that await the new Sophie in America.

RE-CREATING SUBJECTIVITIES

Upon arriving at the airport in the United States, Sophie must take inventory of her embodied memories of Martine, and she cannot quite understand her own reaction in reacquainting with her mother. Instead of immediately acclimatizing Sophie to English, Martine speaks to her in Haitian Creole to make her feel comfortable. However, Sophie is reticent to respond to her mother in Creole, only nodding in response to her questions at the outset of their initial interaction. Her silence exposes her immediate discomfort with Martine, and the feeling of being in the new space of America surrounded by strangers. When Sophie sees Martine, she notices how frail her mother appears, which becomes a metaphor of Martine's poor emotional and physiological health to her daughter. Although this initial scene with Martine and Sophie is brief, it exposes multiple layers of their complex relationship and foreshadows their inability to communicate effectively with one another and Martine's declining mental stability. In attempts to erase the image of physical weakness that Sophie sees, Martine constantly tells her not to be afraid, to show her young daughter that she has strength enough for them both in this new chapter of their lives. Once Sophie reaches her new home in New York, she begins to feel secure enough to answer some of her mother's questions about Tante Atie and family friends. As Martine relaxes, the tone of the conversation shifts to the importance of Sophie's role in America as a young Haitian woman, and the significance of getting a good education: "You are going to work hard here. [. . .] You have a chance to become the kind of woman Atie and I have always wanted to be. If you make something of yourself in life, we will all succeed. You can raise our heads."[18] In this conversation, Martine uses the language of strength and nation building in the United States to offset the image of physical frailty that her body projects to her child.[19] She asserts her role and dominance as Sophie's mother and places the matrilineal legacy of the impending success of Haitian women on Sophie's presence in America.

Her mother's comments show that Sophie's successes will benefit not only the Caco women but also Haiti more generally, because she is a symbol of the country. However, in telling Sophie that she must work hard on her schooling in the United States, Martine unconsciously admits to both her own and Atie's failings as Haitian women who wanted to make more of their lives. Clare Counihan argues that Sophie's journey in America "challenges both the impermeability of state boundaries and geographical fixity of national memory, and the novel's depiction of migration undermines the American myth of immigration as historyless self-reinvention."[20] Consequently, Sophie can never exist as a tabula rasa in America because of her relationship to her mother, grandmother, and aunt. In effect, she is not given the decision to parse out her existence in the United States on her own because she is still bound to the familial and communal expectations of Haitian values. Even though Sophie and Martine reside in a different geopolitical space, Haiti still governs and impacts their private lives in the new country.

I define the middle ground for Sophie in the United States, as Hartman also describes, as the scar between a person's native land and their physical presence in America. This is the space between her Haitian obligations to family and her American individualism. Although Sophie recognizes the gravity of her mother's statement about commitment to success for the benefit of the family, her connection to the middle ground often makes her feel marginalized from both her national identity in Haiti, Ifé, and Atie, and the American individualism she seeks. As she settles into her new home in New York, Sophie sees a picture of her mother and Tante Atie holding a baby; she says: "[I]t was the first time in my life that I noticed that I looked like no one in my family. I did not look like them when I was a baby and I did not look like them now."[21] Seeing this image concretizes Sophie's feelings of being an outsider in her family, and it reminds her of the image of fatherlessness once again.[22] This is also Sophie's first deep episode of shame, because she realizes that she has the face of Martine's rapist. This moment is pivotal and illustrates the difficulty of starting over for immigrant Haitian women inside the shadow of national memory. The image marks the mental and emotional matrilineal gap as permanent for Sophie and Martine. It also solidifies their distance as mother and daughter when Sophie begins to comprehend the meaning of the picture—it triggers an emotional shift of discontinuity for her. I contend that this discontinuity is the first moment Sophie consciously realizes the rupture with her past self and her need to enter a more present version of her subjectivity. Sophie has trouble reconciling the multiple roles in her life—immigrant, new American, daughter—because, somehow, to her each title still means that she has no home and no form of belonging.

As nightfall approaches, having seen the picture, Sophie starts to experience the depths of this discontinuity and crisis of belonging. In the midst of her own dislocated experience, Sophie must also grapple with her mother's problems. As Sophie lies in the dark that night, she hears Martine screaming as though someone were trying to kill her:

> I rushed over, but my mother was alone thrashing against the sheets. I shook her and finally woke her up. When she saw me, she quickly covered her face with her hands and turned away. "Are you all right?" I asked her. [. . .] "It is the night" she said. "Sometimes I see horrible visions in my sleep. [. . .] The nightmares they come and go."[23]

Waking her mother from the nightmare deeply solidifies Sophie's experience with discontinuity because, in addition to the new roles she must inhabit in America, she must now also become a caretaker of Martine. Danticat illustrates that Sophie's concern for her mother, and the idea of her Haitian obligation to family, removes Sophie's autonomy and her ability to make independent decisions at an early juncture in the novel. With Tante Atie, Sophie astutely performed the role of a child, by going to school and doing household chores to keep the home clean. Danticat demonstrates that Sophie's only responsibility was occasionally helping Tante Atie learn to read, but this was not her primary duty or obligation in the home. Conversely, on arrival in the United States, Sophie's role drastically changes; she inherits the status of caretaker for her mother during moments of sustained trauma in a more obligatory manner. Her attempts to comfort her mother seem ineffectual, because tears continue to trickle down Martine's face as she drifts back to sleep. Danticat illustrates that Sophie does not necessarily recognize how to function in the role of caretaker for her mother in this new space of America, and this is an important point in how I am orienting the idea of discontinuity. Sophie has trouble growing accustomed to this fracture, which moves her from childhood innocence to maturity at an extremely quick speed.

NEW NATION HOMEMAKING

Sophie's fears of remaining an outsider in America solidify when she meets her mother's lover, Marc. The three of them visit Miracin's, a Haitian restaurant, so Sophie can better acquaint herself with Marc and the local Haitian eatery. At dinner, Sophie attempts to create a connection to homemaking and listens in on the political conversations of Haitian nationals shouting back and forth at each other.[24] While they quarrel about the *konbit* system, local transportation, and the quality of food in America compared to Haiti, Sophie cannot help but remember that "in the marketplace in Haiti, whenever people were arguing, others would gather around them and watch and laugh at the colorful language."[25] The exchange between the older immigrants reminds Sophie of a space of normalcy in her home country, because it recreates the community she shared with Atie in Croix-des-Rosets. Danticat uses Sophie's reflective remembrance of home in this scene to frame multiple narratives of the working class, the educated, and the impact of American imperialism in Haiti.[26] The conversation illuminates that although some Haitian citizens take pride in the progress of their country, others believe that there are shortcomings in Haiti's insularity. Danticat shows how Sophie's perspective as a child underexposes her to the complexities of her national identity, but her lack of knowledge fosters an affinity for her memory of the country and her sense of belonging.

As voices and sounds of home envelop Sophie, her anxiety begins to ease. However, when her mother introduces her to the waiter, who tries to see Martine's likeness in Sophie, she thinks: "[H]e looks at us for a long time. First me, then my mother. I wanted to tell him to stop it. There was no resemblance between us. I knew it."[27] Sophie had been feeling akin to the other Haitian nationals in the room, including her mother and Marc; the waiter's reaction to her appearance causes this feeling of belonging to dissipate. Instantly, Sophie understands her contradictory status as an outsider within this small community. Following Harris-Perry, I argue that because shame is a response to social rejection, Sophie sharply comprehends this shame as an evaluation of the self. When the waiter misinterprets her looks to be what she perceives as abject, she immediately feels isolated from everyone in the restaurant.[28] This, then, creates deeper shame for Sophie and exacerbates the distance between her and Martine. In response to the sensation of shame, Sophie tries to stuff her mouth with Haitian food and stay quiet in order to mark her inclusion and belonging.[29]

Realizing her own marginalization at the young age of twelve forces Sophie to find a way to erase her connection to the political violence of the cruel Haitian regime. Peter Stearns asserts that "with shame people tend to shrink, and characteristically seek to hide because of the emotional dilemma involved. [. . .] Shame emerges when the child feels that parental love may be threatened or withdrawn; it is this that calls the whole self into question."[30] The waiter not recognizing Sophie's looks to be akin to Martine's makes her feel publicly shamed and immediately reignites the emotional dilemma of belonging for the young girl. Sophie declares, "My mother now had two lives: Marc belonged to her present life, I was a living memory from the past."[31] Given that Sophie did not grow up with Martine, she feels neglected by a mother who has not had an active role in her life thus far. Martine's intimacy with Marc greatly impacts the emotional affinity between Martine and her daughter. To the young Sophie, Marc interrupts the establishment of any early rapport between herself and her mother. This passage empha- sizes Sophie's disillusionment with her budding relationship with Martine. Although she perceives her place in her mother's life as an emotional crutch, she also discerns the mounting difficulty that will arise from in her displace- ment from Haiti and Atie. Moments before the incident with the waiter, Sophie observes displacement as a side effect of migration, which she does not necessarily deem negative. After the episode, however, she senses that displacement articulates a heaviness that she has yet to fully dissect and in- terpret as a young, Black immigrant girl.

RECUPERATING LOSSES FROM THE NATION

For seven years in America, Sophie denies herself the opportunity to live her life as her own because of her duty to her mother, aunt, and grand- mother, until she meets Joseph, who convinces her that being an individual in America can help her achieve goals independent of Martine's approval.[32] As a result, Sophie begins disobeying her mother and, in the process, dam- ages their already fragile relationship. In order to remedy her own feelings of shame for what she interprets as neglect for her mother, Sophie returns to Haiti. The feeling of isolation and the weight of shame about concretizing their separation follow Sophie on her visit to see Tante Atie and Grandmè Ifé. She notes that, during the taxi ride to La Nouvelle Dame Marie, the sun slaps her face as though she has done something wrong.[33] Counihan argues that "the novel cannot bear to either remember or forget what it is to be Haitian,"[34] and Danticat illustrates the impact of this statement when Sophie's taxi driver indicates the importance of retaining vestiges of national memory: "People who have been away from Haiti fewer years than you, they return and pretend they speak no Creole." Sophie responds, "Some people need to forget." The taxi driver says, "You do not need to forget." Sophie agrees: "I need to remember."[35] Counihan emphasizes that this brief conversation reveals the dislocations of diaspora—caught between desires, people who have been away from Haiti can neither stay away nor return to Haiti as home. The middle ground that Sophie occupies has cast her not only as a perpetual outsider in her own family but also as an exiled foreigner in her home country.

As an adult returning to Haiti voluntarily, Sophie requires a different, more assertive version of herself that demands answers about a family history and a nation she never questioned in the past. Sophie's unremitting navigation into deconstructing the practice of virginity testing in the Caco family begins to redefine her embodied shame and transforms her relationship to her autonomy. In order to gain perspective about her own problems with shame and communication, Sophie listens to stories her grandmother tells her about the lark, the girl, and the man with the stained sheets.[36] She does not quite understand them and finally musters the strength to ask her grandmother why she performed the testing at all. Ifé responds,

> If your child is disgraced, you are disgraced . . . the mother is responsible for her purity. If I give a soiled daughter to her husband, he can shame my family. [. . .] The burden was not mine alone . . . you must know that everything a mother does, she does for her child's own good. You cannot always carry the pain. You must liberate yourself.[37]

Ifé's truth resonates with Sophie deeply, and the Erzulie statue she hands her symbolizes their shared connection to Haiti.[38] Ifé affirms that the burden is not hers alone, which is why women pass the practice down to their daughters through each generation.[39] Now, with a child of her own, Sophie sees both sides of Ifé's argument, and weeps for the pain she has suffered and the unconscious burdens she may pass to her daughter, Brigitte. Her grandmother admits to the flaws of virginity testing and how it sacrifices the value of their allegiance to Haitian mores.[40] Danticat frames Ifé's revelation about testing as a means to demystify the troubled history of a nation rooted in the control of women's bodies.

CONFRONTING TRAUMA

After Sophie confronts Ifé, she recognizes how deeply Haiti as a country internalizes Western colonial constructs of femininity. Danticat strategically constructs this intergenerational scene in order to demonstrate the moment these two Caco women regain control of their own narratives—particularly Sophie. Even though Ifé tells Sophie to exorcise her pain, she does not give Martine and Atie the same advice because of their strained relationships. She gives Sophie permission to release herself from the complex burdens of Haiti and to remove her child from the emotional violence that overshadowed the Cacos for generations. Sophie finally faces her mother in La Nouvelle Dame Marie and begins to confront familial trauma. Her grandmother's words about releasing her pain resonate when she sees her mother, and she senses her "old sympathy coming back."[41] Her feelings of empathy for her mother do not deter her from asking the same questions of accountability she asked of Ifé about virginity testing. Martine agrees to tell Sophie why she tested her on the condition that she never ask about it again, and explains, "because my mother had done it to me . . . I realize standing here that the two greatest pains of my life are very much related . . . The testing and the rape. I live both every day. I want to be your friend . . . because you saved my life many times."[42] This dialogue between Sophie and Martine creates a joint space for confronting shame and redefining the purpose of shame in their lives. Sophie in particular has a much greater understanding of how to cope with the social stigma of shame and the positive ramifications it has in healing her intimate relationships with Martine, Atie, and Ifé.[43] Sophie makes space for Martine to join her in recuperating from the social ills that plague the history of their beloved nation.

Martine is less invested in subversive psychological healing of the past. By meeting Sophie in her homeland, it is clear that Martine hopes to recoup the severed portions of their relationship by revisiting their love for a country that unites them. For Sophie, their reunion in Haiti repositions her respect for her mother, while also remedying some of her shame around virginity testing. However, Martine's visit to Haiti reawakens painful memories of the violent regime that led to her rape. Martine is an emblematic transnational child of suffering, both because her rape took place in Haiti and because the United States allowed it to happen. In Haiti, shame is inescapable for the Caco women because they are victims to the legacy of their nation. They each internalize the unmediated ideologies of the Haitian authorities that force them to believe that their own subjugation is for the benefit of the country. During Martine and Sophie's departure from Haiti, a disabled older Haitian woman tells them to find peace; these words foreshadow for the reader how Sophie and Martine choose to look for that peace. As a first stride toward tranquility, Sophie shares with Martine that she suffers from bulimia. However, because Martine still has difficulty processing trauma, she shrugs off the confession: "[Y]ou have become very American . . . you are different. [. . .] I want things to be good with us now."[44] This signals that Martine does not understand their differences, yet she wants to connect with her daughter nevertheless. Her attitude still creates some dissonance for Sophie, but Sophie comprehends that her mother is trying to change.

COPING WITH HEALING

When they return to America, Martine and Sophie continue to try rebuilding from the scars of the past. Martine apologizes to Sophie about burning her belongings after she left because of her own shame. Martine confesses that she believed Sophie would return to her humiliated, soaking in shame and begging for another chance. Martine attempts her journey toward peace by being transparent with Sophie about her pregnancy with Marc. She admits that she does not want the child, because lingering trauma of the rape still haunts her memories. Sophie encourages her to have the child because it will be a second chance to be a mother, but Martine cannot see past the pain Haiti created for her. She tells Sophie: "I've had the second chance of my life by being spared from death from this cancer. I can't ask too much."[45] Sophie struggles to understand her mother's decisions but decides to let Martine confront them on her own. She returns to Rena, her therapist, and rejoins the other two members of her sexual phobia group; together, she and these other two women of the diaspora endeavor to fix the small, broken pieces of themselves in order to be free.[46] Further framing her connection with the African diaspora, Rena is an initiated Santería priestess. The women in Sophie's support group seek healing for their embodied traumas as women of color from other women of color; thus, they desire to restore their communities by helping one another. Unlike her mother, Atie, and Ifé, Sophie insists on narrating her trauma en route to the cure. As Sophie finds ways to name and define her debilitating shame for productive purposes in order to not repeat harmful generational behaviors, Martine drowns under the weight of shame's obligations on her in mind, body, and soul. Martine commits suicide as the only and final way she knows to confront the psychological toll of national memory and the gravity of shame. After her mother is laid to rest, Sophie returns to the cane fields in order to reclaim the collective memory of her family, and to rename both her and her mother's final journeys to Haiti as the journeys of two women who repurposed shame for their own liberation.

NOTES

1. See Simone A. James Alexander, "M/othering the Nation: Women's Bodies as Nationalist Trope in Edwidge Danticat's *Breath, Eyes, Memory*," *African American Review* 44, no. 3 (Fall 2011): 373–90; and Masoumeh Mehni, "Analyzing the Problematic Mother-Daughter Relationship in Edwidge Danticat's *Breath, Eyes, Memory*," *Journal of Caribbean*

Literatures 7, no. 1 (Spring 2011): 77–90, for more information about the mother-daughter relationships in the text.

2. Virginity testing (in *Breath, Eyes, Memory*) is a practice in which a person places two fingers inside a woman's vaginal canal to check if her hymen is still intact (not broken), and that she thus remains a virgin.

3. Here, I am defining macro trauma as a large-scale figurative and literal wound that each Caco woman copes with as a Haitian citizen. I frame the macro trauma as an injury caused by a physical and emotional shock, which is thoroughly unhealed for each woman at the beginning of the novel.

4. See Benedetta Faedi Duramy, *Gender and Violence in Haiti: Women's Path from Victims to Agents* (New Brunswick, NJ: Rutgers University Press, 2014) for more information on the normalization of violence against Haitian women in the countryside and urban slums of Haiti.

5. Embodied memory is characterized here as a verb, which means to cause an idea to become part of a body and the memories of that body; to unite in one body in a complex unity. I am referencing how the traumatic political, physical, and national memories are attached to the bodies and memories of the Caco women in Danticat's text.

6. Edwidge Danticat, *Breath, Eyes, Memory* (New York: Vintage Books, 1994), 16.

7. Danticat, *Breath, Eyes, Memory*, 19–20.

8. Danticat, *Breath, Eyes, Memory*, 21.

9. Danticat, *Breath, Eyes, Memory*, 21.

10. Danticat, *Breath, Eyes, Memory*, 21.

11. Melissa V. Harris-Perry, *Sister Citizen: Shame, Stereotypes, and Black Women in America* (New Haven, CT: Yale University Press, 2011), 104–5.

12. See Joan Dayan, *Haiti, History, and the Gods* (Berkeley: University of California Press, 1995), for more information about the cultural imagination of Haiti.

13. Rural militiamen of Haiti, officially named the Volontaires de la Sécurité Nationale (Volunteers for National Security). They were referred to by locals as Tonton Macoutes, meaning bogeymen of mythic lands.

14. Danticat, *Breath, Eyes, Memory*, 37.

15. See Wien Weibert Arthus, "Haitian International Relations from 1957 to 1971: François Duvalier's Foreign Policy," *Bulletin de l'Institut Pierre Renouvin* 35, no. 1 (April 2012): 157–67 for more information about the elder Duvalier's regime.

16. Here, I utilize the term "fatherless country" to indicate the chaos that the Duvalier regimes (father and son) inflicted on the citizens of Haiti during the 1960s–1980s. The country lacked the steady leadership that should have invested in the interests of the country, leaving the people in a continuous state of disarray.

17. Saidiya Hartman, *Lose Your Mother: A Journey along the Atlantic Slave Route* (New York: Farrar, Straus and Giroux, 2008), 100.

18. Danticat, *Breath, Eyes, Memory*, 44.

19. In encouraging Sophie to become a successful and hardworking woman in America, Martine strongly believes that Sophie will be a direct representative of Haiti.

20. Clare Counihan, "Desiring Diaspora: 'Testing' the Boundaries of National Identity in Edwidge Danticat's *Breath, Eyes, Memory*," *Small Axe* 16, no. 1 (March 2012): 38.

21. Danticat, *Breath, Eyes, Memory*, 45.

22. The image she finds of Atie, Martine, and herself as a small child places Sophie back in a state of emotional turmoil, a feeling of not belonging even within her own family as she embarks on the challenge of also belonging in America. The idea of "fatherlessness" returns as a motif in her life as she looks for and craves love from the men in her life (besides Marc, her mother's lover) rather than the women.

23. Danticat, *Breath, Eyes, Memory*, 48.

24. I utilize the term "homemaking" to mean creating connections to Haiti, while in America, that are both social and political in nature. This practice creates comfort for the young Sophie in New York at the beginning of her stay in the United States.

25. Danticat, *Breath, Eyes, Memory*, 54.

26. See Raphael Dalleo, *American Imperialism's Undead: The Occupation of Haiti and the Rise of Caribbean Anticolonialism* (Charlottesville: University of Virginia Press, 2016).

27. Danticat, *Breath, Eyes, Memory*, 56.

28. I define Sophie's feelings of "abjectness" as an extremely negative experience; Sophie feels like she has no pride in herself, because she believes that she exists outside the sphere of Haitian belonging, unlike the rest of the Haitians in the restaurant, including Marc and Martine.

29. In this scene, like when she first arrives at the airport, Sophie tries to utilize silence as a tool of belonging, since as child she believes that silence creates concealment in her surroundings, rather than openly expressing her sadness, discomfort, or anger at being outside of what others may deem belong to a Haitian national identity. Therefore, hiding behind silence with language and food allows Sophie to remain a member of the Haitian cultural sphere.

30. Peter N. Stearns, *Shame: A Brief History* (Urbana: University of Illinois Press, 2017), 19–20.

31. Danticat, *Breath, Eyes, Memory*, 57.

32. Joseph, in the beginning, is an escape from the shame that dominates Sophie's complex relationship with her mother. He represents for Sophie a symbol of American individualism and helps her assimilate some of her conflicted ideas of self-loathing in her late teenage years.

33. Danticat, *Breath, Eyes, Memory*, 93–94.

34. Counihan, "Desiring Diaspora," 40.

35. Danticat, *Breath, Eyes, Memory*, 95.

36. In the story, the lark sees a little girl and wants to have her, so the lark stops her and asks if she would like a pomegranate: the girl is charmed by the lark. Each time, the lark requests more of the girl, until one day he tricks her into going away. The girl goes home to get the heart the lark has asked of her, but she escapes and never returns to him. The man with the stained sheets cuts the virgin girl's leg after he takes her virginity, because she did not extensively bleed during her first sex, and the man is only concerned that the sheets display sufficient blood to show his honor as a man. However, because of the cut, the girl bleeds to death and thus dies as a result of his foolish pride.

37. Danticat, *Breath, Eyes, Memory*, 157.

38. See Joan Dayan, "Erzulie: A Women's History of Haiti," *Research in African Literatures* 52, no. 2 (Summer 1994): 5–31 for more information about Erzulie, a goddess and spirit of *loa*, of love, of Vodun.

39. Ifé's statement speaks to how nationalism to Haiti is palpably gendered, and reinforces male dominance in the country.

40. When Ifé says that "testing sacrifices the value of their allegiance to Haitian mores," I contend that she means that women deserve to have the same respect within their Haitian identities as men. However, she recognizes the hypocrisy that she has perpetuated in testing her daughters and preserving the system of women's subjugation in the country.

41. Danticat, *Breath, Eyes, Memory*, 169.

42. Danticat, *Breath, Eyes, Memory*, 170.

43. Here, I discuss the positive ramifications of shame, because if shame were not present during the testing practices, Sophie would not have had the courage to confront her mother about the violence of the vaginal testing she committed against her child. The confrontation heals an important aspect of Sophie and Martine's relationship and has positive ramifications, helping them move forward as mother and daughter.

44. Danticat, *Breath, Eyes, Memory*, 180.

45. Danticat, *Breath, Eyes, Memory*, 190.

46. Sophie's sexual phobia group meets at the house of Davina, a middle-aged Chicana who was raped by her grandfather over the course of ten years. The third member is Buki, an Ethiopian college student who was genitally mutilated by her grandmother at puberty. The women are all remnants of the African diaspora and utilize their relationship to console one other in America, a home that does not necessarily belong to them but that they have claimed as their own.

BIBLIOGRAPHY

Alexander, Simone A. James. "M/othering the Nation: Women's Bodies as Nationalist Trope in Edwidge Danticat's *Breath, Eyes, Memory.*" *African American Review* 44, no. 3 (Fall 2011): 373–90.

Arthus, Wien Weibert. "Haitian International Relations from 1957 to 1971: François Duvalier's Foreign Policy." *Bulletin de l'Institut Pierre Renouvin* 35, no. 1 (April 2012): 157–67.

Counihan, Clare. "Desiring Diaspora: 'Testing' the Boundaries of National Identity in Edwidge Danticat's *Breath, Eyes, Memory.*" *Small Axe* 16, no. 1 (March 2012): 36–52.

Dalleo, Raphael. *American Imperialism's Undead: The Occupation of Haiti and the Rise of Caribbean Anticolonialism.* Charlottesville: University of Virginia Press, 2016.

Danticat, Edwidge. *Breath, Eyes, Memory.* New York: Vintage Books, 1994.

Dayan, Joan. "Erzulie: A Women's History of Haiti." *Research in African Literatures* 52, no. 2 (Summer 1994): 5–31.

Dayan, Joan. *Haiti, History, and the Gods.* Berkeley: University of California Press, 1995.

Faedi Duramy, Benedetta. *Gender and Violence in Haiti: Women's Path from Victims to Agents.* New Brunswick, NJ: Rutgers University Press, 2014.

Harris-Perry, Melissa V. *Sister Citizen: Shame, Stereotypes, and Black Women in America.* New Haven, CT: Yale University Press, 2011.

Hartman, Saidiya. *Lose Your Mother: A Journey along the Atlantic Slave Route.* New York: Farrar, Straus and Giroux, 2008.

Mehni, Masoumeh. "Analyzing the Problematic Mother-Daughter Relationship in Edwidge Danticat's *Breath, Eyes, Memory.*" *Journal of Caribbean Literatures* 7, no. 1 (Spring 2011): 77–90.

Stearns, Peter N. *Shame: A Brief History.* Urbana: University of Illinois Press, 2017.

Part III

I Speak Out:
Storytelling and Narrative Structure

Chapter Nine

"THE LISTENING GETS TOO LOUD"

The Reader's Task in Edwidge Danticat's *Brother, I'm Dying*

LAURA DAWKINS

Describing her attempts to interpret her father's brief letters from the United States during her childhood years in Haiti, Edwidge Danticat recalls: "Because he wrote so little, I would try to guess his thoughts and moods from the dotting of his *i*'s and the crossing of his *t*'s, from whether there were actual periods at the ends of his sentences or just faint dots where the tip of his pen had simply landed. Did commas split his streamlined phrases, or were they staccato, like someone speaking too rapidly, out of breath?"[1] The writer's ability to intuit emotional undercurrents in punctuation marks, the omission of punctuation, and subtle nuances of language serves her well when her uncle Joseph's surgery for throat cancer leaves him unable to speak except through a machine, and she again must read and interpret feelings behind a robotic voice: "Like distance, [the machine] masked pain. Still, his pauses were like sobs, the expansion or contraction of his words mechanical traces of sorrow."[2] Danticat's role as an interpreter or "decoder" for her father and uncle expands beyond her family to encompass, through her own experience as well as through the stories passed down to her, all the suppressed and marginalized voices of the Haitian community. Joseph's literal loss of voice invokes the silencing of Haitian voices both in their own homeland and in the diaspora, a silencing Joseph challenges by "jotting things down [. . .] the names of victims [. . .] the condition of their bodies."[3] Like Danticat herself, Joseph reads the sounds of his neighbors in Bel Air as they "beat the darkness" by "pounding on pots and pans and making clanking noises that rang throughout the entire neighborhood," and he "trie[s] to imagine in each clang an act of protest, a cry for peace, to the Haitian riot police, to the United Nations soldiers, all of whom were supposed to be protecting them."[4] Transmitting these messages to Danticat, who pieces stories together from the fragments available, Joseph collaborates on the narrative whose title significantly registers his first-person voice: *Brother, I'm Dying*. Throughout her memoir of her father and uncle, Danticat highlights the importance of the communal voice, defining her own role as that of a mouthpiece or messenger: "I am writing this only because they can't."[5]

Although communal storytelling is a familiar trope in all of Danticat's works, what makes *Brother, I'm Dying* distinctive is the author's attentiveness to the role of the reader—not only Danticat's own task as reader and decoder of her uncle's nonverbal cues and her father's cryptic letters, but also her uncle's self-imposed responsibility to read and decipher the sometimes inchoate voices of his community, as well as our obligation as Danticat's readers to engage actively with her multilayered text. Danticat has frequently insisted upon the intimate bond between reader and writer, sometimes blurring the distinction between the two roles. Responding to Paul Holdengräber's query as to whether "the figure of the writer, in Haiti, is viewed as an important presence," Danticat affirms: "Absolutely, but interesting, much more interesting to me, too, has always been the figure of the reader."[6] As she argues, "for a lot of writers, the reader and the writer overlap a lot," pointing out that, like writing, reading "forces you to step into another body, to step into other skins."[7] This overlap emerges clearly in *Brother, I'm Dying* when Danticat's task of portraying her father and her uncle involves a reciprocal intimacy between writer and subject, a collaboration in which Danticat reads the lives and characters of her family members and then serves as their mouthpiece after their own voices are silenced. The text that is born out of this loving collaboration, Danticat explains, is "not a *me*-moir but a *nou*-moir, a *we*-moir"—a joint creation that, as Régine Michelle Jean-Charles observes, provides a useful framework for "thinking through how the memoir, usually seen as a genre focused on interiority, can become a narrative space for collective political, historic, and social work."[8]

Danticat has acknowledged her role as proxy and interpreter for those who cannot speak on their own behalf, stating, "I wanted to raise the voice of a lot of the people that I knew growing up, and this was, for the most part, poor people who had extraordinary dreams but also very amazing obstacles."[9] Yet she also recognizes her complicated position as a Haitian American attempting to speak for the silenced victims of political terrorism in a homeland she has left behind. As Jean-Charles observes, "Danticat has repeatedly refused the title of the 'voice of Haiti,' pointing out that Haitian experience is far too vast to be captured by one voice."[10] Danticat describes herself as "an insider and outsider in both cultures," an expatriate with a "mixed gaze [. . .] looking at the United States with Haitian eyes and [. . .]

at Haiti with American eyes."[11] Conceding that the insider/outsider has an incomplete perspective, Danticat nevertheless argues that this position also gives her a nuanced and multifaceted outlook on both her culture of origin and her adopted country. Although she admits that the role of insider/outsider "might be an uncomfortable place personally [. . .] it's an extraordinary place artistically because all these things that you are processing mesh. Nuance is important to art and being from different places offers nuance."[12]

In learning to read both her extended family in Haiti and her nuclear family in the United States, Danticat repeatedly underscores the importance of nonverbal communication. Writing to her father, she depends upon him to assume an active role as an interpreter of her unspoken emotions, "decod[ing] the longing in my childish cursive slopes and arches, which were so much like his own."[13] When her parents visit Haiti with her new sibling, Danticat feels envious of her infant brother's bond with her mother but immediately picks up on the consoling message that her mother silently transmits: "I could tell from the way she stopped now and then to run her fingers over both his face and mine that she meant him to be a link between us."[14] She captures the power of such unspoken messages in her eloquent description of one of the last meals her mother prepares for Danticat's desperately ill father:

> When the rice was done, my mother searched a cabinet filled with her special-occasion dishes, the kind she used only when she had company, and pulled out a white porcelain plate with two giant cherries sketched in the middle. The cherries overlapped in a way that made them look like one large heart and as my mother heaped the rice on top of them, they seemed like a coded message from a woman who was beyond taking ordinary moments with her husband for granted.[15]

Just as the lovingly prepared rice attests to her nurture of her dying husband, the image of a heart at the bottom of the bowl silently reinforces her fierce devotion. In Danticat's *The Art of Death* (2017), she observes that Tolstoy "supposedly came up with a series of codes, including eye movements, so that when his time came, he could describe to the people around him what it was like to die."[16] Our hunger to communicate with others, Danticat indicates, defies not only the loss of speech but also the limitations of spoken language itself.

Danticat extends this notion of unspoken communication between family members to embrace the possibility of a charged but wordless connection between the writer and the reader. Describing a book as "an intimate

conversation between two people, one writer and one reader,"[17] she underscores not only the writer's attunement to her silent audience but also the
reader's highly personal responsiveness to the ghostlike reflections of her
own life in the written text. In *The Art of Intimacy*, Stacey D'Erasmo captures
the nature of this intense, unarticulated bond between writer and reader:

> One of the most complex and mobile intimacies produced on the
> page is that between reader and writer. As writers, we engage that
> space between with every letter we put down, every comma, every
> sentence, paragraph, and scene. [. . .] [T]he writer is continually
> engaging an unknowable Other, a protean ghost. [. . .] The topos, the
> meeting ground, for fiction that makes powerful use of the relation-
> ship between reader and writer is white space, which we can simul-
> taneously consider to be white space on the page and the blankness,
> the open air, between reader and writer.[18]

Comparing the link between the writer and reader to the connection between
a testifier and witness, Nancy K. Miller and Jason Tougaw similarly suggest
that what remains unspoken between the two carries an elusive and immea-
surable weight: "Whatever the attachment between writer and reader, there
remains in every act of witness a place of opacity, what [Giorgio] Agamben
calls a 'lacuna' that cannot be illuminated or put into language."[19] Danticat's
implicit analogy between decoding her family's unspoken messages and
the conversation she initiates with her silent readers speaks to her sense of
the powerful voices registering between the lines of the oral or written text.

As Danticat demonstrates in *Brother, I'm Dying*, the voices of silenced
victims of political oppression in Haiti resonate profoundly for those listeners
attuned to their muted reverberations. Describing Joseph's acuity in interpreting unarticulated messages, Danticat suggests that the role of attentive
listener or reader of others' lives also encompasses the duty of witnessing
to collective trauma. Joseph, a Baptist minister in his home village of Bel
Air during the political and social turmoil of the Duvalier regime in Haiti,
discerns anger and fear in the chorus of sounds from the community, but he
gleans a message of hope from the passionate clamor of his roused neighbors:

> He heard something he hadn't heard in some time: people were
> pounding on pots and pans and making clanking noises that rang
> throughout the entire neighborhood. It wasn't the first time we'd
> heard it, of course. This kind of purposeful rattle was called *bat teneb*,
> or beating the darkness. His neighbors, most of them now dead,

had tried to beat the darkness when Fignole had been toppled so many decades ago. A new generation had tried it again when Aristide had been removed both times. [. . .] The din of clanking metal rose above the racket of roof-denting rocks. Or maybe he only thought so because he was so heartened by the *bat teneb*. Maybe he wouldn't die today after all. Maybe none of them would die, because their neighbors were making their presence known, demanding peace from the gangs as well as from the authorities, from all sides.[20]

Deprived of his own voice through cancer, Joseph assumes the responsibility of listening to and recording the voices of his community. As Danticat documents, he serves not only as a witness to the townspeople's mourning rituals but also—like Danticat herself in telling the story of her uncle's life—as a mouthpiece for their collective sorrow: "As soon as the forces left, the screaming began in earnest . . . Amwe, they shot my son. Help, they hurt my daughter. My father's dying. My baby's dead. My uncle jotted down a few of the words he was hearing in one of the small notepads in his shirt pocket. Again, recording things had become an obsession."[21] Reflecting his niece's sense of obligation in detailing Joseph's own ordeals, Danticat's uncle provides a voice for those whose singular experiences of grief might otherwise be lost to history.

Danticat has insisted, "The need to bear witness can feel almost unrelenting after a loved one dies."[22] Yet she also affirms, as do Shoshana Felman and Dori Laub, that witnessing to a traumatic event cannot take place in a vacuum; rather, for trauma victims to experience the healing benefits of testimony, they must speak to a deeply attentive listener. As Felman and Laub argue, "There needs to be a bonding, the intimate and total presence of an *other*—in the position of one who hears. Testimonies are not monologues; they cannot take place in solitude. The witnesses are talking to *somebody*, to somebody they have been waiting for for a long time."[23] In the story "Night Talkers" from Danticat's short-story cycle *The Dew Breaker*, the trauma victim Dany recognizes that, even though he "spoke his dreams aloud in the night, to the point of sometimes jolting himself awake with the sound of his own voice,"[24] his testimony is ineffective because he speaks only to himself—unlike his new acquaintance Claude, who chooses Dany as the "*somebody*" who will listen to his own disturbing story: "Claude was a palannit, a night talker, one of those who spoke their nightmares out loud to themselves. Except Claude was even luckier than he realized for he was able to speak his nightmares to himself as well as to others."[25] Danticat herself, attempting to inhabit Joseph's consciousness when he is preyed upon by gang members in Bel Air, and imagining in scrupulous detail his thoughts and emotions while in danger, serves as an ideal listener and an empathic and engaged participant in her uncle's act of witnessing.

Danticat's task as attentive listener and recorder of her uncle's experiences expands into the role of community mouthpiece after gang members destroy Joseph's meticulous documentation of Bel Air's political violence. Joseph's literal loss of voice as a middle-aged man, prompting the nine-year-old Danticat to "[go] everywhere with him and [speak] for him,"[26] is reenacted years later when his notepads are "trampled, carried away, or burned."[27] Again, Danticat assumes the mantle of proxy for her uncle's silenced voice. As Angela A. Ards has pointed out, the suppression of Joseph's speech as well as the reference to his approaching death in the title of Danticat's memoir widens out to encompass Haiti's state of crisis: "The dying 'I' of the memoir's title is thus a collective one, at once referring to her uncle and father, Haitian brothers who die within months of each other on the soil of the imperial regime that occupied their country at their births, as well as to Haiti's twentieth-century travails."[28] When Joseph meets a tragic death during his internment at the Krome Detention Center in Miami, Danticat allows his fate to stand in for the trauma of all Haitian refugees seeking asylum in the United States, and, in transcribing her conversations with detainees, she serves as witness to their collective pain:

> [One] asked us to tell the world the detainees were beaten sometimes. He told of a friend who'd had his back broken by a guard and was deported before he could get medical attention. [. . .] They were at times so cold that they shivered all night long. They told of the food that rather than nourish them, punished them, gave them diarrhea and made them vomit. They told of arbitrary curfews, how they were woken up at six a.m. and forced to go back to that cold room by six p.m. The shame of being a prisoner loomed large. A stigma most couldn't shake. To have been shackled, handcuffed. [. . .] I'd met a young man from Bel Air. His eyes were red. He couldn't stop crying. His mother had died the week before, he said, and he couldn't even attend her funeral.[29]

By sharing the detainees' testimony, Danticat both carries on her uncle's project of recording the voices of his community and invites her readers' empathic engagement with the victims of political trauma. As Miller and Tougaw contend, "testimony attempts to bridge the gap between suffering individuals, and ultimately communities of listeners, whose empathic response can be palliative, if not curative."[30] As the refugees' "living memorial,"[31]

Danticat ensures that she not only listens to their stories but also keeps their voices alive.

However, as several Danticat scholars have noted, Danticat's autobiographical persona undergoes a dramatic transformation when she begins to document the details of her uncle's death.[32] Danticat relates the events of Joseph's final days with the detached, impersonal tone of a reporter, muting both her own emotional response as well as her apprehension of her uncle's trauma. While Veronica Austen interprets Danticat's reticence as a form of self-protection, Elizabeth Walcott-Hackshaw and Kezia Page both view the author's impersonal style as a deliberate replication of the immigration authorities' clinical detachment, reinforcing through understatement the sense of alienation and isolation that Joseph must have felt during his ordeal.[33] Certainly, Danticat's spare, unadorned narrative captures the incommunicability of trauma as well as the survivor's need to shield herself from the horror of the experience. However, the sparseness of her account also suggests the author's awareness that descriptive details are superfluous, even intrusive, in recounting a trauma of such magnitude. In her tribute to the power of Toni Morrison's prose, Danticat herself indicates her reason for using stark, simple language in her description of her uncle's detention and death. Danticat focuses on the scene of Sethe's infanticide in *Beloved*: "That scene has some of the most deliberately unadorned language in an otherwise densely lyrical novel. The moment is both horrible and powerful enough, Morrison seems to be indicating, that there's no need to sensationalize it further."[34] Danticat goes on to quote Morrison's own reflections on her composition of the scene of Beloved's death: "So if I'm going to imagine what it takes to kill your baby, then I have to put in my arms *my baby*. [. . .] And when that happens—and it's difficult—then the language just pares down. You don't get ornamental with that. You get very still, very clean-limbed, and very quiet, because the event itself is bigger than language."[35] Danticat follows Morrison's lead in *Brother, I'm Dying*, creating an unembellished narrative in which Joseph's tragic experience speaks for itself.

Yet Morrison is not Danticat's only model in constructing her restrained narrative of her uncle's last days. Joseph Dantica himself provides an example for his niece of the powerful impact of understatement. As Danticat has observed, Dantica repeatedly writes down simply the numbers and facts of military atrocities in Bel Air, needing no descriptive details or passionate denunciations to convey their stark horror:

Every morning he got up to count the many bloody corpses that dotted the street corners and alleys of Bel Air. [. . .] In his notebooks, he wrote the names of the victims, the conditions of their bodies, and the times they were picked up, either by family members or by the sanitation service, to be transported to the morgue or dumped in mass graves.[36]

In recounting the destruction of his church at the hands of gang members, Dantica similarly "gave up writing sentences to simply list what had been removed or burned from the church."[37] Like Dantica, Danticat strips her uncle's horrific experience down to a bare statement of facts, implicitly understanding the emotional weight of unadorned truth.

Significantly, by vacating her role as attuned reader and recorder of her uncle's interior consciousness, Danticat transfers that obligation to the reader of her memoir. Morrison has insisted on the reader's responsibility to "work *with* the author in the construction of the book. What's left out is as important as what is there."[38] Danticat strategically allows Joseph's individuality as well as her intimate bond with him to recede into the background as she recounts his final moments. Withholding her own sorrow as well as her imagining of her uncle's pain, the author invites the reader to fill in the blanks—to step into Joseph's skin—as she dispassionately details his interrogation by immigration authorities. This important passage must be quoted at length:

The interpreter had trouble understanding my uncle's voice box, so Officer Castro asked my uncle to move his mouth closer to the phone. As my uncle leaned forward, his hand slipped away from his neck and he dropped his voice box. The records indicate that my uncle appeared to be having a seizure. His body stiffened. His legs jerked forward. His chair slipped back, pounding the back of his head into the wall. He began to vomit. Vomit shot out of his mouth, his nose, as well as the tracheotomy hole in his neck. The vomit was spread all over his face, from his forehead to his chin, down the front of his blue Krome-issued overalls. There was also vomit on his thighs, where a large wet stain showed he had also urinated on himself. [. . .] Fifteen minutes had passed since my uncle first started vomiting. A registered nurse and medic finally arrived. By then my uncle looked "almost comatose," Pratt [Joseph's lawyer] recalled. "He seemed somewhat unconscious and couldn't move." Pratt told the medic and nurse that right before he became ill, my uncle had told him his medication had been taken away. Pratt then turned to Officer Castro and asked if my uncle could be granted humanitarian parole given his age and condition. "I think he's faking," the medic said, cutting Pratt off. To prove his point, the medic grabbed my uncle's head and moved it up and down. It was rigid rather than limp, he said. [. . .] When Maxo [Joseph's son] arrived, he ran to his father and seeing him slumped over in the wheelchair and leaning over the side, began to cry. [. . .] "He wouldn't be like this if you hadn't taken away his medication," Maxo said, sobbing. "He's faking," repeated the medic. "He keeps looking at me." Later that morning, in the Krome medical unit, my uncle's condition worsened and according to Krome records, he was transported to Miami Jackson Memorial Hospital with shackles on his feet.[39]

By inserting journalistic phrases such as "the records indicate"[40] and "according to Krome records"[41] into her description of her uncle's ordeal, Danticat assumes the position of the distanced observer, accordingly compelling us to step into the role that she has abandoned: that of attentive and compassionate reader and interpreter of the scene she depicts.

Danticat understands the difficulty of the task she imposes on her reader. In *Create Dangerously*, she suggests that the role of the empathic and engaged listener can at times become a crushing burden: "I listen for everything. [. . .] I listen too closely and sometimes the listening gets too loud."[42] Asking her readers to assume this burden, she transforms them from passive recipients of her words into active agents who struggle to inhabit the writer's own consciousness as well as the consciousness of the traumatized subjects she depicts. Recounted matter-of-factly by the distanced author, Joseph's seizures, his vomiting, his loss of bladder control, and his pain become unbearable to the empathic reader who has stepped into Danticat's role. "Too loud" listening indicates that the listener or reader has engaged so fully with the subject that the trauma the narrator describes becomes his or her own.

By enabling her reader to take on the role of empathic listener, Danticat underscores, through dramatic contrast, the refusal of the immigration authorities to read Joseph's state of crisis. As Austen observes, Danticat "emphasize[s] that her uncle's death was caused by a system that assumed the hubris that it could and did know Joseph Dantica, a system that could, for instance, declare with no recorded self-consciousness, doubt, or regret that Dantica was 'faking' his illness, despite his vomit and altered state of consciousness proving the contrary."[43] Equipped with inflexible stereotypes about Haitian refugees, the authorities neither see nor hear the suffering individual placed before them. For the reader who has come to know Joseph through Danticat's intimate and sensitive portrayal, the callous obliviousness of his interrogators provokes a bottomless anger and sorrow. "Listening too loud," Danticat suggests, is the ethical alternative to willed insensibility, and she demands that her readers assume this moral imperative.

Danticat has frequently affirmed the value of what Morrison calls "participatory reading." Morrison has argued, "Two people are busy making the story. One is me and one is you and together we do that, we invent it together and I just hold your hand while you're in the process of going there and hearing it and sharing it."[44] Similarly, referring to a scene in her novel *Claire of the Sea Light* in which young children play a circle game that requires "switch[ing] places during different moments of [a] song," Danticat states, "I imagine the reader joining that circle, if you will, as he or she tries to understand what is happening in the town at that moment."[45] Danticat suggests in *Create Dangerously* that during an intense reading experience, ego boundaries between writer and reader dissolve: "I sometimes wonder if in the intimate, both solitary and solidary, union between writers and readers a border can really exist."[46] She expands on this notion in citing the reflections of the Haitian Canadian writer Dany Laferrière:

> [Laferrière] talks often about this experience of the reader, of a reader who repatriates the writer. [. . .] When he wrote a novel called *Je suis un écrivain japonais*, "I'm a Japanese writer," saying that if I'm read by a Japanese reader, I become a Japanese writer. [. . .] He says, these writers of course they were repatriated, Whitman, Cervantes—[he] has a whole list—otherwise, what were they doing in my room? They were living with me under the blanket with a pillow.[47]

Recalling Morrison's conviction that the writer and reader ideally become "inward toward the other," Danticat has suggested that the author and her reader establish a one-on-one rapport: "That's how it works: one person at a time holding one book, so the whole process is full of intimacy."[48] Felman and Laub compare the reader to a trauma witness's listener, maintaining, "Acts of witness bind teller and listener through what Wendy Chun calls a 'contract of listening' [. . .] not unlike the one binding writer and reader in autobiographical acts."[49] Asserting that in *Brother, I'm Dying* she "wanted to have the reader become a part of my family,"[50] Danticat accordingly confers on that reader the duty of a family member to respond with heartsick fury to her beloved uncle's needless death.

Although Danticat maintains that reading is an "intimate conversation" between "one writer and one reader," she also affirms in her epilogue to *Krik? Krak!* that "heading on a journey with the reader"[51] requires that one become attuned to a chorus of voices, "those whose fables and metaphors, whose similes, and soliloquies, whose diction and *je ne sais quoi* daily slip into your survival soup."[52] Remembering the myriad female voices of her family and community—the "kitchen poets"—Danticat celebrates the "thousand women urging you to speak through the blunt tip of your pencil . . . ask[ing] for your voice."[53] Brenna Munro has observed, "Danticat's work engages, in an unusually sustained and nuanced fashion, with the relationship between written narratives and oral culture. She seems compelled by the border between orality and writing, and, appropriately enough as a transnational writer, attempts to reimagine that border."[54] By blurring the distinction between reader and listener and between writer and reader, Danticat imagines a narrative space in which the creation of the text becomes a communal project. Yet Munro cautions, "To imagine that a printed text can revive or continue orality is of course a contradiction in terms."[55] She describes Danticat's quest to transfer voice onto page as an act of violence, a futile attempt to bridge an unbridgeable gap:

> In a kind of magical synesthesia, orality and writing merge in the image of the "blunt" pencil that speaks. Her mother also describes the young Danticat silently writing in terms of sound: "But then she's not being quiet. You hear this scraping from her. Krik? Krak! Pencil, paper. It sounds like someone crying." These sounds, however—scraping, cracking, and crying—evoke acts of violence more than they do a speaking human voice. [. . .] [T]hese croaking sounds also bring our attention to the way in which the silence of writing cannot easily be equated with the voice, and the ways in which literature cannot simply replicate an oral culture.[56]

According to Munro, a writer "cannot be a griot,"[57] cannot do what Henry Louis Gates Jr., by contrast, has identified as a central feature of African diasporic narrative: "The paradox of representing, of containing somehow, the oral within the written."[58]

Yet for Danticat, the progression from the call-and-response interplay within a vibrant oral culture to stationary words on the page lies in the imagination of the reader as he or she participates with the writer in the making of the narrative. In an interview conducted soon after the publication of *Brother, I'm Dying*, Danticat calls the text of her memoir "my tears on the page," acknowledging, "The only way I knew to grieve them [her father and uncle] was to write about them."[59] The crying sound of her pencil, therefore, need not represent a painful transition from orality to text, as Munro argues, but rather the writer's attempt to translate her visceral emotional responses onto the blank page. An empathic and attuned reader, Danticat indicates, will share the writer's act of mourning and will accordingly hear, touch, see, and feel these "tears on the page." In *Brother, I'm Dying*, Danticat demonstrates how both her father's and her uncle's verbal and nonverbal messages, as well as the combined voices of her Haitian and American communities—all of which she must read with care—inspire and sustain her as she constructs her "*we*-moir." However, Danticat suggests that the final responsibility to make the text come alive remains with the reader: "When [readers] read a piece of literature that we've [Haitian writers] written, we become closer to them. We are now part of them when the art stays with them. They then come closer to meeting us, and closer to the different layers of who and what we are."[60]

Danticat's notion of the active and responsible reader informs all of her work, both fiction and nonfiction. Her writing demands a participatory witness who must work with the author to make meaning of the text. She requires the reader of *Brother, I'm Dying* to "listen too loud"—to step into the skins of Danticat's loved ones and read their lives in the spaces she leaves open—and thus inhabit rather than simply observe and interpret the experiences that sear them. Enabling her reader to engage empathically not only with her uncle and her father but also with the Haitian victims whose fates her uncle Joseph transcribed so meticulously, Danticat passes on to this reader the responsibility that Joseph bequeathed to her: to raise the voices of the brutally silenced, carrying their stories and their legacies into the larger world. As she affirms in the closing pages of her memoir, "It is not our way to let our grief silence us."[61]

NOTES

1. Edwidge Danticat, *Brother, I'm Dying* (New York: Vintage Books, 2007), 23.

2. Danticat, *Brother, I'm Dying*, 135–36.

3. Danticat, *Brother, I'm Dying*, 139.

4. Danticat, *Brother, I'm Dying*, 172–73.

5. Danticat, *Brother, I'm Dying*, 26.

6. Maxine Lavon Montgomery, *Conversations with Edwidge Danticat* (Jackson: University Press of Mississippi, 2017), 81.

7. Montgomery, *Conversations with Edwidge Danticat*, 83.

8. Régine Michelle Jean-Charles, "Of Memories and Men: The Ethics of Life Writings in Edwidge Danticat's *Brother, I'm Dying* and Jamaica Kincaid's *My Brother*," in *Writings*

on *Caribbean History, Literature, Art and Culture: One Love*, ed. Irline François (Newcastle upon Tyne: Cambridge Scholars Publishing, 2018), 128–50.

9. Montgomery, *Conversations with Edwidge Danticat*, 8.

10. Jean-Charles, "Of Memories and Men," 138.

11. Bonnie Lyons, "An Interview with Edwidge Danticat," *Contemporary Literature* 44, no. 2 (Summer 2003): 29–57.

12. Montgomery, *Conversations with Edwidge Danticat*, 119.

13. Danticat, *Brother, I'm Dying*, 24.

14. Danticat, *Brother, I'm Dying*, 91.

15. Danticat, *Brother, I'm Dying*, 260.

16. Edwidge Danticat, *The Art of Death: Writing the Final Story* (Minneapolis: Graywolf Press, 2017), 30.

17. Montgomery, *Conversations with Edwidge Danticat*, 139.

18. Stacey D'Erasmo, *The Art of Intimacy: The Space Between* (Minneapolis: Graywolf Press, 2013), 91–92.

19. Nancy K. Miller and Jason Tougaw, introduction to *Extremities: Trauma, Testimony, and Community*, ed. Nancy K. Miller and Jason Tougaw (Urbana: University of Illinois Press, 2002). In "Art as Engagement: Violence, Trauma, and the Role of the Reader in Edwidge Danticat's *The Dew Breaker*," *Contemporary Women's Writing* 8, no. 2 (July 2014): 189–205, Birgit Spengler links the reader's role in *The Dew Breaker* with that of the empathic witness or therapist. As she explains, "Danticat's aesthetic strategies to communicate the characters' inner dilemmas also turn the reader into an ersatz trauma worker who is called upon to help in the process of making sense of the fragmented stories and symptoms of a traumatized subject. [. . .] In this attempt, the reading experience resembles a victim's way of coping with trauma, and a therapist's attempt to make sense of its symptoms" (196).

20. Danticat, *Brother, I'm Dying*, 172–73.

21. Danticat, *Brother, I'm Dying*, 176.

22. Danticat, *The Art of Death*, 158.

23. Shoshana Felman and Dori Laub, *Testimony: Crises of Witnessing in Literature, Psychoanalysis, and History* (New York: Routledge, 1992), 70–71.

24. Edwidge Danticat, *The Dew Breaker* (New York: Vintage Books, 2005), 120.

25. Danticat, *The Dew Breaker*, 120.

26. Lyons, "An Interview with Edwidge Danticat," 193.

27. Danticat, *Brother, I'm Dying*, 187.

28. Angela A. Ards, *Words of Witness: Black Women's Autobiography in the Post-*Brown *Era* (Madison: University of Wisconsin Press, 2015), 112.

29. Danticat, *Brother, I'm Dying*, 212–13.

30. Miller and Tougaw, introduction to *Extremities*, 11.

31. Montgomery, *Conversations with Edwidge Danticat*, 90.

32. See, for example, Veronica Austen, "Empathetic Engagement in Danticat's *Brother, I'm Dying*," *Ariel* 44, nos. 2–3 (April–July 2014): 29–57; Kezia Page, *Transnational Negotiations in Caribbean Diasporic Literature: Remitting the Text* (Abingdon, Oxon.,

England: Routledge, 2011); and Elizabeth Walcott-Hackshaw, "Home Is Where the Heart Is: Danticat's Landscapes of Return," *Small Axe* 12, no. 3 (October 2008): 71–82.

33. Austen argues that Danticat's "larger purpose of human rights advocacy" requires that she establish her credibility "by offering only documented facts rather than an imagining of what her uncle's experiences must have entailed" ("Empathetic Engagement," 39). She also suggests that Danticat's restrained narrative "necessarily speaks to trauma's inherent stilting, if not utter silencing, of emotional expression," since immersion in the traumatic experience "would be overwhelming and even psychically harmful" (42). By contrast, Walcott-Hackshaw and Page contend that Danticat reproduces the authorities' impersonal rhetoric as a way of underscoring the callousness of their response to her uncle's crisis.

34. Danticat, *The Art of Death*, 102.

35. Danticat, *The Art of Death*, 103.

36. Danticat, *Brother, I'm Dying*, 139.

37. Danticat, *Brother, I'm Dying*, 214.

38. Toni Morrison, "Rootedness: The Ancestor as Foundation," in *Black Women Writers (1950–1980): A Critical Evaluation*, ed. Mari Evans (New York: Doubleday, 1984), 339–44.

39. Danticat, *Brother, I'm Dying*, 232–36.

40. Danticat, *Brother, I'm Dying*, 232.

41. Danticat, *Brother, I'm Dying*, 236.

42. Danticat, *Create Dangerously: The Immigrant Artist at Work* (Princeton, NJ: Princeton University Press, 2010), 36.

43. Austen, "Empathetic Engagement," 47.

44. Danille Taylor-Guthrie, ed., *Conversations with Toni Morrison* (Jackson: University Press of Mississippi, 1994), 231.

45. Montgomery, *Conversations with Edwidge Danticat*, 164.

46. Danticat, *Create Dangerously*, 16.

47. Danticat, *Create Dangerously*, 15. Reflecting on Laferrière's statement, Danticat writes: "Is there a border between Antigone's desire to bury her brother and the Haitian mother of 1964 who desperately wants to take her dead son's body out of the street to give him a proper burial, knowing that if she does this she too may die?" (*Create Dangerously*, 16). She declares, "Even without globalization, the writer bound to the reader, under diabolic, or even joyful, circumstances can possibly become an honorary citizen of the country of his readers" (15).

48. Montgomery, *Conversations with Edwidge Danticat*, 139.

49. Felman and Laub, *Testimony*, 11.

50. Montgomery, *Conversations with Edwidge Danticat*, 196.

51. Montgomery, *Conversations with Edwidge Danticat*, 212.

52. Danticat, *Krik? Krak!* (New York: Vintage Books, 1996), 220.

53. Danticat, *Krik? Krak!*, 222.

54. Brenna Munro, "Letters Lost at Sea: Edwidge Danticat and Orality," in *Echoes of the Haitian Revolution, 1804–2004*, ed. Martin Munro and Elizabeth Walcott-Hackshaw (Mona, Jamaica: University of the West Indies Press, 2008), 122–33.

55. Munro, "Letters Lost at Sea," 123.

56. Munro, "Letters Lost at Sea," 127–28.

57. Munro, "Letters Lost at Sea," 125.

58. Henry Louis Gates Jr., *The Signifying Monkey: A Theory of African-American Literary Criticism* (New York: Oxford University Press, 1988), 130–31.

59. Montgomery, *Conversations with Edwidge Danticat*, 49.

60. Montgomery, *Conversations with Edwidge Danticat*, 121.

61. Danticat, *Brother, I'm Dying*, 266.

Chapter Ten

READING EDWIDGE DANTICAT'S ESSAYS IN LIGHT OF HER FICTION

Diaspora, Ethics, Aesthetics

LUCÍA STECHER AND THOMÁS ROTHE

After publishing several novels, short stories, a travel book, and a memoir on her father and uncle, Edwidge Danticat released her first book of essays in 2010: *Create Dangerously: The Immigrant Artist at Work*. Several of the articles collected in this book had previously appeared in the *New Yorker*, the *Progressive*, or the *Miami Herald*, or were presented at conferences, attesting to Danticat's position within the US public sphere as a respected observer of issues related to Haiti. The book focuses largely on artists of the Haitian diaspora, illustrating how most of them have permanently renewed a political commitment to their home country despite living abroad. Seven years later, in 2017, Danticat published another book of essays, *The Art of Death: Writing the Final Story*, inspired by her mother's recent passing. In this contribution to Graywolf Press's "The Art of" series on literature and literary criticism, Danticat relies on the essay genre not only to reconstruct her mother's life but also to confront illness and dying on a larger scale. Here, Danticat questions the possibilities of writing about death, representing this absolute experience in words and speaking of something that is never a writer's own experience, not even in the case of death diaries or accounts of near-death experiences.

In this chapter, we discuss both volumes of essays, reading them alongside Danticat's fiction in order to illustrate central aspects of her larger literary project. Our analysis highlights how Danticat's essays revisit certain topics and discursive strategies that appear throughout her fiction, revealing consistencies and transformations in her ethical and aesthetic proposals. Among these issues, we discuss the implications of writing about Haiti from a diasporic locus of enunciation, the search for literary voices and forms that allow Danticat to speak about Haiti without attempting to speak for Haitians, and aesthetic explorations that convey intersections between the oral and written traditions as well as Haitian Creole and US standard English.

The essay genre, as Liliana Weinberg suggests, is "a class of non-fictional and predominantly interpretative prose texts, which represent a responsible process of thinking and representing the world, its issues and problems, formulated from an author's personal and specific perspective"[1] (2014, 62). Originating in sixteenth-century France, the genre's name comes from *essai*, meaning a "trial" or "attempt," similar to the Spanish *ensayo*, the same word for "rehearsal." Randi Saloman points out that the genre "offers freedoms of movement and association, and an ability to balance truth and fiction, that are untenable in other formats" (2013, 56). Within Caribbean literature, Norval Edwards argues that the essay is often blurred with other genres such as "memoir and literary and cultural criticism, social and political commentary, and ruminations on race, history and nationalism," forming a critical tradition introduced by George Lamming and C. L. R. James (Edwards 2011, 116). We believe that the essay genre is especially productive for Danticat, since it offers a space to reflect on her already vast literary work, the ethical and aesthetic challenges implied in writing about Haiti from the diaspora, and her position within US, Haitian, and transnational literary fields. Just as her fiction incorporates many real-life experiences, her essays are often articulated around autobiographical elements, including her career as a writer, which guide her reflections on the meaning of art and writing in contexts of migration and political violence.

COMMUNICATING VESSELS: FICTION AND ESSAY

In "New York Day Women," one of the stories included in Danticat's second book, *Krik? Krak!* (1996), the narrator learns of her mother's secret outings to Manhattan and decides to follow her to observe her routine. Although the mother belongs to a Haitian cultural universe, with traditional values and strict disciplinary measures, she confidently strides through the busy urban streets, window shopping and indulging in fast food. The narrator then realizes that her mother's life is much more complex than the image revealed at home and begins to appreciate her mother's traditional knowledge, despite some of its oppressive qualities, particularly regarding gender values. The mother figure, therefore, provides a vital connection to the cultural universe of Haiti from within the United States, connecting the narrator with a cultural tradition that offers both valuable and repressive qualities.

As Rocio Davis has shown, *Krik? Krak!* can be read as a short story cycle that refashions stories from the Haitian oral tradition, particularly those Danticat absorbed while living in Haiti (Davis 2001, 68). Danticat's attention to form and social concerns appears explicitly in this book as two aspects that characterize her broader literary production. On the one hand, she invests importance in narrating through different voices and perspectives. On the other, she poses complex issues of personal and collective memory, and critical views of Haitian history and politics, migration, and tensions between tradition and modernity. This first volume of stories helps situate her more contemporary work, since many of the issues she deals with in her early fiction reappear later in her essays. For instance, "New York Day Women" evokes several aspects we will discuss in Danticat's essays, such as representing others in narrative, cross-sections of memories of Haitian oral traditions, the United States as a destination for emigrants, and critical perspectives that recognize complexities and contradictions in Haitian culture.

In the epilogue to *Krik? Krak!*, the narrator reflects on writing as a space to confess and connect loose ideas: "When you write, it's like braiding your hair. Taking a handful of coarse unruly strands and attempting to bring them unity" (1996, 220). Writing is also a dangerous occupation in a country like Haiti, since "writers don't leave any mark in the world. Not the world where we are from. In our world, writers are tortured and killed if they are men. Called lying whores, then raped and killed, if they are women" (221). Writing from the United States allows Danticat to reflect on the risks that writers face in Haiti, aware that she does not directly face the same difficulties. Such a degree of separation grants her certain liberties to criticize social structures that perpetuate injustice in Haiti—liberties wielded by a sense of responsibility to use her legitimacy as a widely read author in the English-speaking world.

The idea of literature and art as perilous activities is central to *Create Dangerously*. The essays collected in this book reveal the richness and complexity of Haitian art and artists, many of whom fled into exile to avoid death or political persecution in Haiti. From exile, writers, journalists, painters, and artists of all kinds produce discourses and symbolic representations committed to transforming their country. Danticat, who forms part of this community of diasporic artists, reflects on the borders that divide and connect Haitians living in their country and abroad, on the challenges of confronting negative stereotypes of Haitians (without lessening her critique of the profound problems afflicting Haiti), and on the role of art in transforming society. She also contemplates her own literary production, in terms of both her personal history and the collective experience of belonging to a group of writers who, since the 1980s in the United States, have been referred to as ethnic writers (Rivero 1989). She is conscious of the demands she and her peers confront, such as adhering to the stereotypical image of what it means to be Haitian, telling stories representative of a national community, and articulating collective more than individual voices. As we will discuss, these pressures of authenticity are voiced through self-critiques and, in some ways, function as an element of self-censorship. Danticat's essays provide a space to discuss how these restrictions have influenced her writing, and to reflect on their limits and the pressures of authenticity.

In *Create Dangerously*, Danticat writes extensively of her first novel, *Breath, Eyes, Memory* (1994), which provoked mixed reactions among the Haitian community in the United States. The novel narrates the story of Sophie Caco, a twelve-year-old Haitian child who emigrates to the United States to join her mother, fictionalizing crucial aspects of Danticat's life: her own migration to the United States at the age of twelve, and her experience of leaving the aunts and uncles who raised her until she was able to join her parents in New York. One central topic in the novel is the virginity test Sophie's mother forces upon her—a humiliating and violent custom involving vaginal penetration with a foreign inanimate object, passed on from one generation to another by the women in her family. In an attempt to confront the traumas of her past, Sophie decides to return to Haiti, which frees her from the cultural oppression inherited through her mother.

The second essay in *Create Dangerously*, "Walk Straight," recounts a trip to Danticat's family's ancestral village, Beauséjour, tucked into the mountains of Haiti's Ouest Department, where her great-grandparents are buried and where only her elderly aunt Ilyana still lives: "I have come to see just how far we have trekked in less than two generations, from Léogâne's rural hamlet of Beauséjour to Miami and New York City, from the valley to skyscrapers. I have come to see an aunt whom I have seen only once before in my life, when I was eight years old, because she has literally refused to come down from the mountain" (2010, 22). In documenting her journey to Beauséjour, Danticat intertwines reflections on her experience of publishing *Breath, Eyes, Memory* and its wide reception after being included in Oprah's Book Club. Many Haitian residents in the United States accused Danticat of betraying her country, contributing to its negative international image, and downright lying. In the essay, Danticat discusses the latter accusation so as to defend the fictional aspect of her literature, her right to construct characters with personal and unique stories, and her rejection of self-censorship. These ideas materialize in the letter she writes to the novel's protagonist, Sophie, while visiting her great-grandparents' graves. In the letter, included in "Walk

Straight" and published as an epilogue in subsequent editions of the novel, she writes, "I feel that this is the only place in the world where I truly belong" (33). In addition to claiming her right to invent a character like Sophie—with her own "peculiarities, inconsistencies, [her] own voice" (34)—Danticat affirms her right to be considered and accepted as a Haitian, despite living in the United States. The recognition she demands also implies the ability to write, speak, and voice her opinions on Haiti without being expected to represent all Haitians. The essay, therefore, provides a form, nonexistent in the novel or short story, that allows for a self-critical exercise. More than Danticat's own humble characterization of "airing [. . .] dirty laundry" (33), the essay genre exposes her creative process and, in doing so, demands a level of interaction or complicity with the reader.

Danticat's work has progressively incorporated a wide variety of narrative voices in order to expand her representation of Haitian experiences. In a more recent novel, *Claire of the Sea Light* (2013), the narrative is based on a choral structure that not only illustrates contrasting perspectives but also asserts the aesthetics of oral storytelling techniques. In this novel, she also introduces a peculiar metaliterary aspect through the character of Louise George. As the host of a radio program, *Di Mwen* (Tell Me), Louise collects the stories of everyone who lives in Ville Rose, a fictitious town that also appears in several of Danticat's short stories and represents a microcosm of Haiti. Louise, a solitary woman who suffers from a strange menstrual condition in which she bleeds from her mouth, functions as the town's ears and amplifier: her radio show broadcasts interviews with regular people, generating a space for circulating local news, gossip, and sometimes different versions of the same story. During her periods, Louise stays at home writing "[h]er book [which] had begun as an extension of the show, but had grown into a type of choral piece. She called it to herself a collage à clef" (124). Danticat invites us to read her novel as if it were Louise George's book, a place to compile and retell the stories of the people of Ville Rose. However, this communal structure revolves around one main character, Claire of the Sea Light (Claire Limyè Lanmè in Creole, Claire Lumière la Mer in French), who runs away after discovering her father's plans to have her live with a wealthy woman. Such circumstances address the complex issue of child servitude through the concept of Haiti's *restavèk*,[2] all the while questioning literature's potential to spread social awareness in a country with high illiteracy rates. The essay "I Am Not a Journalist," included in *Create Dangerously*, also draws attention to the *restavèk* when describing the life work of journalist Jean Dominique. Danticat recalls how Dominique, in an attempt to educate rural families about the horrors of child labor, asked Haitian film director Rassoul

Labuchin "to develop screenplays [...] that meant something to the Haitian people" (2010, 45). Throughout *Create Dangerously*, Danticat asks how literature can also tell stories that mean something to Haitian people. While there is no definitive answer to this question, we believe that it forms an important part of the ethical and aesthetic concerns that guide Danticat's writing.

ACCIDENTS OF LITERACY

Danticat's essays explicitly reflect on literature, narrative forms, and the possibilities of reaching various audiences. One recurring issue is the tension that her decision to pursue a career in writing caused in a family that never encouraged books or reading. Unlike most twentieth-century Haitian writers,[3] Danticat was born into the poorest echelons of society, where high rates of illiteracy still persist; however, she was surrounded by a rich oral tradition that she integrates into her writing through the use of Creole and stylistic storytelling elements. In this sense, Danticat has expressed how important it is for her to have her stories translated into Creole and broadcast on radio shows in Haiti. In *Create Dangerously*, she reflects on this experience:

> It was as if the voice in which I write, the voice in which people speak Creole that comes out English on paper, had been released and finally I was writing for people like my Tante Ilyana, people who did not read, not because they did not have enough time or because they had too many other gadgets and distractions, but because they have never learned to. (2010, 50)

The internal conflict of writing about Haiti in English finds solace in a process of translation, which in itself is twofold: between two languages and between written and oral forms. This is the only way to reach many of Danticat's family members who cannot read, such as her aunt Ilyana, who insists on referring to her as a journalist instead of a writer.

Aside from the challenge of writing in a country with high levels of illiteracy, Haitian writers face the hegemonic effects of French colonialism on Haitian culture. Throughout the twentieth century, Haitian intellectuals have dealt with this situation of neocolonial cultural submission, which, in the first decades of the century and in the context of the US invasion of Haiti in 1915, Jean Price-Mars identified as the Haitian elite's expression of cultural bovarism. "Daughters of Memory," an essay from *Create Dangerously*, is situated within this same critical vein. Here, Danticat recalls the

Francophile character of Haiti's education system, which preferred French classics over literature written by Haitian-born writers. Only after she moved to Brooklyn, where she found refuge from school bullies in the public library, did she discover Haitian novels that would be decisive in her education, first as a reader and later as a writer. All the authors she would come to admire—Jacques Roumain, Jacques Stephen Alexis, Marie Vieux-Chauvet, Jan J. Dominique—either fled into exile or died as a consequence of writing in Haiti during the twentieth century. Whether the country was governed by foreign occupation or homegrown dictators, the Haitian cultural field has developed amid opposing forces that exalt French literature, impose very real dangers for Haitian authors, and curb local literary production through censorship, persecution, or assassination.

Conscious that her books have a much larger public and impact than those written by many of her compatriots, Danticat pays tribute to Haitian artists and denounces the brutalities committed against them throughout the country's history. "I Am Not a Journalist," for instance, tells the story of Jean Dominique, an exiled radio journalist who was assassinated upon his return to Haiti. The essay reproduces parts of Danticat's conversations with Dominique, allowing her to define her own position within the Haitian diaspora and compare her sense of belonging and authorial legitimacy to Dominique's. Passionately devoted to his country, Dominique illustrates the complexities of those who are forced to leave Haiti and become a *dyaspora*, the polysemic Creole term used for any Haitian living abroad. As Danticat elaborates, "My country, I felt, both as an immigrant and as an artist, was something that was then being called the tenth department. Haiti then had nine geographic departments and the tenth was the floating homeland, the ideological one, which joined all Haitians living outside of Haiti, in the *dyaspora*" (2010, 49). As with many residents of Haiti's "tenth department," Danticat insists on her right to participate in the public debate around problems afflicting her home country. In each of the essays compiled in *Create Dangerously*, she argues for the need to legitimize this diasporic space of enunciation where she locates her own literary production.

A BRIDGE TO THE OTHER SIDE OF THE WATER

Life and death are two inextricably linked topics that appear throughout Danticat's writing. In her nonfiction, this is evident in the memoir, *Brother, I'm Dying* (2007), where she revisits the deaths of her father and uncle as a means to come to terms with two paternal figures who strongly impacted her life. Several years later, she faced her mother's illness and death, experiences she examines in *The Art of Death*. The definitive absence of her mother leads Danticat to reflect on other moments when the two were separated, in particular during the eight years when she remained in Haiti while her parents lived in New York. Just as the mother-daughter relationship is a major theme in Danticat's early narratives, absence and loss constantly merit attention in her writing. In the first chapter of *The Dew Breaker* (2004), for example, the narrator parallels the function of literature to the role of masks in Egyptian mortuary art—both stand in for absent people. This idea resurfaces in *Create Dangerously*, along with the association between diaspora and death as situations of prolonged or definitive absence. The Haitian expression *lòt bò dlo* (the other side of the water) refers to people who have either migrated abroad or died. Danticat's literature in general, and her essays in particular, testify to her belief that the written or spoken word can help rebuild bridges to connect those who are on either side of the water. As Anne Brüske argues, Danticat shapes death and the diaspora as thematically and aesthetically linked phenomena of absence. At the center of these phenomena is the void provoked by the disappearance of those who migrate or die, but who remain alive in the memory and imagination of their loved ones. Following Thomas Macho, Brüske describes the "presence of absence" as a fundamental element in Danticat's poetics (Brüske 2019).

While *The Art of Death* clearly displays a continuation of Danticat's literary project, several new aspects distinguish this book from her previous work, one of the most striking differences being the universe of literary references. Here, she reaches far beyond Haiti to contemplate the narrative strategies and ethical challenges of dealing with death, engaging with writers from around the world, such as Dylan Thomas, Haruki Murakami, Anton Chekhov, Simone de Beauvoir, and Albert Camus, as well as a long list of US writers, including Anne Sexton, Sylvia Plath, Zora Neale Hurston, Joan Didion, and Toni Morrison. African American women writers have been especially important for Afro-Caribbean women who enter the US literary field. Lucía Stecher has observed this relationship with regard to authors such as Jamaica Kincaid, Michelle Cliff, and Danticat:

Black Caribbean women who immigrate to the United States are not expected to become writers, let alone devote their lives to literature as a profession. However, the already existing tradition of African American women writers strongly influenced Cliff, Danticat, and Kincaid to become writers. Authors like Maya Angelou, Audre Lorde, Paule Marshall, Alice Walker, Zora Neale Hurston, and, especially,

Toni Morrison, allowed them to enter a genealogy of writers who defied the odds set against them as black women. These writers laid a path for them to travel, explore, strengthen, and widen; they also provided a connection to the African diaspora, associating their own migration experiences with those imposed upon their African ancestors centuries before. (Stecher 2016, 12–13)

Deprived of reading Haitian authors during her childhood, Danticat grew up as a literary orphan, a sensation accentuated by the death of Marie Vieux-Chauvet, who could have been a literary parent, as she recounts in "Daughters of Memory." *The Art of Death*, however, leaves little doubt that Toni Morrison has taken on the role of a literary mother: the essays in this book frequently quote Morrison and closely study her fictionalized scenes of death. As an African American author whose work has been translated into many languages and reaches audiences far beyond the United States, Morrison provides a point of reference for Danticat to position her own work within the larger African diaspora without forfeiting either a culturally diverse group of readers or her Haitian origins. When Morrison passed away in 2019, Danticat published an article in the *New Yorker* as a tribute to the life and work of both Morrison and Paule Marshall, who passed shortly after. There, she reflects on Morrison's definition of an ancestor not necessarily as family but as a spiritual presence incorporated into much of African American literature. As a teenager, Danticat identified with these ideas, which were prevalent among her family; she writes, "Growing up, [. . .] I had been assured, and reassured, that our ancestors were always with us, no longer in body but always in spirit" (Danticat 2019). Seen from this perspective, Danticat turns the apparent absence of being *lòt bò dlo* into a powerful tool for maintaining connections with her cultural origins and her literary mentors.

Danticat also looks to other women writers for insight into dealing with their mothers' deaths, finding a bond of sisterhood with Zora Neale Hurston, Simone de Beauvoir, and Mary Gordon. Although they differ in style and perspective, Danticat once again fixates her attention on the orphan figure. In "Circles and Circles of Sorrow," she writes that "we have all been orphaned, except by our words, which we eventually turn to in order to make sense of the impossible, the unknowable" (2017, 135). Her reflections on their essays, which she refuses to describe as mere memoirs, defend writing as a healing mechanism to bear the weight of such loss. She continues:

We want to write not just of our mothers' deaths but of their lives too and of the ways, beyond the obvious, that our lives and theirs were linked. We want to share the connections that we have built with our mothers, be they through books, clothes, or words. We want to write of the disconnections too. We want to write our mothers not only as our mothers but as people, lovers, women who had a beginning that did not include us but who are now pulling us along with them into their ending. Writing, we hope, might make all this easier to grasp, even though we cannot change the outcome. While I am reading these other daughters' accounts, their mothers become my mother. (135)

Danticat seems to argue here that, if one is faced with the loss of a parent, literature (in terms of both writing and reading) fills in as a mentor figure, somewhat of a twist on the idea that books are a writer's children.

MANMAN'S LANGUAGE, OR
TRANSLATING THE MOTHER TONGUE

When Danticat writes in *The Art of Death* that "past horrors give us a language, or a basis on which to create a new language, to define new disasters" (2017, 57–58), she seems to pinpoint a crucial element in her intellectual project. Perhaps her migration from Haiti to the United States as an adolescent and the death of her mother are not past horrors but rather life-changing experiences based on trauma, such as poverty, dispossession, and the irreplaceable loss of a loved one, which demand a new language to fully comprehend their meaning. In this specific quotation, included in the essay "Dying Together," Danticat references the September 11, 2001, attack on the Twin Towers in New York, one of the more significant national tragedies in recent US history. While she shares the terror and mourning, she also steps back from US exceptionalism to distinguish herself as an outsider who has survived similar tragedies: "Those of us who were from countries that have been, in their own way, on the edge of destruction, could now be counselors to our previously sheltered friends, but only barely" (2017, 56).

Far from posing a new dilemma, the question of how to adequately speak or write of collective horrors such as genocide is a common theme in modern literature from around the world, ranging from Holocaust writers like Primo Levi to testimonial narratives and essays inspired by the Southern Cone's wave of dictatorships in the latter half of the twentieth century. However, in *The Art of Death*, Danticat returns to Morrison for insight, quoting a text Morrison wrote directly following the attacks: "Speaking of the broken and the dead is too difficult for a mouth full of blood. [. . .] I must be steady and I must be clear, knowing all the time that I have nothing to say—no words stronger than the steel that pressed you into itself; no scripture older or more elegant than the ancient atoms you have become" (cited in Danticat 2017, 59). Morrison recognizes the inadequacy of her own words, yet she must write to grasp some sort of meaning amid confusion and fear. While US citizens often imagine political violence and state-orchestrated massacres as foreign problems, Danticat's acute awareness of these issues is informed by having spent her childhood in Haiti and, as such, understanding her place within the Caribbean community, which also allows her to identify similar experiences in Latin America. These concerns arise in both her fiction and nonfiction, as in *The Farming of Bones* (1998), a historical novel dealing with the so-called Parsley Massacre of 1937, and in *The Art of Death* through her reflections on Gabriel García Márquez's *One Hundred Years of Solitude*, specifically his fictional rendering of the 1928 massacre of United Fruit Company workers in Colombia. Danticat questions how to ethically write about inconceivable horror, trauma, or loss, and how to represent experiences that are much more transcendental than language itself. In returning to Morrison, Danticat discusses her aesthetic decisions in the infanticide scene of *Beloved*, in which Sethe, a runaway slave, kills her baby daughter instead of allowing her to grow up in slavery. In "Condemned to Die," Danticat examines Morrison's need to imagine the baby killed in the novel as her own child, an exercise that led her to strip down the language. Due precisely to such compressed, unadorned language, Danticat identifies "the arc of Sethe's swing [as] the emotional center of that scene for me, and, indeed, the heart of the novel" (2017, 104). The poetics of creating such a powerful image with minimal language urges readers to reevaluate art's reliance on ornament and love's foundation on joy.

Reflecting on the death of her mother inevitably leads Danticat to confront her cultural identity as belonging to both Haiti and the United States. While she negotiates this diasporic middle ground throughout her entire career, *The Art of Death* provides a space for considering the implications of writing in a language unable to captivate the subtleties of Haitian culture. Given that much of her relationship with her mother exists in Haitian Creole, Danticat engages in various acts of translation in order to convey her mother's personality. Whether literally translating dialogue or culturally translating beliefs and humor, this task is fraught with difficulties, as when Danticat discusses the cassette tape her mother recorded in the months leading up to her death. Although most of the content is withheld from the reader, Danticat highlights that her mother only speaks in English once to say "I love you okay" (2017, 12). Considering this sole phrase along with the rest of the cassette, Danticat translates her mother's words back into Haitian Creole in order to interpret them in English through several versions: "And to me, she keeps saying, '*Met fanm sou ou*.' 'Be your own woman'; 'Be a strong woman.' [. . .] Be the woman I raised you to be" (2017, 12–13). Aware of her mother's limited English, Danticat assumes the role of a translator, selecting, interpreting, and representing her mother's words across languages and mediums of expression. She also explicitly values her family's oral tradition as a legitimate means for intellectual production and cultural transfer, claiming it as a major source in her writing.[4]

These Creole phrases and their approximate translations attest to Danticat's understanding that translation can never be entirely faithful. As Emily Apter has shown, untranslatability characterizes the processes of language contact, and mistranslation can in fact encourage the development of new meaning. She argues that "translation failure demarcates intersubjective limits, even as it highlights that 'eureka' spot where consciousness crosses over to a rough zone of equivalency or crystalizes around an idea that belongs to no one language or nation in particular. Translation is a significant medium of subject re-formation and political change" (Apter 2006, 6). Danticat never attempts to render phrases and ideas from Haitian Creole word-for-word in English. Rather, different cadences of speech and forms of Creole seep into her writing, as is most clearly conveyed by the prayer she writes from her mother's perspective, included near the end of the volume. Although she admits that her "mother had a singular and wicked sense of humor, one that's hard to convey in translation" (2017, 159–60), this prayer written in the form of a letter attempts to capture such subtleties, such as wishing that her children knew where she had hid money and her good wig for the funeral. Significantly enough, the only Creole word in this text is *manman*, the word for mother.

Though she is not a professional translator, Danticat's predicament of negotiating between Haitian and US culture has forced her to think about translation. In her discussion of Gregory Rabassa's renderings of García Márquez's novels, she explains: "A translation is as much the work of the translator as it is of the writer" (2017, 68). While all communication can be considered a process of translation, as George Steiner would say—"[T]o understand is to decipher. To hear significance is to translate" (1998, xii)— Danticat's writing raises questions about interlinguistic translation and the cultural and political implications that stem from mediating between two cultures separated by a hierarchy of power. Rendering Haitian Creole into US standard English not only operates under the logic of translating from a marginal to a dominant language, a process that can involve certain degrees of violence, including the appropriation of non-Western cultures, skewed representation, and the dilution of cultural difference; but also poses an ethical problem given the long history of US intervention in Haiti. Danticat ultimately attempts to accommodate a mainstream English-language audience while infusing her texts with specificities of Haitian culture, including the language. These essays literally transcribe her mother's voice onto paper and translate her words into English, making her life and legacy public. Returning to the account of September 11, 2001, Danticat asserts that "[d]ying en masse, especially on television, makes death—the most private of departures—public, national, global" (2017, 55). We would add to this list that death made public is also a political act, and in this sense Danticat's decision to publish a series of essays on the basis of her mother's death exposes the life of a Haitian immigrant in the United States at a particular moment of mounting anti-immigrant rhetoric. Both mother and daughter belong to both Haiti and the United States; both mother and daughter negotiate, write, translate, and create a new language to comprehend the multifaceted aspects of life—and death—in any country.

FROM WOUNDS TO WORDS: STORYTELLING AS A FORM OF HEALING

As a novelist, Edwidge Danticat brings an element of storytelling to her nonfiction that lures readers in, captivating a wide audience to showcase her own literature and discuss neglected social and political issues, such as Haitian immigration to the United States. She uses the essay to position herself as an author and intellectual within the US and Haitian public spheres and also to promote Haitian art and literature, both in Haiti and in the diaspora. As in her fiction, the choral or polyphonic structures in her essays seek to combine her own voice with those of other authors, constructing a more communal rather than individual perspective. The translational aspects in her writing also reveal an ensemble-like creative process as well as the subjective and political implications of language. By locating Danticat's essays within the broader context of her work, we have explored how she constantly searches for new means to reflect on her situation as a diasporic writer, and the ethical and aesthetic proposals that such a stance entails. Both *Create Dangerously* and *The Art of Death* take as their premise traumatic experiences in order to defend writing as a form of healing personal and collective wounds. This pursuit of language negotiates between the mother and adopted tongues, between oral speech and writing, between past horrors and future hope.

NOTES

1. Our translation, as in other cases unless otherwise indicated.

2. *Restavèk* comes from the French term *rester avec*, meaning "to stay with." In Haiti, peasants sometimes send their children to live with distant family or acquaintances in urban areas to perform domestic work in exchange for education and food; the practice resembles a modern form of child slavery (Cadet 2001).

3. As elsewhere in the Caribbean and in Latin America, Haiti's literary field has traditionally been restricted to elites, who during the nineteenth and most of the twentieth centuries had relatively exclusive access to education and print culture (Dalleo 2011; Rama 2004).

4. We see an example of this in *Breath, Eyes, Memory*, where the mother character corresponds with her family in Haiti through recordings on cassette tapes sent in the mail.

BIBLIOGRAPHY

Apter, Emily. 2006. *The Translation Zone: A New Comparative Literature*. Princeton, NJ: Princeton University Press.

Brüske, Anne. 2019. "*Lòt bò dlo*: Raumproduktion im Zeichen von Tod, Diaspora und Sprachlosigkeit in Edwidge Danticat's *The Dew Breaker* (2004)." In *Raumproduktion zwischen De- und Reterritorialisierung in karibisch-diasporischen Gegenwart-sliteraturen der USA*, by Anne Brüske. Unpublished manuscript.

Cadet, Jean-Robert. 2001. "Restavèk." In *The Butterfly's Way: Voices from the Haitian Dyaspora in the United States*, edited by Edwidge Danticat, 12–22. New York: Soho Press.

Dalleo, Raphael. 2011. *Caribbean Literature and the Public Sphere: From the Plantation to the Postcolonial*. Charlottesville: University of Virginia Press.

Danticat, Edwidge. 1994. *Breath, Eyes, Memory*. New York: Vintage Books.

Danticat, Edwidge. 1996. *Krik? Krak!* New York: Vintage Books.

Danticat, Edwidge. 1998. *The Farming of Bones*. New York: Soho Press.

Danticat, Edwidge. 2004. *The Dew Breaker*. New York: Alfred A. Knopf.

Danticat, Edwidge. 2007. *Brother, I'm Dying*. New York: Vintage Books.

Danticat, Edwidge. 2010. *Create Dangerously: The Immigrant Artist at Work*. Princeton, NJ:: Princeton University Press.

Danticat, Edwidge. 2013. *Claire of the Sea Light*. New York: Alfred A. Knopf.

Danticat, Edwidge. 2017. *The Art of Death: Writing the Final Story*. Minneapolis: Graywolf Press.

Danticat, Edwidge. 2019. "The Ancestral Blessings of Toni Morrison and Paule Marshall." *New Yorker*, August 17. https://www.newyorker.com/books/page-turner/the-ancestral -blessings-of-toni-morrison-and-paule-marshall.

Davis, Rocio G. 2001. "Oral Narrative as Short Story Cycle: Forging Community in Edwidge Danticat's *Krik? Krak!*" *MELUS* 26, no. 2 (June): 65–81. https://doi.org/10.2307 /3185518.

Edwards, Norval. 2011. "The Foundational Generation: From *The Beacon* to *Savacou.*" In *The Routledge Companion to Anglophone Caribbean Literature*, edited by Michael A. Bucknor and Alison Donnell, 111–23. Abingdon, Oxon., England: Routledge.

Rama, Ángel. 2004. *La ciudad letrada*. Santiago: Tajamar Editores.

Rivero, Eliana. 1989. "From Immigrants to Ethnics." In *Breaking Boundaries: Latina Writing and Critical Readings*, edited by Asunción Horno-Delgado, Eliana Ortega, Nina M. Scott, and Nancy Saporta Sternbach, 189–200. Amherst: University of Massachusetts Press.

Saloman, Randi. 2013. " 'Unsolved Problems': Essayism, Counterfactuals, and the Futures of *A Room of One's Own.*" *Tulsa Studies in Women's Literature* 32, no. 1 (Spring): 53–73. http://www.jstor.org/stable/43653364.

Stecher, Lucía. 2016. *Narrativas migrantes del Caribe: Michelle Cliff, Jamaica Kincaid y Edwidge Danticat*. Buenos Aires: Ediciones Corregidor.

Steiner, George. 1998. *After Babel: Aspects of Language and Translation*. 3rd ed. Oxford: Oxford University Press.

Weinberg, Liliana. 2014. "Ensayo y humanismo." *Co-herencia* 11, no. 20 (January–June): 59–76. https://publicaciones.eafit.edu.co/index.php/co-herencia/article/view /2447/2315.

Chapter Eleven

HOME EXILE, LANGUAGE, AND THE PARATEXT IN *ANACAONA: GOLDEN FLOWER* AND *MAMA'S NIGHTINGALE: A STORY OF IMMIGRATION AND SEPARATION*

CÉCILE ACCILIEN

Since the 1960s and 1970s, feminist scholars such as Audre Lorde, bell hooks, Alice Walker, Toni Morrison, and Barbara Christian have embraced the notion that "the personal is political and the political is personal" in their writings while also challenging the American literary canon—especially when and how women of color are represented in literature and literary theory. Following some of these scholars, Edwidge Danticat views the personal as political and vice versa, as reflected throughout her writings in different genres and for different audiences. As a writer, immigrant, woman, and mother, Danticat has emphasized the intergenerational transmission of history and culture. In a May 2018 interview in the *New Yorker*, she discusses her short story "Without Inspection" about two undocumented immigrants.[1] She states that when she first moved to Miami nearly two decades earlier, she was aware of the recurring news stories of immigrants who come to the United States via boat. She connects that short story not only to Haitian immigrants (who come to Miami and are usually sent back to Haiti because they are considered "economic refugees," as opposed to Cubans, who are seen as "political refugees") but also to the countless numbers of construction workers (many of whom are immigrants) who fall while building expensive, elite hotels in Miami. Danticat explicitly relates the everyday reality in which she lives to US immigration policies. Thus, the lives of immigrants, with their different and complex stories, are crucial in Danticat's narratives.

In chapter 3 of the essay collection *Create Dangerously: The Immigrant Artist at Work*, Danticat reflects on the complex negotiation of being an immigrant and her inner struggle with the notion of *dyaspora*, the Kreyòl word for Haitians living outside of Haiti. This term, which may be used to describe Danticat's identity as an insider-outsider, nomad, refugee, or immigrant, also characterizes her two main characters in the chapter, Anacaona and Saya. Furthermore, dyaspora draws together images of exile, home, and language. The paratextual elements in the two books that I discuss create a space for Danticat to accept, affirm, and even embrace the definition of the diaspora that Jean Dominique, a well-known Haitian journalist, provided to her—"people with their feet planted in both worlds."[2]

This chapter analyzes the themes of exile, home, and language in *Anacaona: Golden Flower* and *Mama's Nightingale: A Story of Immigration and Separation* through their paratextual elements. These elements further enable Danticat to bring forth her own personal connection to the stories and these themes. For example, in the section about the author, Danticat asserts her fascination with Anacaona, a fifteenth-century Taíno *cacica*, ever since she was a young girl to demonstrate why writing the story is so valuable to her. She also directly links Anacaona's life to hers by telling readers that her mother was born in Léogâne, the town believed to have been the center of Xaraguá, where Anacaona ruled as queen. Danticat notes: "Thus in some very primal way, Anacaona has always been in my blood and I remain, in the deepest part of my soul, one of her most faithful subjects."[3] Likewise, through the paratext in *Mama's Nightingale*, she connects her own journey as a young girl who was separated from her parents in the United States to the story of Saya, who is also separated from her mother.

Throughout her children's book *Mama's Nightingale: A Story of Immigration and Separation*[4] and in her young adult novel *Anacaona: Golden Flower, Haiti, 1490*, Danticat introduces readers to the complex realities of immigration and separation. *Anacaona: Golden Flower*, part of Scholastic Press's Royal Diaries series, recounts the story of young Queen Anacaona, an important figure in Haiti's history and culture. Danticat grants Anacaona a Taíno voice to tell her story, a different one from that found in Christopher Columbus's diaries. As Anacaona is a Native Caribbean woman from a culture that did not have a written language in the fifteenth century,[5] Danticat reintroduces her voice and accords her agency. Danticat uses Taíno words such as *cacique*, *opia*, and *tabacú*[6] and provides a glossary. She presents Anacaona's family tree and information about other notable leaders in the kingdom of Xaraguá such as Cotubanama and Guarionex. Likewise, in *Mama's Nightingale*, Danticat inserts Kreyòl words and phrases such as *tanpri kite bon ti nouvèl pou nou* (please leave us some good news) and *wosiyòl* (nightingale) to further Haitianize the text and thus emphasize the role of language in maintaining culture and identity.

The paratextual elements in both books not only reinforce themes such as immigration, exile, and home but also prepare readers to receive the text in a particular way. In the introduction to *Paratexts*, Gérard Genette maintains the following about the text and its links to the paratext:

> A literary work consists, entirely or essentially, of a text, defined (very minimally) as a more or less long sequence of verbal statements that are more or less endowed with significance. But this text is rarely presented in an unadorned state, unreinforced and unaccompanied by a certain number of verbal and other productions, such as an author's name, a title, a preface, illustrations. And although we do not always know whether these productions are to be regarded as belonging to the text, in any case they surround it and extend it, precisely in order to *present* it, in the usual sense of this verb but also in the strongest sense: to *make present*, to ensure the text's presence in the world, its "reception" and consumption in the form . . . of a book.[7]

Following Genette's theory and definition of the paratext as being "a threshold," "a zone between text and off-text, a zone not only of transition but also of transaction: a privileged place of pragmatics and a strategy, of an influence on the public,"[8] I argue that these paratextual elements reinforce the veracity of the stories and contribute to the authority and visibility that Danticat provides not only to Haiti but also to two marginalized groups: women and children. The paratext also allows Danticat to insert her own history and that of her family. In the author's note for *Mama's Nightingale*, she describes her separation from her parents at an early age due to their emigration to the United States. In *Anacaona: Golden Flower*, in the biographical section, Danticat notes that she was always interested in Anacaona "because [Anacaona] was a woman who was not only a warrior, poet and storyteller but also one of [Haiti's] first diplomats."[9] Moreover, like Danticat herself, both Anacaona and Saya are immigrants.

Danticat's author's note in *Mama's Nightingale* deliberately brings awareness to issues of immigration. She inserts her own narrative into the story to make it feel more intimate. In a section in the back of the book, Danticat reveals that she moved to the United States when she was twelve years old; she experienced life as an immigrant child and understands Saya's sense of loss, anxiety, and separation. Danticat uses this opportunity to teach parents and children about immigration. She notes, "According to the United States' Department of Homeland Security's Immigration and Customs Enforcement (ICE), the people Saya refers to as the immigration police, over 70,000 parents of American-born children have been jailed and deported in recent years. This book is dedicated to those children, who, like Saya, are dreaming of the day when their mother, or father, or both parents, will come home."[10] In the story, Saya tells readers that for the past three months her mother has been at "Sunshine Correctional, a prison for women without papers."[11] In an ironic twist, "Sunshine" is now equivalent to prison. The United States is not El Dorado, the land of wealth, but rather a place that separates parents from children and prevents people from achieving their dreams. Furthermore, having Saya wait for a cassette tape gives the story a feeling of déjà vu and historical continuity. Ultimately, Saya's story demonstrates that aggressive immigration enforcement and hostility toward immigrants has been ongoing in the United States; the story could just as easily have been set in 2019 as in 1985. Perhaps Danticat wants to further connect Saya's longing for her mother to her own childhood through the image of cassette tapes, the media through which Danticat stayed in contact with her parents in the 1970s.

In her 2019 essay in *World Literature Today* "'All Geography Is within Me': Writing Beginnings, Life, Death, Freedom, and Salt," Danticat reflects upon the power of words and the importance of the cassette tapes for her when she was separated from her parents. She notes:

> One way I used to communicate with my parents was through letters . . . but we also communicated through cassettes that we sent back and forth with people who were traveling between New York and Port-au-Prince. . . . When [their] letters and cassettes found their way to me from Brooklyn to Port-au-Prince, I again realized how words—both written and spoken—can transcend geography and time. My mother could tell me stories—once upon a time—in my mind. And I knew, because she later told me this, that she was imagining every day of my life, then would dream of whatever indispensable thing she thought I needed to know, things she believed that only she could tell me.[12]

Paratextual elements are just as crucial in *Anacaona: Golden Flower*. Before the novel's beginning, in the author's note, Danticat acknowledges and legitimizes ways in which Taíno people kept their stories alive.[13] She notes that "Anacaona's Taíno people . . . passed on their stories, myths, cultural practices, and ways of healing through songs, dances, and ballads that were performed at their feasts and celebrations, called *areitos*. Even though the Taínos had no written language, they had petroglyphs—rock paintings and pictographs through which they kept records of their lives."[14] Ultimately, she affirms that petroglyphs are as valid as other forms of writing.

On the hardcover edition of *Anacaona: Golden Flower*, the word "ANA-CAONA" is written in large print, "Golden Flower" in medium-size print, and "Haiti, 1490" in smaller print, directing readers' attention. At the top of the cover in an elaborate gold-colored font are the words "The Royal Diaries," alerting readers that Anacaona will be at the center of the novel as the storyteller. Moreover, her picture adorns the cover, portrayed as a young lady holding a spear standing regally in what appears to be a flower-filled jungle. The title creates a certain expectation for readers: we know that Anacaona's perspective and voice will tell the story. Critic Barbara Herrnstein Smith asserts that "texts, like all the other objects we engage with, bear the marks and signs of their prior valuing and evaluation by our fellow creatures and are thus, we might say, always to some extent pre-evaluated for us."[15] Both *Mama's Nightingale* and *Anacaona: Golden Flower* are assessed for readers. The summary section of *Anacaona* asserts: "Beginning in 1490, Anacaona keeps a record of her life as a possible successor to the supreme chief of Xaraguá, as wife of the chief of Maguana, and as a warrior battling the first white men to arrive in the West Indies, ravenous for gold."

The back cover of *Mama's Nightingale* describes the story as follows: "A little girl discovers her words can change the world." The book's summary states: "When Saya's mother is sent to jail as an illegal immigrant, she sends her daughter a cassette tape with a song and a bedtime story, which inspires Saya to write a story of her own—one that just might bring her mother home." This is a beautiful and hopeful message about the complexity of immigration. However, current reality of immigration in the United States, whereby children are separated from their parents, offers a grim picture in which children are disempowered and traumatized.[16] We must also interrogate the problematic use of the term "illegal immigrant."[17]

One of the most powerful aspects of the paratext in *Anacaona: Golden Flower* is that only in the two-and-a-half-page epilogue do we read about the Spanish invasion of Hispaniola led by Christopher Columbus and Chief Caonabó's resulting captivity. Rather, Danticat focuses on the Taíno and Anacaona's story: the Spaniards' greed and cruelty is an afterthought and does not define the culture and story of the Taínos, their strength and their fight for freedom.[18] By telling Anacaona's story through her diary, Danticat inscribes her voice as a woman and a Taíno into the historical canon of the Native Caribbeans. She also demonstrates the dynamic and vibrant culture that existed before the arrival of the Spanish colonizers. By centering the story on Anacaona and her life in Xaraguá and Maguana, Danticat recenters history and places Anacaona—and, through her, the Taínos—at the center of history, where they belong.

The paratext also allows us to learn about Taíno culture and to understand the lineage of the royal family. In the "Historical Note," Danticat depicts the complexity of the relationship between the Caribs or Kalinas and the Taínos before the Spaniards arrived. She does not romanticize life in Xaraguá, the region where Anacaona reigned. Likewise, through Saya, Danticat challenges the too often simplistic representation of Haitian immigrants, especially Haitian children immigrants, as only poor and hungry people.

Immigration is a crucial theme in Danticat's work. Although some may view her as an example of an immigrant who appears to embody the mythos of the so-called American Dream, she remains aware and critical of the price of this dream. In her work overall and in *Mama's Nightingale* in particular, she presents the immigration crisis as a problematic global phenomenon. Immigration is one of the most critical humanitarian issues of our time. Saya's nostalgia for her mom is similar to that of countless other children, making Danticat a writer who can appeal to various types of readers and communities. Aminatta Forna, the Sierra Leonean Scottish writer, notes: "Writers do not write about places, they write about people who happen to live in those places."[19] Saya evokes a displaced child from France, Syria, Ethiopia, Italy, Mexico, or Israel who is in search of home. The current acute immigration crisis in the United States, whereby children are sent to foster care while their parents are in detention, makes Danticat's story even more relevant. The Donald Trump administration's zero tolerance policy has directly impacted children and put them in situations of emotional and physical trauma. As of October 2019, hundreds of children remain in detention, shelters, or foster care and ineligible for reunification or release. Headlines from mainstream newspapers such as the *New York Times* read: "Detentions of Child Migrants at the U.S. Border Surge to Record Levels" and the like. It is a human rights disaster. While federal officials claim that they are reuniting families, an Associated Press investigation shows through court documents and immigration records that some judges are granting custody of migrant children to American families without the approval or notification of the parents.[20] Children ranging from two to seventeen years of age have appeared before judges in federal court.[21] Children's rights are not respected in the context of the 1989 United Nations Convention on the Rights of the Child, which protects all children. By removing children from their families, an action that is always traumatic, the United States violates these children's rights. Saya could have easily been one of those children separated from both parents and a ward of the state if her father had not been living in the United States as a citizen and able to take care of her.

Like Saya, Anacaona confronts the issue of immigration, since she had to leave her home in Xaraguá to be with her husband Caonabó in Maguana. However, her sense of exile is different from Saya's. Anacaona misses Xaraguá but feels welcome in Maguana. While visiting the villages in Maguana, she notes:

> Wherever we stop to rest, we are offered many gifts: hammocks, canoes, and birds. . . . In one day, we have collected so much more than we could use. . . . Caonabó says that these gifts are really mine. The people offer them to me to make me feel welcomed. But I don't need gifts to feel welcomed. The warm manner in which people have treated us already shows that they are happy to see me.[22]

This contrasts with Saya's feeling of exile and anxiety due to her mother's absence from home. When Saya visits her jailed mother, the guards make her feel unwelcome:

> "Gotta go, folks," one of the guards says when it's time to take Mama away. I kick and I scream and beg to stay with her. Tears run down Mama's face as she is led away. The two guards on either side of her give me very stern looks. One of them tells Papa not to bring me again until I can behave myself.[23]

The guards' attitude signifies a lack of compassion for immigrants, as both Saya and her mother are viewed as unwelcome immigrants. As I noted earlier, this problem has only intensified, as evident from current US immigration policy.[24] In response, Saya uses the figure of the *wosiyòl*, the Kreyòl word for nightingale, her mother's nickname for her, to deal with her pain while her mom is kept from her.

In spite of the warm welcome bestowed upon her, Anacaona misses home. She is lonely and feels like a stranger. She states: "Though Caonabó's advisers and servants show much respect, no one shows friendliness toward me. It is as if friendliness, which I am in need of most, is beyond my stature."[25] Even though she has a life of luxury, Anacaona's sense of displacement manifests itself deeply. Similarly, Saya feels like she is in exile due to her physical and emotional separation from her mother. Both Anacaona and Saya try to create a home for themselves, but the process is fraught.

In "Transnational Migrants: When 'Home' Means More Than One Country," sociologist Peggy Levitt notes:

The assumption that people will live their lives in one place, according to one set of national and cultural norms, in countries with impermeable national borders, no longer holds. Rather, in the 21st century, more and more people will belong to two or more societies at the same time. . . . Transnational migrants work, pray, and express their political interests in several contexts rather than in a single nation-state. Some will put down roots in a host country, maintain strong homeland ties, and belong to religious and political movements that span the globe. These allegiances are not antithetical to one another.[26]

Saya's mother tries to create a home for her by keeping her presence alive through the stories she sends on cassette tapes; as Saya listens to her mother singing about the *wosiyòl*, her mother is transported to her bedroom. The bedtime stories keep her connected to her mother and to Haiti, passing on Haitian cultural traditions: "In Mama's Haitian stories, a *wosiyòl* is a beautiful nightingale who loves the taste of a sweet cottony fruit called a soursop. Just like I do. The *wosiyòl* also keeps a mean old witch from eating little children by distracting them with a beautiful song."[27] By using the story of the mother nightingale on a journey looking for a rainbow in the sky to find her way home, Saya's mother helps her to understand that she is looking for something—for the documentation she needs as an immigrant—so that she can return home to Saya and her father. Saya can imagine her there: "I close my eyes and imagine Mama lying next to me as she leans in to whisper the nightingale's story in my ear. I imagine Mama tucking me in, kissing me good night, then going to sleep in the next room with Papa."[28] Her mother sends a tape every week with a new story. The stories keep Saya hopeful and help her cope with the void and the loneliness: "Sometimes the stories are as sad as melted ice cream. Other times they are as happy as a whole day at the beach."[29] These stories are a form of resistance and survival for both Saya and her mother.

Likewise, Anacaona creates a home for herself in Maguana. She is intentional about carving out a space for herself and creating her own community: "I told Caonabó about my desire to work with Simihena and some of the other carvers in Maguana and he said I should take charge of all such work in Maguana."[30] Both Anacaona and Saya have rituals that help them in their search for home and belonging. Anacaona sometimes returns home through her daydreams and imagination, and her new interest in wood carving. She collaborates with Simihena, one of the Maguana women she has befriended. One of the strategies she uses to remember home is carving the people she loves:

I was staring at my shadow in the ground when it came to me. Why not carve ourselves? Simihena will carve Simihena. I will carve Anacaona. I will carve my memories of my ancestors. . . . I will also carve the living people who are missing from my life: Bibi and Baba and my uncle and even Behechio. . . . I will carve Caonabó's strong and handsome image. I will carve images of caves, of the way our world was created. And in addition to all that, I will make ceremonial chairs, effigy vessels, ceramic flasks . . . all images of frogs, fish and birds carved into them. Nothing will be carved in Maguana that will not bear the mark of Anacaona's heart or hand.[31]

This statement may be read as if Anacaona believes that in order to truly belong, she must possess and dominate the land. However, in Taíno culture, harmony and respect for nature is essential, and the environment is reflected in various art forms.[32] Danticat intended to represent Anacaona as someone who feels so close to nature that she becomes a part of it as she finds a way to belong. Just as Saya does not feel like she belongs in her home due to her mother's absence, Anacaona, too, feels like she does not completely belong in Maguana. Through Anacaona, Danticat teaches readers about the flourishing of fifteenth-century Taíno culture in the land known today as Haiti. In fact, Haiti is a Taíno word that means "mountainous land." Anacaona's reflections on her artistic talent support the fact that the Taíno had achieved a relatively high level of socioeconomic development. Their works of art as petroglyphs were made by engraving the walls of caves and river rocks. This is the tradition that Anacaona maintains in her meticulous descriptions of the carving that she plans to execute.

Saya also creates home through her mother's stories and her own writing. The beloved story of the nightingale is based on a well-known song rooted in Haiti's musical patrimony. The song's lyrics state:

Ti zwazo kote ou prale
Mwen prale kay fiyèt lalo
Fiyèt Lalo kòn manje timoun
Si ou ale la manje ou tou
Brik kolobrik, brik kolobrik
Wosiyòl maje korosòl

Little bird, where are you going?
I am going to Lalo's house.
Lalo eats little birds; if you go, she will eat you, also.

> Make noise, Nightingale, make noise, Nightingale.
> Nightingale eats soursop fruit.

Fiyèt Lalo is a female bogeyperson who eats little children. The nightingale uses her beautiful voice to keep witches and bogeypeople like Fiyèt Lalo from eating kids. Like the nightingale in popular Haitian folktales that protects children from Fiyèt Lalo, Saya, by writing a letter, helps to protect her mother and eventually bring her home. Through the power of words, Saya, her papa, and others from the community help plead her mother's case to the judge. This part of the story is also a statement about the power not only of words but of community. When Saya's mother returns home, Saya asks her to read the story about the nightingale who goes through the rainbow to get home. The story ends when "a smart and brave little nightingale helps her mommy find the right rainbow trail . . . and the mommy follows it home."[33] Saya and the nightingale become one and the same. The rainbow is a symbol found in many cultures with various myths associated with it. Among the most common is that of messenger. For Saya and her mother, the rainbow becomes a sign of a bright future that leads the mother to find her way home. Saya also embodies the *wosiyòl* who protects children by now protecting her mother through the letters that she writes. Like Saya, Danticat in the author's note states that she grew up in a family that was separated by immigration. Just as Saya is unable to understand the notion of "the right papers" that keep families apart, Danticat explains that as a young child living in Haiti she could not comprehend why she could not join her parents living in the United States because they did not have "the right papers." Danticat also describes how she and her brother used to play writing games and create documents that could reunite her with her parents. Both she and Saya used writing as a tool to express their sadness and remain connected to their family and home.

For Danticat, as for Saya and Anacaona, home is interwoven with language. Their cultural and linguistic identity are intrinsically linked. Anacaona's cultural background as a Xaraguán remains the mark of her identity. For Saya, her link to Haiti through Kreyòl and folktales is her lifeline. Language is an important ritual for both. The words, thoughts, and phrases that they repeat regularly (whether to themselves or to others) become a ritual that keeps them connected to home, at once tangible and conceptual. For Saya, her mother's voice and stories attempt to fill the void that she feels. The Kreyòl words and phrases on the answering machine and on the cassette tapes connect Saya directly to her mother; among the Kreyòl expressions dear to Saya repeated throughout the story are: "*Tanpri kite bon ti nouvèl pou nou*" (Please, leave us a little bit of good news); "*Yon istwa dodo pou Saya*" (A bedtime story for Saya); and "You know Saya, Mama loves you *anpil, anpil,* very very much." *Wosiyòl,* the nickname Saya's mother gives her, is another link to Haiti. But the disembodied voice alone is not enough—home means primarily having her mother in the house and having Haitian culture as a central and visible part of her life.

By using Kreyòl words and phrases in the text alongside English translations or explanations, Danticat creates a *métissage* that allows the two languages to interact with one another with a high level of fluidity. Thus, Danticat is legitimizing the Kreyòl language and not forcing the reader to choose, just as the immigrant should not have to choose between two countries. Rather, she creates a space to embrace both countries and cultures in an organic manner. Using Kreyòl and not French is also a way to relieve/release the ongoing tension between the languages, which are Haiti's two official languages. Kreyòl, a language of revolution and freedom, is still considered by many as inferior to French, the language of the colonizers and the elite. In *Anacaona: Golden Flower,* Danticat includes a glossary of the various Taíno words used in the book. Since this is a young adult novel, she uses a strategy that is different from that of *Mama's Nightingale.* However, it is clear that both works emphasize the place of indigenous languages in Haitian culture.

Even though *Mama's Nightingale* is a children's story, it is very candid and realistic. Danticat presents the reality of immigration for children who are victims of the system like their parents. The story describes the various steps that Saya's father takes in trying to publicize her mother's story, such as contacting newspapers and writing to the judge and to immigration officials. The story ends on a positive note with the mother returning home. The immigrant is not just a victim, because she has agency and is empowered. Importantly, Saya has her own agency, since she writes to her mother as well. This empowerment is reflected in the ending. Saya writes: "I like the way Mama's and my story ends, too. I like that it is our words that brought us together again."[34] It is crucial to have the power to use words to fight against injustice and oppression. Danticat uses her craft as a writer to "create dangerously,"[35] denounce inequity, and tell stories of cultures that had no written languages, like that of the Taínos.

From the first chapter of *Anacaona: Golden Flower,* Danticat interweaves Taíno words throughout the story. On the first page of the diary, Anacaona writes: "In my language, the Taíno language, *ana* means 'flower' and *caona* means 'golden.' Thus I am called the 'golden flower.' "[36] Taíno words, set in italics, are interwoven throughout the text. Words such as *opia* (spirit), *siani* (married woman), *mayohaboa* (drum), and *niguas* (insects) are used interchangeably with English. As she did with *Mama's Nightingale*, Danticat uses this technique to help legitimize the Taíno language as a mode of expression with ongoing linguistic and cultural relevance. It is also imaginable that the art and hieroglyphs described by Anacaona are another manifestation of the linguistic and cultural diversity of the Taíno people.[37] They serve as historical documentation. As Danticat states in *Anacaona: Golden Flower*, "Taíno artifacts are being discovered all the time. With each piece found, the story of the Taíno people gets more and more specific, more and more defined."[38] Their legacy remains in the names of various towns (such as Mayagüez and Coamo) in Caribbean islands such as Hispaniola (Haiti and the Dominican Republic) and Puerto Rico.[39] The names of foods, trees, and plants are also reminiscent of Taíno culture. This serves to remind readers that Taíno presence, history, and culture are still part of these islands. Since around the turn of the twenty-first century, there has been growing interest in the cultural and genetic legacies of Native peoples as demonstrated by museum exhibits as well as individuals and organizations who are affirming their Taíno identity.[40]

Taking the stories of Anacaona and Saya, separated by more than five hundred years, Danticat demonstrates that the human condition of immigration, exile, and the search for home is as complex and painful in 2015 as it was in 1490. Furthermore, she challenges the Eurocentric narrative that typically describes the encounter between Europeans and Taínos, as well as the simplistic narrative of the immigrant. Danticat presents the fluidity of identity that becomes evident as one creates a home in a new place, as well as the ruptures and discontinuities that such a process brings with it. By giving voice to a young girl and young woman, she brings forth the stories of survival, resilience, transformation, and hope of those who are too often trapped at the margins of history. Through paratextual elements, she inserts her own narrative into those of Saya and Anacaona, as her story as an immigrant woman is intertwined with theirs.

NOTES

1. Deborah Treisman, "Edwidge Danticat on Her Caribbean Immigrant Experience," *New Yorker*, May 7, 2018, https://www.newyorker.com/books/this-week-in-fiction/fiction -this-week-edwidge-danticat-2018-05-14.

2. Edwidge Danticat, *Create Dangerously: The Immigrant Artist at Work* (Princeton, NJ: Princeton University Press, 2010), 51.

3. Edwidge Danticat, *Anacaona: Golden Flower, Haiti, 1490*, 1st ed. (New York: Scholastic, 2005), 181.

4. Edwidge Danticat and Leslie Staub, *Mama's Nightingale: A Story of Immigration and Separation* (New York: Dial Books, 2015).

5. Encyclopedia Britannica, "Taino People," https://www.britannica.com/topic/Taino; and Encyclopedia Britannica, "Native American Art," https://www.britannica.com/art/Native-American-art.

6. *Cacique* means chief, *opia* refers to the spirit of the ancestors or the dead, and *tabacú* means tobacco.

7. Gérard Genette, *Paratexts: Thresholds of Interpretation*, trans. Jane E. Lewin (Cambridge: Cambridge University Press, 1997), 1.

8. Genette, *Paratexts*, 2.

9. Danticat, *Anacaona: Golden Flower*, 179.

10. Danticat and Staub, *Mama's Nightingale*, n.p. The book does not contain page numbers, as is common in children's book.

11. Florida's nickname is the Sunshine State.

12. Edwidge Danticat, "'All Geography Is within Me': Writing Beginnings, Life, Death, Freedom, and Salt," *World Literature Today* 93, no. 1 (Winter 2019): 59–65, https://www.worldliteraturetoday.org/2019/winter/all-geography-within-me-writing-beginnings-life-death-freedom-and-salt-edwidge-danticat.

13. Robert M. Poole, "What Became of the Taíno?," *Smithsonian Magazine*, October 2011, https://www.smithsonianmag.com/travel/what-became-of-the-taino-73824867/.

14. Danticat, *Anacaona: Golden Flower*, 3.

15. Barbara Herrnstein Smith, "Value/Evaluation," in *Critical Terms for Literary Study*, ed. Frank Lentricchia and Thomas McLaughlin, 2nd ed. (Chicago: University of Chicago Press, 1995), 183.

16. Vivian Yee and Miriam Jordan, "Migrant Children in Search of Justice: A 2-Year-Old's Day in Immigration Court," *New York Times*, October 8, 2018, https://www.nytimes.com/2018/10/08/us/migrant-children-family-separation-court.html.

17. While this phrasing seemingly attempts to make the issue of immigration relevant and intelligible to mainstream readers, it falls into the trap of classifying some people as "illegal" immigrants and creating a binary of us versus them and good versus bad. The term "undocumented immigrant" is preferable.

18. The story of the Taíno is generally told from the perspective of the Spanish colonizers. See Poole, "What Became of the Taíno?"

19. Aminatta Forna, "Don't Judge a Book by Its Author," *Guardian*, February 13, 2015, https://www.theguardian.com/books/2015/feb/13/aminatta-forna-dont-judge-book-by-cover.

20. Chris Mills Rodrigo. "AP: Migrant Children May Be Adopted after Parents Are Deported," *The Hill*, October 9, 2018, https://thehill.com/policy/international/americas/410653-ap-migrant-children-may-be-adopted-after-parents-are-deported.

21. Yee and Jordan, "Migrant Children in Search of Justice."

22. Danticat, *Anacaona: Golden Flower*, 93–94.

23. Danticat and Staub, *Mama's Nightingale*, n.p.

24. Among Danticat's well-known nonfiction works are *Create Dangerously: The Immigrant Artist at Work*, a collection of introspective essays published in 2010; and

Brother, I'm Dying, a 2007 memoir in which Danticat depicts her uncle, who was denied entry to the United States, jailed, and died in a hospital in Florida. Both books critically address US immigration laws and their impact on ordinary people.

25. Danticat, *Anacaona: Golden Flower*, 97.

26. Peggy Levitt, "Transnational Migrants: When 'Home' Means More Than One Country," Migration Policy Institute, October 1, 2004, https://www.migrationpolicy.org /article/transnational-migrants-when-home-means-more-one-country.

27. Danticat and Staub, *Mama's Nightingale*, n.p.

28. Danticat and Staub, *Mama's Nightingale*, n.p.

29. Danticat and Staub, *Mama's Nightingale*, n.p.

30. Danticat, *Anacaona: Golden Flower*, 99.

31. Danticat, *Anacaona: Golden Flower*, 101–2.

32. Encyclopedia Britannica, "Native American Art."

33. Danticat and Staub, *Mama's Nightingale*, n.p.

34. Danticat and Staub, *Mama's Nightingale*, n.p.

35. The idea of "creating dangerously" for Danticat is a way to describe part of the role of the immigrant artist, who has a responsibility to write about what is happening in their country. In the context of this chapter, Danticat is helping both Saya and Anacaona create dangerously in order to represent their respective communities.

36. Danticat, *Anacaona: Golden Flower*, 5.

37. Encyclopedia Britannica, "Native American Art."

38. Danticat, *Anacaona: Golden Flower*, 180.

39. Poole, "What Became of the Taíno?"

40. The Smithsonian Institution's National Museum of the American Indian had a special exhibit titled "Taíno: Native Heritage and Identity in the Caribbean." The exhibit was from July 28, 2018, to November 12, 2019. For more information, visit: https:// americanindian.si.edu/explore/exhibitions/item?id=966

BIBLIOGRAPHY

Danticat, Edwidge. "'All Geography Is within Me': Writing Beginnings, Life, Death, Freedom, and Salt." *World Literature Today* 93, no. 1 (Winter 2019): 59–65. https:// www.worldliteraturetoday.org/2019/winter/all-geography-within-me-writing-begin nings-life-death-freedom-and-salt-edwidge-danticat.

Danticat, Edwidge. *Anacaona: Golden Flower, Haiti, 1490*. 1st ed. New York: Scholastic, 2005.

Danticat, Edwidge. *Create Dangerously: The Immigrant Artist at Work*. Princeton, NJ: Princeton University Press, 2010.

Danticat, Edwidge, and Leslie Staub. *Mama's Nightingale: A Story of Immigration and Separation*. New York: Dial Books, 2015.

Encyclopedia Britannica. "Native American Art." https://www.britannica.com/art/Native -American-art.

Encyclopedia Britannica. "Taino People." https://www.britannica.com/topic/Taino.

Forna, Aminatta. "Don't Judge a Book by Its Author." *Guardian*, February 13, 2015. https://www.theguardian.com/books/2015/feb/13/aminatta-forna-dont-judge-book-by-cover.

Genette, Gérard. *Paratexts: Thresholds of Interpretation*. Translated by Jane E. Lewin. Cambridge: Cambridge University Press, 1997.

Levitt, Peggy. "Transnational Migrants: When 'Home' Means More Than One Country." Migration Policy Institute, October 1, 2004. https://www.migrationpolicy.org/article/transnational-migrants-when-home-means-more-one-country.

Poole, Robert M. "What Became of the Taíno?" *Smithsonian Magazine*, October 2011. https://www.smithsonianmag.com/travel/what-became-of-the-taino-73824867/.

Rodrigo, Chris Mills. "AP: Migrant Children May Be Adopted after Parents Are Deported." *The Hill*, October 9, 2018. https://thehill.com/policy/international/americas/410653-ap-migrant-children-may-be-adopted-after-parents-are-deported.

Smith, Barbara Herrnstein. "Value/Evaluation." In *Critical Terms for Literary Study*, edited by Frank Lentricchia and Thomas McLaughlin, 177–85. 2nd ed. Chicago: University of Chicago Press, 1995.

Treisman, Deborah. "Edwidge Danticat on Her Caribbean Immigrant Experience." *New Yorker*, May 7, 2018. https://www.newyorker.com/books/this-week-in-fiction/fiction-this-week-edwidge-danticat-2018-05-14.

Yee, Vivian, and Miriam Jordan. "Migrant Children in Search of Justice: A 2-Year-Old's Day in Immigration Court." *New York Times*, October 8, 2018. https://www.nytimes.com/2018/10/08/us/migrant-children-family-separation-court.html.

Chapter Twelve

"QUIETLY, QUIETLY"

Thinking and Teaching the Global South through Edwidge Danticat's Intertextual Writing, Reading, and Witnessing

JENNIFER M. LOZANO

Known for writing that powerfully interweaves her own personal identity and experiences with a larger, public, and political identity, Edwidge Danticat is a master at navigating what she calls Haiti's "tenth department" or the "floating homeland"[1]—an ideological space that joins all Haitians living in the diaspora. This "tenth department" comes to life powerfully in Danticat's nonfiction writing through intertextual writing strategies that draw from a multiplicity of locations and voices and render new (hi)stories and collective memory. These intertextual writing strategies not only reflect Danticat's insider/outsider position but also facilitate her role as a self-described "witness." As she explains, "I think of myself as a witness: a person who can report on what I'm seeing and who can report on what others are saying. [...] And the way I witness is through this work of writing."[2] This reportage necessarily requires Danticat's careful intertwining of multiple voices and stories that sensitize her to listening and intimacy as much as to speaking and authority. It is from this unique position that Danticat can speak the untold stories of Haiti, its diaspora, and, increasingly in recent years, the Global South.

In this chapter, I will provide an overview of the Global South as a critical concept and examine how Danticat's work engages with this concept in a way that can inform a critical pedagogy for the literature classroom. I suggest that Danticat's approach to intertextual writing, reading, and witnessing—or what I call her "intertextual Global South thinking"—can provide a model for scholar-teachers to better understand the Global South as an epistemological and pedagogical project, and facilitate this project for students in the United States (see the end of this chapter for sample reading list). I will focus specifically on Danticat's first and similarly titled essay from her nonfiction collection *Create Dangerously: The Immigrant Artist at Work* (2010), but whenever possible I will refer to her larger body of work, a rich and regular publishing history in widely circulated periodicals, which echoes her role as a Global South witness for marginalized voices and experiences.

THE PROBLEM OF THE GLOBAL SOUTH

In his introduction to the collection *The Global South and Literature*, Russell West-Pavlov describes the idea of the Global South as, at best, "various forms of political, environmental, social, and epistemological agency arising out of the erstwhile colonized nations—what was once known as the Third World"; and, at worst, "a new master narrative that homogenizes real diversity."[3] Regardless, by the turn of the twenty-first century, in academic discourse the term had largely taken the place of "Third World" by continuing to index a geopolitical space not at the helm of Euro-American capitalism nor a primary beneficiary of its spoils, while shifting the "axis of analysis" from a North-South orientation to a South-South one.[4] Central to this South-South orientation is a move away from a model of center-periphery exchanges to periphery-periphery ones.[5] As Alfred J. López explains, the Global South marks "the mutual recognition among the world's subaltern of their shared conditions at the margins of the brave new neoliberal world of globalization."[6] For Danticat, this perspective is evident in her more flexible understanding of diaspora that does not adhere to a rigid, linear progression from nation and home to the unbelonging of the Global North. As Nadège Clitandre explores at length in her monograph *Edwidge Danticat: The Haitian Diasporic Imaginary*, Danticat's writing testifies to the mutually constitutive quality of both nation and diaspora, which requires that she pay careful attention to (trans)local spaces, memory, community, and other typically national features that continue to bear diasporic significance.[7] In the words of Clitandre: "Danticat's diasporic consciousness does not privilege diaspora (e.g., the global) at the expense of the nation and its localized narratives."[8] It is this particular diasporic consciousness that makes Danticat's intertextual writing so powerful in its work of witnessing the often "multilocational, multihistorical, and multinational" lives of the Haitian diaspora.[9] It is also this quality of her writing that resonates with a Global South emphasis on a deterritorialized subaltern subjectivity.

If, as I suggest, a Global South analytic is useful for understanding Danticat's intertextual and translocal writing practices, it is important to explain the intellectual traditions that inform (but are still distinct from) a Global South paradigm and why the latter is advantageous for our contemporary moment. Rather than understanding the Global South as a new buzzword for the "Third World" or "Postcolonial Studies" as West-Pavlov expresses in his introduction, Anne Garland Mahler explains the emergence of a Global South framework as "an attempt to recover a latent [tricontinental] ideological legacy that has been lost, or at least overlooked, in the all encompassing frame of postcolonial theory."[10] In her 2015 article "The Global South in the Belly of the Beast: Viewing African American Civil Rights through a Tricontinental Lens," Mahler specifically connects the Global South's emphasis on a deterritorialized subaltern subjectivity to the ideology that informed the 1966 Tricontinental Conference in Havana and the formation of Organization of Solidarity with the People of Asia, Africa, and Latin America. The alliance included representatives from liberation movements across eighty-two different nations and "quickly became the driving force of international political radicalism."[11] Importantly, this tricontinental ideology did not just focus on formerly colonized nations but extended subaltern solidarity to African Americans in the United States.[12] The transatlantic slave trade (and, thus, the Caribbean) in particular was of great significance to tricontinental ideology, which understood African Americans as deeply connected to imperialism despite their geographic location in the West.[13] While postcolonial studies intends to study all cultures emerging from a colonial experience, the field has tended to emphasize formerly colonized Asian and African nations with less focus on Latin America and the Americas as a whole.[14] Global South studies, thus, has built from the anticolonial work of postcolonial studies while still departing from its geographic and ideological limitations that reinforce the "colonial fictions of North-South."[15] By deterritorializing empire and destabilizing colonial racial divisions, the Global South is more adept at addressing the culture and experiences of those living with and responding to the contemporary failures of globalization (and its imperial roots) across the world's many "souths." This is an especially important paradigm for writers from the Caribbean like Danticat who have, at times, fallen outside the postcolonial frame but who have maintained a capacious tricontinental expression of their experiences and political subjectivity.

Without this history of the ideological roots of the Global South, however, it is easy to misunderstand the concept, as well as the work of Global South writers. As a case in point, students in my graduate-level Global South literature class at a predominantly white institution struggled to follow and understand the intertextual, (trans)local connective leaps that Danticat makes in *Create Dangerously*. In this nine-person, master's-level seminar, students grappled with the complex affect of wanting to privilege the so-called Global

South, while also experiencing frustration and guilt about being privileged residents of the Global North. Part of their response, I hypothesize, has to do with my framing of the class primarily with West-Pavlov's introduction with a few other critical touchstones. Despite this text's singular presence at the intersection of literary studies and Global South studies, it could not (nor should it have to) bear the weight of the multidisciplinary histories and practices that the Global South indexes. This lack of theoretical anchoring likely exacerbated students' ambivalent "Global North" perspective. Turning instead to a few foundational interdisciplinary pieces (such as those by López and Mahler) to pair with Danticat's lived practice of Global South witnessing in her writing is a crucial move toward developing a more accessible Global South pedagogy.

DANTICAT'S INTERTEXTUAL GLOBAL SOUTH THINKING

In her collection of essays *Create Dangerously* and especially the first, similarly titled chapter, Danticat describes and addresses an a/effect of diaspora that resonates with my students' concerns. It is in this first chapter that I anchor my analysis of Danticat's intertextual writing, reading, and witnessing, or her intertextual Global South thinking. Here, Danticat turns to literature to articulate this a/effect by contrasting the despair of the Haitian resident and the joy of the exile depicted in the classic Haitian novel *Masters of the Dew* by Jacques Roumain. She explains: "Délira's despair and Manuel's hope make for a delicate balance, of which I am reminded each time I return to Haiti: the exile's joy and the resident's anguish—it can also be the other way around, the resident's joy and the exile's anguish—clashing."[16] This passage precedes and helps contextualize Danticat's description of the reaction by Jean Dominique, the late and beloved Haitian journalist and Danticat's friend, to the suffering in Haiti as he experiences it from the diaspora. Danticat, Dominique, and my students all intuit a disconnect resulting from their respective distance from the Global South and their imbrication in the systems that continue to perpetuate unequal development and opportunities. Of course, the frustration and upset my students feel are but faint echoes of Danticat's and Dominique's, yet there is a small connection here that I hope a Global South pedagogy can draw out, and that Danticat's life and work is committed to quietly developing.[17]

It is through the creative process, and writing in particular, that Danticat enacts an intertextual Global South thinking and forges connections across otherwise cavernous global differences. Drawing our attention to creation

myths at the outset of her essay, she explains the significance of these stories
that "haunt and obsess" all writers.[18] For her, it is the brutal execution of
Haitian political leaders Marcel Numa and Louis Drouin under the François
Duvalier regime, and how, although occurring well before she was born, their
stories impacted her own life and diasporic imaginary. It is through stories,
both oral and written, that she is transnationally and transgenerationally
linked to Haiti. Danticat then circles back to what she calls "the biggest
creation myth of all, the world's very first people, Adam and Eve," and how
their exile (rather than death) facilitated the telling and circulation of even
more stories.[19] Linking back to this Judeo-Christian creation story at the
outset of a highly intertextual chapter (and book) that moves seamlessly from
artists such as Camus, Pierre Corneille, and Shakespeare to Frantz Fanon,
Aimé Césaire, Graham Greene, and Haitian writers Marie Vieux-Chauvet,
Frankétienne, and Louis-Philippe Dalembert, among others, Danticat casts a
net of creators that is wide and daringly inclusive. This is intertextuality not
solely as allusion or influence, but as geographic and temporal reticulation.
For although the subtitle of her essay is "The Immigrant Artist at Work," the
first-person narration of this piece shifts from the singular ("I") to plural
("we") near its conclusion. And while the "we" may refer to "immigrant
writers" whose work it is to create these reticulations, Danticat suggests
that all readers participate in creation stories, either as writers themselves
or as listeners and tellers. In fact, she even considers whether a border can
"really exist in the intimate, both solitary and solidary union between writers and readers."[20] This inclusive, transborder writer-reader relationship is
central to understanding Danticat's intertextual Global South thinking and
her relationship to diaspora, as well as our own role as readers and writers
approaching Danticat's and other Global South writing.

As I've alluded, one way scholars have approached understanding the
significance of Danticat's intertextual writing strategies is by considering
how they help her retheorize diaspora. Clitandre's monograph in particular elaborates the significance of Danticat's writing and reading strategies
for retheorizing the concept of nation and diaspora as dialogic.[21] Importantly, Clitandre also connects Danticat's relational approach to diaspora
as part of a "consciousness of expansiveness" that is fundamental to Black
women's writing.[22] This practice of expansiveness can also be connected
to women of color feminist writing that works to connect people across
differences and geopolitical boundaries. With the anthology as a pivotal
form for women of color feminist writing, and Cherríe Moraga and Gloria
Anzaldúa's collection *This Bridge Called My Back: Writings by Radical Women
of Color* as a touchstone for this connective, creative work, proponents of

this tradition[23] are still renowned for, as Barbara Smith explains, deciding that "as women, feminists, and lesbians of color we had experiences and work to do in common, although we also had our differences."[24] Similarly, through its proliferation of Haitian and diasporic voices, Danticat's writing creates what Clitandre calls an "endless knowledge of relation within the world's totality and projects that attempt to destabilize all totalitarian structures of thought."[25] Although Clitandre's study focuses primarily on the dialogic connection of Haitian and Haitian diasporic voices in Danticat's work, her deep knowledge of Danticat's attention to wide-reaching connectivity prompts her acknowledgment in the quotation above that Danticat's intertextual thinking includes more than Haitian voices. While this approach may seem overly accommodating, the ability to represent a Global South way of thinking—that is, thinking in a way that decenters the Global North, but still acknowledges its existence and seeks moments of translocal solidarity—is crucial to overcoming "totalitarian structures of thought" that otherwise reduce writing by marginalized people to segregated, devalued categories. It is this relational expansiveness that I am interested in mining from Danticat's theoretical and reflective work to serve as a guide for a Global South pedagogy.

Drawing from this impulse of expansion, the call or challenge of Danticat's essay is, as she explains, "to create dangerously for people who read dangerously."[26] Her call to do this, however, is not bound by location, identity, or situation. As she explains,

> So though we may not be creating as dangerously as our forebears—though we are not risking torture, beatings, execution, though exile does not threaten us into perpetual silence—still while we are at work bodies are littering the streets somewhere. People are buried under rubble somewhere. Mass graves are being dug somewhere. [. . .] And still many are reading and writing, quietly, quietly.[27]

Implicit even in the repetitious call to "create dangerously for people who read dangerously," there is a distinct but close relationship between creator and reader. This relationship is further echoed by the unspecified "many" readers and writers and the undisclosed "somewhere" that are not reflective of a specific national, ethnic, or regional belonging, but on the awareness, connection, and care for such a (deterritorialized) place—on an imaginative capacity. Immigrant artist or otherwise, Danticat's call can apply to those in the United States or to those who, like Danticat's relatives, were forced to read "quietly, quietly" during the devastating Duvalier dictatorship.

Danticat's intertextual Global South thinking does not necessitate that she *become* one of those experiencing extreme oppression, but rather that her sense of time, place, and history can accommodate her connection to and relationship with multiple sites of belonging and unbelonging in the Global South; more importantly, Danticat understands that these sites are not immutably severed or inconsequentially connected. Clitandre's study of Danticat's diasporic imaginary that accommodates both nation and the scattered networks beyond the nation beautifully elucidates this aspect of her writing and activism. In considering her Global South intertextual thinking, however, we can also surmise that her diasporic imaginary is shaped not only against the home nation-state and its literary legacies but also against a world literary and artistic sphere that includes dominant voices and cultures. Danticat, therefore, models a way to facilitate a Global South conversation that amplifies the voices of marginalized figures, especially women, in a relational, local-global dialectic. In this model, dominant global voices like Camus's are deployed in service of more silenced ones. After all, part of the title of her book *Create Dangerously* is inspired from a Camus lecture, and it is Camus's play *Caligula* that she claims helped her Haitian relatives face the circumstances of the Duvalier regime when they could not document or respond to it themselves.[28] Even more importantly, in Danticat's circuitous retelling of the origin of her book's title, she relays that her connection to Camus, and to her family's literary lineage, is itself speculative and derived from her father's deathbed recollection of Haiti's banned books and its citizens' illicit readings. Deducting from her father's hazy descriptions, Danticat makes the connection to *Caligula* herself, and she recovers the play and its significance for understanding Haitian and her own history. In this scenario, the flow of knowledge and knowledge production is not unidirectional (North to South), but multidirectional. This is, to use Walter Mignolo's phrase, the Global South as "a place (or places) from which to speak" our interconnected realities in unconventional ways and formats.[29] With Danticat's intertextual Global South thinking as an example of a Global South epistemological project, we can now ask ourselves: how can we, too, participate in or contribute to this space and develop platforms and research that do not dominate marginalized voices but help amplify them?

CRAFTING A GLOBAL SOUTH SYLLABUS

With the above question as a guiding force for a Global South and literature class, my revised reading schedule would begin with a section called

"Interrogating the Global South as Interpretive Lens," which would put forth several scholars' theoretical explanations of the term and foreground the need to critically interrogate new theoretical concepts. This section would still incorporate, for instance, West-Pavlov's introduction but would also include other voices such as Mahler's brief keyword entry "What is the Global South," included in the University of Virginia's ever growing Global South studies digital platform (https://globalsouthstudies.as.virginia.edu/); López's introduction to the first issue of the *Global South* scholarly journal; as well as marginalized voices of women of color such as Danticat who have been implicitly considering the Global South for many years. Students will summarize the readings as well as provide their own interpretation and review of how the author engages with the concept and what it means for the scholars' work. These ongoing responses will allow students to internalize and complicate their understanding of the Global South. With this unit as a foundation, students should learn that critical terms are always being created and contested, and that who/when/how a person is speaking about a term or concept matters as much as what is being said. By ending with a discussion of Danticat's generous Global South intertextual thinking, students will hopefully feel more comfortable entering a scholarly debate as conscious, reflective participants who are aware of their creative potential, responsibility, and the "endless knowledge of relation" they can contribute to in solidarity with the Global South.[30]

Danticat's essay can also model ways to think about literature and culture from a Global South perspective. When discussing "Create Dangerously," instructors can draw attention to the following: (1) Danticat's care relationship toward literature, (2) the agency and volition she ascribes to Global South readers, and (3) her disruption of time, space, nation, and geography for generative, deterritorialized Global South imaginings. Toward the first point, in her essay and throughout the *Create Dangerously* collection, writing and reading are described as activities that require extreme care and consciousness, if not outright bravery. As she explains, to create dangerously is to "writ[e], knowing in part that no matter how trivial your words may seem, someday, somewhere, someone may risk his or her life to read them."[31] While this may seem like a platitude, in the context of her essay's concern with reading and writing and her larger career-wide engagement with ideas such as writing as healing, writing as testimony, it is indicative of her unique Global South perspective that foregrounds the transborder intimacy of the writer-reader relationship, as well as the future-making project of writing and reading, which are both crucial for a Global South pedagogy invested in analyzing power and forging solidarities. Danticat's Global South intertextual thinking shows us the sociality of literature and storytelling that Black women and women of color have always known, but that is not always conveyed in the classroom.

Following Danticat's focus on the writer as sustainer or nurturer, her intertextual thinking also stresses the urgency and life-sustaining qualities of writing and reading as opposed to only the power structures of exchange and circulation. Of course, the incorporation of Camus, Sophocles, and Osip Mandelstam into the lives and minds of Haitians has much to do with the global circulation of these texts and their relative political safety as classics compared to writing by Haitians who were persecuted along with their readers under the Duvalier regime.[32] While it is absolutely correct to read this circumstance as indicative of the unequal world literary marketplace and political economy, in the context of Danticat's essay, it is also, ironically, a testament to the usefulness of world literature and its ability to generate this type of transborder, intimate, and nourishing readership. Danticat's many and diverse literary references are not oriented or valued by time, nation, or identity but on their ability to attest to the significance of creating and speaking oneself into new formations of history.[33] In Danticat's words, the value of reading Camus in Duvalier-era Haiti was "to be convinced that words could still be spoken, that stories could still be told and passed on."[34] From this perspective, the circulation of texts from around the globe do not have to speak for the Global South subject, but hold space for them to also create. As she explains: "Somewhere, if not now, then maybe years in the future, we may also save someone's life (or mind) because they have given us a passport, making us honorary citizens of their culture."[35] These are bold words from Danticat that shift our focus from our presentist understanding of cultural politics to the care acts of creating and reading for a Global South future.

Danticat's perspective also zeroes in on the volition of the Global South reader who *elects* to make the nonlocal author and their text "honorary citizens" of the reader's culture. The Global South reader is not assumed to be a passive subject ready to be enlightened by a canonical outside text, but a volitional participant in accepting the world of the book, welcoming it into the local culture, and adding to its creative impact. Danticat further illustrates this point by contemplating her Haitian Canadian friend and author Dany Laferrière's statement that "when a Japanese reader reads my book, I immediately become a Japanese writer."[36] This gives tremendous agency and significance to a reader-writer relationship that is collaborative and disrupts colonial models that replace local culture with an imperial one. This has also often been the orientation of globalization and its attendant neoliberal policies and values that stunt the growth of local resources, culture, and economy in favor of the "free market" while fetishizing token aspects of a given culture.[37] In line with a Global South understanding of power, Jodi Melamed's work on the racial logics of "neoliberal multicultur-alism" attests to the way US universities and literary studies departments in particular incorporate racial difference (e.g., diversity) in limited and capitalist ways. Specifically, students are introduced to racial difference via literature to expose them to a shallow understanding of cultural difference (both in the United States and abroad) that they can then internalize and use to demonstrate global competency in their future roles within the workings of global capitalism.[38] It is important, thus, that a Global South pedagogy and syllabus include literature and culture from Global South artists who demonstrate a willingness and attentiveness to South-South collaborations; and that the theoretical pieces to interpret primary texts are not solely or predominantly from Western scholars.

With regard to primary texts to support a Global South pedagogy, dia-sporic writers such as Danticat often provide important perspectives on the parallel operations of power in different Global South locations and times. Moreover, with Danticat's intertextual Global South thinking as a model, students should feel prepared to think critically about how artists repre-sent the Global South, to explore Global South narratives across diverse media, and to identify pressing concerns. This work can involve addressing narrative silences, uncovering marginal histories, and looking for intertex-tual nodes of Global South storytelling that exist beyond the primary text. Daniel Alarcón's *Lost City Radio* and Junot Díaz's *The Brief Wondrous Life of Oscar Wao* are excellent texts to consider the way that the Global South and its histories are remembered, represented, and imagined (both inside and outside the United States), while still considering the very acute silences these texts reproduce. Although both texts thematize a collective amnesia that often plagues regions of the Global South, they also perpetuate other silences, particularly pertaining to the voices and experiences of women of color. At the same time, following the contours of an increasingly networked and globalized society, students can be encouraged to consider how these primary texts intersect with readers through other media that extend and complicate the writer-reader relationship. Interested students could, for example, consider the Global South reach and impact of Alarcón's bilingual podcast Radio Ambulante and its relation to his literary work, or the reader-writer intimacy of the fan-based wiki "The Annotated Oscar Wao" (http://www.annotated-oscar-wao.com).

Also important for a Danticat-inspired Global South pedagogy is the development of a publicly accessible archive of a class's critical responses and research projects. Danticat publishes regularly in well-circulated periodicals and gives countless interviews, which she's described as a "shadow of the [literary] work" that allows her to continue to make connections that she may not have otherwise made.[39] As she explains, this practice is part of creating dangerously and, more specifically, her work of witnessing. Similarly, if we want to engage the Global South in a meaningful way, we must be willing to make our work visible and create dangerously as well. Making scholarship and ideas public also highlights how we participate in intertextuality and the creation of an expansive "knowledge of relation" through our citational practices.[40] The easiest way to develop such a visible and archived space is through the use of a class website that is publicly accessible. A simple and free WordPress blog would adequately meet these needs. Alternatively, the class could incorporate the use of open source digital humanities tools, such as Scalar, that provide a more robust web platform for online publishing of scholarly research.[41] In either of these platforms, students can incorporate hashtags as metadata for the topics discussed. Additionally, as preparation for a final research paper, students can be given the option to contribute a keyword entry to the University of Virginia's Global South Studies website. In partnership with the *Global South* scholarly journal, student entries are peer reviewed and possibly selected to appear on the university's website, further amplifying the impact of Global South studies and students' role in contributing to its ongoing dialogue. Through these readings and assignments, students can hopefully understand that we can and do play a role in the way that we think and write about the Global South in our own lives and in our academic spheres.

CONCLUSION

In her role as a public intellectual, Danticat continues her witnessing through regular contributions to the *New York Times* and the *New Yorker* magazine. A vivid example of her intertextual Global South thinking can be seen in a *New York Times* piece from November 2017 entitled "Edwidge Danticat: Dawn after the Tempests." In this piece, Danticat turns to her favorite writers to understand the places and people of the Caribbean who were devastated by Hurricanes Irma and Maria while weaving in her own experience, or lack thereof, with these places. She begins with Audre Lorde's "Grenada Revisited: An Interim Report" as a guide for thinking about and seeing Grenada with her own eyes, familiar as they are with Haitian imagery. When Danticat's thoughts turn to Dominica, she anchors her connection to the island through writer Jean Rhys. It is through Rhys and Jamaica Kincaid that Danticat knows and cares for Dominica and incorporates their images and experiences into her own. In this way she continues, meditating on Puerto Rico's riches and losses through the writing of Esmeralda Santiago and the words of San Juan mayor Carmen Yulín Cruz Soto, and even surmising the undocumented words of the indigenous islanders, the Arawak and Taíno people.

Danticat concludes her piece with words from Grenadian poet Merle Collins's poem "Because the Dawn Breaks," which echoes her own essay title—"Dawn after the Tempests." Not only does Danticat's intertextuality here showcase the depth of feeling and connection that can emerge from a long-standing writer and reader relationship, but she uses her public voice in this essay to bring forth the voices of other Caribbean and Global South writers. In Danticat's piece, these writers' words are cared for and nourished and are, perhaps, the "dawn after the tempests"—with the title's plural s suggesting a future in which these words are already a balm. While I am only scratching the surface of Danticat's full oeuvre, her intertextual Global South thinking is both evident and powerful. As Clitandre has documented, it has shaped her more capacious understanding of diaspora and her role as a diasporic writer. Moreover, as I suggest here, Danticat offers us a framework from which to think about a world literary and cultural sphere, and how we can center marginalized histories and people by using our own voices and writing to create powerful temporal and geographic reticulations. Danticat's voice and work are as much about nurturing as they are corrective, offering up forgiveness and hope at the same time that they "quietly, quietly" weave a net of relations for a differently imagined tomorrow.

NOTES

1. Renee H. Shea, "'Stretching the Limits of Silence': Witness and Resistance in Edwidge Danticat's Nonfiction," *World Literature Today* 93, no. 1 (Winter 2019), https://www.worldliteraturetoday.org/2019/winter/stretching-limits-silence-witness-and-resistance-edwidge-danticats-nonfiction-renee-h.

2. Jake Brownell, "'I Am a Witness': A Conversation with Edwidge Danticat," KRCC Converge Lecture Series Podcast, October 31, 2018, https://www.krcc.org/post/i-am-witness-conversation-edwidge-danticat.

3. Russell West-Pavlov, "Toward the Global South: Concept or Chimera, Paradigm or Panacea?," in *The Global South and Literature*, ed. Russell West-Pavlov (Cambridge: Cambridge University Press, 2018), 1, 7.

4. West-Pavlov, "Toward the Global South," 5.

5. As West-Pavlov explains, the term "Third World" first emerged to describe the nonaligned nations that met at Bandung in Indonesia in 1955 to consider an alternative to the "First World of Euro-American capitalism and the Second World of Soviet- and Chinese-aligned communism" ("Toward the Global South," 4). It should also be noted that in academic communication, the term "Global South" first emerged not in the humanities but in the realms of "development, environmentalism, international relations, and finance" (6).

6. Alfred J. López, "Introduction: The (Post)global South," *Global South* 1, no. 1 (Winter 2007): 3.

7. Likewise, as Clitandre explains, Danticat's relational understanding of nation and diaspora extends to her understanding of the local and global as intertwined and mutually constitutive. This crucially shapes Danticat's interest in globalization as "closeness, exchange, and exposure." Nadège T. Clitandre, *Edwidge Danticat: The Haitian Diasporic Imaginary* (Charlottesville: University of Virginia Press, 2018), 3.

8. Clitandre, *Edwidge Danticat: The Haitian Diasporic Imaginary*, 3.

9. Clitandre, *Edwidge Danticat: The Haitian Diasporic Imaginary*, 2.

10. Anne Garland Mahler, "The Global South in the Belly of the Beast: Viewing African American Civil Rights through a Tricontinental Lens," *Latin American Research Review* 50, no. 1 (2015): 96.

11. Mahler, "The Global South," 95.

12. Mahler, "The Global South," 97.

13. Mahler, "The Global South," 109–10.

14. Mahler, "The Global South," 110.

15. López, "Introduction: The (Post)global South," 5.

16. Danticat, "Create Dangerously," 46.

17. In a 2007 interview for *Callaloo*, Danticat expounds on the connective effect of globalization on national literature, identity, and culture, explaining: "Globalization makes these villages, most of these villages, come closer together. [. . .] And also it makes it possible for writers to read other writers, to be aware of what other writers are doing. [. . .] [I]f there is anything positive to draw from globalization, I think culturally there is more exchange, and so I think it's harder to pin down what makes a national literature." Nancy Raquel Mirabal, "Dyasporic Appetites and Longings: An Interview with Edwidge Danticat," *Callaloo* 30, no. 1 (Winter 2007): 30.

18. Danticat, "Create Dangerously," 5.

19. Danticat, "Create Dangerously," 5.

20. Danticat, "Create Dangerously," 16.

21. Clitandre, *Edwidge Danticat: The Haitian Diasporic Imaginary*, 2.

22. Clitandre, *Edwidge Danticat: The Haitian Diasporic Imaginary*, 2–3.

23. It's important to note that Danticat has also been an editor for several anthology projects including two anthologies on Haitian writing: *Haiti Noir* (2011) and *Haiti Noir 2: The Classics* (2014). She is also the sole editor of another anthology of Haitian writers, *The Butterfly's Way: Voices from the Haitian Dyaspora in the United States* (2001).

24. Barbara Smith, "A Press of Our Own Kitchen Table: Women of Color Press," *Frontiers* 10, no. 3 (1989): 11.

25. Clitandre, *Edwidge Danticat: The Haitian Diasporic Imaginary*, 10.

26. Danticat, "Create Dangerously," 10.

27. Danticat, "Create Dangerously," 18.

28. Danticat, "Create Dangerously," 8; and Elvira Pulitano, "An Immigrant Artist at Work: A Conversation with Edwidge Danticat," *Small Axe* 15, no. 3 (2011): 41.

29. Walter Mignolo, quoted in West-Pavlov, "Toward the Global South," 7.

30. Clitandre, *Edwidge Danticat: The Haitian Diasporic Imaginary*, 10.

31. Danticat, "Create Dangerously," 10.

32. Danticat, "Create Dangerously," 9.

33. In this essay ("Create Dangerously") alone, Danticat makes a total of twenty-one literary references, nine of which are to Haitian artists. A significant body of Danticat scholarship echoes her interest in new formations of history by focusing on memory, testimony, and healing in her work; see Maria Rice Bellamy, "More than Hunter or Prey: Duality and Traumatic Memory in Edwidge Danticat's *The Dew Breaker*," *MELUS* 37, no. 1 (Spring 2012): 177–97; Yan Xu, "To Narrate Is to Be: Edwidge Danticat's The Farming of Bones," *Forum for World Literature Studies* 6, no. 2 (2014): 218–29; Jennifer Harford Vargas, "Novel Testimony: Alternative Archives in Edwidge Danticat's *The Farming of Bones*," *Callaloo* 37, no. 5 (Fall 2014): 1162–80; and Judith Misrahi-Barak, "Biopolitics and Translation: Edwidge Danticat's Many Tongues," *International Journal of Francophone Studies* 17, nos. 3–4 (November 2014): 349–73.

34. Danticat, "Create Dangerously," 8.

35. Danticat, "Create Dangerously," 10.

36. Danticat, "Create Dangerously," 15.

37. David Harvey, *A Brief History of Neoliberalism* (Oxford: Oxford University Press, 2007); and Arlene Dávila, *Culture Works: Space, Value, and Mobility across the Neoliberal Americas* (New York: New York University Press, 2012).

38. Jodi Melamed, "Making Global Citizens: Neoliberal Multiculturalism and Literary Value," in *Represent and Destroy: Rationalizing Violence in the New Racial Capitalism*, by Jodi Melamed (Minneapolis: University of Minnesota Press, 2011), 137–78.

39. Pulitano, "An Immigrant Artist at Work," 58.

40. This is a perfect opportunity to direct students to the Cite Black Women webpage (https://www.citeblackwomencollective.org) and movement.

41. For an example of a class Scalar project, see the Women of Color Feminism: Then and Now project (https://scalar.usc.edu/works/women-of-color-feminism-then-and-now/index) created by a graduate class of mine in 2019. Through the plugin hypothes.is, students can also annotate their peers' writing in Scalar.

BIBLIOGRAPHY

Bellamy, Maria Rice. "More than Hunter or Prey: Duality and Traumatic Memory in Edwidge Danticat's *The Dew Breaker*." *MELUS* 37, no. 1 (Spring 2012): 177–97.
Brownell, Jake. "'I Am a Witness': A Conversation with Edwidge Danticat." KRCC Converge Lecture Series Podcast, October 31, 2018. https://www.krcc.org/post/i-am-witness-conversation-edwidge-danticat.

Clitandre, Nadège T. *Edwidge Danticat: The Haitian Diasporic Imaginary*. Charlottesville: University of Virginia Press, 2018.

Danticat, Edwidge. *Create Dangerously: The Immigrant Artist at Work*. New York: Vintage Books, 2011.

Danticat, Edwidge. "Create Dangerously: The Immigrant Artist at Work." In *Create Dangerously: The Immigrant Artist at Work*, by Edwidge Danticat, 1–20. New York: Vintage Press, 2011, 1–20.

Danticat, Edwidge. "Dawn after the Tempests." *New York Times*, November 6, 2017.

Dávila, Arlene. *Culture Works: Space, Value, and Mobility across the Neoliberal Americas*. New York: New York University Press, 2012.

Harford Vargas, Jennifer. "Novel Testimony: Alternative Archives in Edwidge Danticat's *The Farming of Bones*." *Callaloo* 37, no. 5 (Fall 2014): 1162–80.

Harvey, David. *A Brief History of Neoliberalism*. Oxford: Oxford University Press, 2007.

López, Albert J. "Introduction: The (Post)global South." *Global South* 1, no. 1 (Winter 2007): 1–11.

Mahler, Anne Garland. "The Global South in the Belly of the Beast: Viewing African American Civil Rights through a Tricontinental Lens." *Latin American Research Review* 50, no. 1 (2015): 95–116.

Melamed, Jodi. "Making Global Citizens: Neoliberal Multiculturalism and Literary Value." In *Represent and Destroy: Rationalizing Violence in the New Racial Capitalism*, by Jodi Melamed, 137–78. Minneapolis: University of Minnesota Press, 2011.

Mirabal, Nancy Raquel. "Dyasporic Appetites and Longings: An Interview with Edwidge Danticat." *Callaloo* 30, no. 1 (Winter 2007): 26–39.

Misrahi-Barak, Judith. "Biopolitics and Translation: Edwidge Danticat's Many Tongues." *International Journal of Francophone Studies* 17, nos. 3–4 (November 2014): 349–73.

Pulitano, Elvira. "An Immigrant Artist at Work: A Conversation with Edwidge Danticat." *Small Axe* 15, no. 3 (2011): 39–61.

Shea, Renee H. "'Stretching the Limits of Silence': Witness and Resistance in Edwidge Danticat's Nonfiction." *World Literature Today* 93, no. 1 (Winter 2019). https://www.worldliteraturetoday.org/2019/winter/stretching-limits-silence-witness-and-resistance-edwidge-danticats-nonfiction-renee-h.

Smith, Barbara. "A Press of Our Own Kitchen Table: Women of Color Press." *Frontiers* 10, no. 3 (1989): 11–13.

West-Pavlov, Russell. "Toward the Global South: Concept or Chimera, Paradigm or Panacea?" In *The Global South and Literature*, edited by Russell West-Pavlov, 1–22. Cambridge: Cambridge University Press, 2018.

Xu, Yan. "To Narrate Is to Be: Edwidge Danticat's *The Farming of Bones*." *Forum for World Literature Studies* 6, no. 2 (2014): 218–29.

Part IV

"Create Dangerously": Trauma, Resilience, and the Way Forward

Chapter Thirteen

EDWIDGE DANTICAT

The Ethics of Disobedient Writing

ISABEL CALDEIRA

> But who does not know of literature banned because it is interrogative;
> discredited because it is critical; erased because alternate?
> —TONI MORRISON, 1993, NOBEL LECTURE

> Tyrants know there is in the work of art an emancipatory force, which is
> mysterious only to those who do not revere it.
> —ALBERT CAMUS, 1988 (1960), "CREATE DANGEROUSLY"

> The general remembers the tiny green sprigs
> men of his village wore in their capes
> to honor the birth of a son. He will
> order many, this time, to be killed
>
> for a single, beautiful word.
> —RITA DOVE, 1983, "PARSLEY"

DISOBEDIENT WRITING

Edwidge Danticat starts the first chapter of *Create Dangerously*[1] with a story of disobedience that resulted in a death penalty. She recalls the execution by François "Papa Doc" Duvalier's regime of Marcel Numa and Louis Drouin, two young men who had joined the organization Jeune Haiti (Young Haiti) to fight against the Duvalier dictatorship. Their story, she says, haunts her like a creation myth: the dissent, the self-exile, the return, the guerrilla war, and the ultimate self-sacrifice for the freedom of the nation. For her, the story of these patriots "involves a disobeyed directive from a higher authority and a brutal punishment as a result" (Danticat 2010, 5). It reminds her of the Adam and Eve creation myth; both stories involve disobedience, defiance of authority, and the consequent punishment. By juxtaposing the biblical parable with the historical episode in Haiti, Danticat reveals her ethical posture as a storyteller to use the symbolic power of words to confront power and authority, reclaim the memory of facts, and thus fight against the oblivion of history: "Reading, like writing, under these conditions is disobedience to a directive in which the reader, our Eve, already knows the possible consequences of eating that apple but takes a bold bite anyway" (2010, 10). She reminds us that it was Eve and not Adam who dared to disobey. In fact, she represents women as most daring in their fight for freedom and self-determination.

Toni Morrison—an author Danticat has elected as a model[2]—has also delved into the biblical creation myth and its implied meanings. When she started writing her novel *Paradise* (1997), the question that triggered her was "why paradise necessitates exclusion" (Farnsworth 2008, 156). Mulling over the idea of paradise, Morrison ponders human contradiction; while to reimagine paradise means "yearnings for freedom and safety; for plenitude, for rest, for beauty; [. . .] the search for one's own space, for respect, love, bliss," it also means a craving for borders, exclusivity, and privilege (Morrison 2014).[3] She sees in the idea of paradise (which necessitates exclusion) the key to understanding human ambivalence, encompassing as it does both the negativity of exclusion and the positivity of the capacity to dream. In her interpretation, the everlasting social exclusion of the Other reenacts the authoritarian banishment of the disobedient in the biblical creation myth. And she extrapolates this idea to those who *can*—their power defined by "*my* way, *my* land, *my* borders, *my* values" (Streitfeld 1998)—and hence build borders to keep out the ones who do not conform to their hegemony. For Morrison, therefore, the way we imagine paradise reflects how our human imagination is constrained by our social and political positionings. As she reflects on our contradictions and limitations as human beings, she leaves us a moral lesson for a better world: "We [humans] are the only ones who can imagine paradise, so let's start imagining it properly, so that it isn't about *my* way, *my* land, *my* borders, *my* values, and keeping out you and you and you" (Streitfeld 1998).

In Edwidge Danticat's writing, I find a similar thesis. She leads us, however, to another layer of meaning in the foundational myth: disobedience defines our humanity, although it may cost us banishment, exclusion, and ultimately death. Hence, human beings betray their true nature when they exchange conformity for safety. Both in her fiction and in her public interventions she is well aware of her job as a writer-as-citizen,[4] the one who accepts the mission "to create dangerously," or, in Toni Morrison's articulation, the one who accepts the "response-ability" (Morrison 1992, xi). As Danticat once declared in an interview in 2016: "[F]or me personally, there is no separation between the work I do as a writer and my personal commitment as a citizen" (Montgomery 2017, 205). Thus, I propose to analyze her work as a form of ethical response to the Other in defense of the rights of freedom and citizenship, against the oblivion of historical memory and the abuses of power.

THE WRITER AS INTERPOSER

Writers such as Edwidge Danticat and Toni Morrison who are not willing to compromise with social injustice and inequality use their writing to fight for social change and make literary production an act of political disobedience for the sake of freedom, equality, and, ultimately, humanity. Danticat's ethical posture is indeed comparable to Morrison's, for whom the job of the writer is "the serene achievement of, or sweaty fight for, meaning and response-ability" (Morrison 1992, xi). Along the same line, Gayatri Chakravorty Spivak in her essay "Responsibility" (1994) stresses the ethical responsibility—or accountability—and answerability that the intellectual bears to the Other, or the subaltern (22). She defines responsibility as "all action undertaken in response to a call [. . .] that cannot be grasped as such." Response, she remarks, involves not only " 'respond[ing] to,' [. . .] but also the related situations of being answerable for" (22).[5] This concern fits well the conception of writing of these two writers-as-citizens. Both have a serious and responsible social positioning toward their job: writing as "a defiant political act" (Morrison 2014), an act of citizenship. Danticat's writing contributes to defending her people's right to full citizenship. *Haiti Noir*, an anthology of short fiction she edited in 2010, for example, makes clear her concern in redeeming the humanity of a people ravaged by colonialism by showcasing Haitian creativity and dignity against all odds. As Toni Morrison says in *Burn This Book* (2009), "A writer's life and work are not a gift to mankind; they are its necessity. [. . .] Certain kinds of trauma visited on peoples are so deep, so cruel, that unlike money, unlike vengeance, even unlike justice, or rights, or the goodwill of others, only writers can translate such trauma and turn sorrow into meaning, sharpening the moral imagination" (4). Danticat conveys an identical feeling but in a state of much more unquietness, even self-conflict when she questions the relevance of her own writing in relation to overwhelming and devasting aspects of reality, such as the earthquake of 2010 in Haiti: "I feel I have to struggle even more with this idea that [. . .] it pales, you know this notion that what you're writing pales in comparison to what's really happening and this thing I wrestle with myself all the time, like 'Does it matter? Does it fit?' [. . .] '[W]hat is the purpose, what is the purpose of this?'" (Montgomery 2017, 94). In *The Origin of Others* (2017), Morrison formulates the possibility opened by fiction to address the Other and the Other in the self: "Narrative fiction provides [. . .] an opportunity to be and to become the Other. The stranger. With sympathy, clarity, and the risk of self-examination" (91). This also reminds me of Danticat speaking of art as a possibility to convey empathy with the Other: "[A]rt in general forces you to step into another body, to step into other skins" (Montgomery 2017, 95). Danticat surely fulfills these intellectual demands in the way she practices her job, combining writing and militancy: "I remember reading something by Toni Cade Bambara where she says that writing is the way she participates in the struggle. And it's not the only way, you need boots on the ground, but writing is most at our disposal" (Montgomery 2017, 172). She uses her tools as a writer not only to give visibility to the lives of Others but to redeem and regenerate a dominant vision of the Haitian as Other: "We deserve to have our full humanity and the complexity of our lives fully explored" (Chen 2019). But what I think is most revealing is that she sometimes uses the first-person plural because she feels othered, too: "[W]e're still deprived of complexity. [. . .] I am allowed more complexity if people know— [. . .] I am allowed that if people know that I come from this great culture, [. . .] [i]t makes me a more complex human being" (Montgomery 2017, 95–96).

Danticat has always found an important inspiration in the people of Haiti, in the numerous examples of human resistance they have shown throughout history—a "legacy of resilience and survival." In Haitians' "reverence for readers and for reading" (Montgomery 2017, 82), even when reading and writing were acts of disobedience, Danticat feels that she has learned her office as a writer: "Create dangerously, for people who read dangerously. This is what I've always thought it meant to be a writer. [. . .] Somewhere, if not now, then maybe years in the future, we may also save someone's life, because they have given us a passport, making us honorary citizens of their culture" (Danticat 2010, 10). As an immigrant away from home and from the experience of daily life in Haiti (an insider/outsider; Chen 2019), she faces inner conflicts and self-doubts about her moral responsibility to represent Haitian people, mainly when she is addressed as the face of a ravaged Haiti. But she feels the need to always speak up (Montgomery 2017, 182), for, as she once said: "Part of my role is to try to keep people's awareness up" (Montgomery 2017, 136). *Create Dangerously* is witness to Danticat's political posture and sense of accountability.[6] Although she left her country while still a child, she has always been back and forth, never losing the sense of Haiti as her homeland (Montgomery 2017, 155). In Miami, where she lives with her family, she has chosen to inhabit Little Haiti, where she can find a replica of the sounds of Kreyòl, the smells of Haitian food, and the right products to buy.

As an immigrant in the United States, Danticat always keeps alert to what concerns her home nation: "Forgetting is a constant fear in any writer's life. For the immigrant writer, far from home, memory becomes an even deeper abyss" (2010, 65). Camus's idea that to create dangerously means "creating as a revolt against silence" was thus very inspiring to her (2010, 11). Her ethical positioning toward history, nation, and power defines her as an "honorary citizen" (10) of a more humane and democratic world. That is her way of responding to the call of the deprivation of Haitian people, their history of tyranny and abuse under the Duvaliers, the long-standing scenario of poverty and dependence, and the geo-economic vulnerability of their island to natural catastrophes. To this may be added the conflictual history between Haitians and Dominicans, as a cruel legacy of colonialism, which caused the division of the island under different powers. All this offers the drama that furnishes her fiction.

Furthermore, Danticat believes in literature's capacity to build human bridges in a global world deprived of justice and civil rights, a world where, borrowing from Marleine Bastien, it is "a crime to dream" (Danticat 2005a).[7] She invariably expresses a sense of hope: "All of us who want to see a better future for our nations need to fight the toxicologies of the past by practicing the simple revolutionary techniques of contact, compassion and critical solidarity" (André 2014). I see in her fiction a concern to balance scars with bridges, a willingness to overcome conflict and difference, to find hope in togetherness (Montgomery 2017, 176). Her observation in relation to the divisions between Dominicans and Haitians—"Often in the dialogue we bring up our historical scars, but not our historical bridges. Because our neighbors are solely defined by what they did to us, rather than what we can do together" (Montgomery 2017, 176)—also reveals that her ideological positioning is of (re)conciliation rather than conflict. She uses her position as a writer to act as interposer[8]—one who puts herself in between, to put into words inter-dictions to dismantle interdictions, attempting to build bridges over the boundaries erected by power.

THE WRITER-AS-CITIZEN

I will now explore a few examples from Danticat's fiction to support the idea that her use of writing to confront authority in a struggle against the powers that exclude—what I call an ethics of disobedience—establishes her as a writer-as-citizen. In one of the stories included in *Krik? Krak!* (1996), "Children of the Sea," a young man flees impending death at the hands of the Tonton Macoutes for being a political dissident following the military coup that ousted President Jean-Bertrand Aristide in 1991. His lover, a young girl, and her parents are also fleeing Port-au-Prince in order to avoid persecution. The narrative is built as an exchange of letters between the two young lovers, letters that will never reach their addressee. Looking at this exchange of letters, April Shemak argues that Danticat "portrays a number of inter-dictions for Haitians fleeing violence" (Shemak 2011, 72). Shemak focuses on refugees in the Americas and how they face the US interdiction policy in the asylum process and are thus impeded from producing their testimonies. She uses the concept of "inter-diction" to represent that impediment, their silencing. In their name, so to say, "writers-as-witnesses" (245), as she calls them, attempt to narrate the transnational stories of those silenced voices (41). Shemak analyzes the narrative structure of "Children of the Sea" as a narrative "inter-diction," playing with the meaning of interdiction as prohibition. For her, the fact that the names of the characters in Danticat's short story are not revealed suggests a kind of protection from interdiction, making their testimonials a representation of the silenced voices of all the undocumented Haitians.[9]

Although her reasoning has a different purpose, Shemak's play with the homophony of interdiction/inter-diction was very inspiring for the development of my argument.[10] Danticat often writes about dissidence against dictatorship in Haiti and the boldness that that requires, as she does in *Create Dangerously*. Individuals—such as Marcel Numa and Louis Drouin, the two young men who paid with their lives for their fight against the Duvalier dictatorship—are excluded from citizenship and representation, which certainly reduces their capacity to act. However, those who are not willing to conform still resist through dissent. As a consequence, they may be punished or interdicted, in the sense of being excluded or othered. Going a little further beyond Shemak's play with those meanings, I underline that the letters written by the two lovers in "Children of the Sea" are dead letters. Therefore, the act of *inter + dicere* only works between writer and reader, which accentuates the interdiction imposed by the dictatorship that forced the separation of the two young lovers. It is only at the fictional level, through the meanings conveyed by the imagined dialogue between the young man and the young girl, that interdiction is ultimately subverted and resignified—interdiction becoming inter-diction, silencing imposed by the political power becoming voice, death becoming survival. The writer puts herself in the position of interposer, to pass the message on, reminding us of the words of Toni Morrison cited above: "[O]nly writers can translate such trauma and turn sorrow into meaning, sharpening the moral imagination" (Morrison 2009, 4). I relate this position of interposer to the idea of in-betweenness that Danticat so often mentions—starting with the sense of being caught between the two worlds of Haiti and the United States, as with the hundreds of thousands of Haitians referred to by the Kreyòl word *dyaspora*,[11] and torn between three languages (Kreyòl, French, and English). But she goes much further in her artistic ambition "to look for that in-between place" (Montgomery 2017, 95) and be able to convey it, exposing the complexity and ambivalence of the Haitian people behind the simplism of stereotypes that usually fix their representation in other people's minds:

> I want to send people down all these paths, to know more, and art on some level, I think, grants us that complexity, because you're looking at the thing, but you also have to, if you're a careful reader, if you're a careful viewer, you have to take the next step and go—but where does that come from? Who are those people who created that? [. . .] [A]nd so I want to claim that complexity for people who I think are sometimes simplistic—looked at in a very simplistic and pitying way. (Montgomery 2017, 96)

As I argued earlier in this chapter, to break the silence is felt by the writer-as-citizen to be an act of responsibility toward the Other. Having chosen in her work to address many of the troubles faced by Haitian people throughout history, Danticat pays utmost attention to devalued people (Montgomery 2017, 79) and shows a constant self-questioning as it relates to the truth in an attempt to voice their hardships (Danticat 2010, 159; Spivak 1988; Spivak 1999).[12] Danticat imparts it very clearly: "The only thing writers can do in those types of situations is, if they choose, to add their voices to those others who bear witness to that type of violence, those types of crimes, that kind of injustice" (Montgomery 2017, 141). But she is also deeply aware of her location as an insider/outsider (Chen 2019). Danticat calls that choice the "immigrant work ethic" (Montgomery 2017, 137), reminding us of her sense of responsibility (Spivak 1994, 22) or response-ability (Morrison 1992, xi).

THE FARMING OF BONES:
HISTORICAL SCARS AND HISTORICAL BRIDGES

In Edwidge Danticat's ethics of disobedience, I identify a very deep commitment to human rights and the preservation of memory for the survival of a
people's soul as the writer questions the structures of power. Her novel *The
Farming of Bones* (1998) is a good example of the representation of authority
and interdiction that subject the most vulnerable people to try to stifle their
indelible capacity to dream. The plot develops around the 1937 persecution
and massacre of thousands of Haitian migrants in the Dominican Republic
under President Rafael Trujillo's orders. Political propaganda justified the
acts as a way to protect the local Dominican population, who complained
about crescent depredations by Haitians living among them; it is significant
that Trujillo ordered his soldiers to use machetes so that the slaughtering
could be attributed to the campesinos.[13] This traumatic experience found
its tragic, commemorative plaque in the name of the border river between
Haiti and the Dominican Republic, the Massacre River (El Masacre), which
offered its waters to entomb the bodies of many of the Haitian victims. An
irony of history lies in the fact that the name of the river refers not to the
tragic episode of the 1937 massacre under Trujillo but to a former massacre,
the battle between French and Spanish colonizers in their fight for dominion
over the island. In this way, the history of violence for possession and exclusion, division and hate, which so well describes colonialism, is reenacted by
subsequent powers that perpetuate the logic of racial and ethnic discrimination and racial division of labor. It is worth recalling that Trujillo was himself
mixed blood, but he wanted to hide the fact. After all, he represented a white
Creole bourgeoisie that had accessed power in the wake of Spanish decolo-
nization, basing their power on claims of white ancestry (Dhar 2005–2006,
189). Haitians were othered for their Blackness, and the massacre was justified as a de-Africanization of the country (Balaguer 1983; Strongman 2006,
39). According to Border of Lights, an organization commemorating the
seventy-fifth anniversary of the massacre in 2012: "The massacre cemented
Haitians into a long-term subversive outsider incompatible with what it
means to be Dominicans" (Phillip 2015). This stigma has been encrusted
in poor Haitians who cross the border to the Dominican Republic in their
struggle for survival and then are stigmatized, persecuted, and excluded.

When Danticat was doing research for *The Farming of Bones*, she visited
the Massacre River and recalls: "Between Haiti and the Dominican Republic flows a river filled with ghosts" (2005b, 7). She refers to that experience
in the preface she wrote in 2005 for the English translation of a novel by

Haitian writer René Philoctète, *Le peuple des terres mêlées* (1989), which was translated into English as *Massacre River*. Philoctète's original title refers to the mixed (*mêlée*) population living on the border between Haiti and the Dominican Republic, originating in the several colonizations that divided the island,[14] while the English translation directly refers to the historical setting of the novel. The novel's plot exposes the drama of an abusive power's cruel interruption of that mixture, which had naturally taken place among working people who shared their lives unmindful of their origin, ethnicity, or any other difference. Operation Cabezas Haitianas (Haitian Heads), ordered by power-mad Generalissimo Trujillo, was the interdiction imposed on a group just because of their Haitian origin, even on those who had been born on the Dominican side of the island. The soldiers shouted, "Perejil! [Parsley!] Perish! Punish!" Haitians tried to pronounce the word *perejil* correctly, but if they failed, they were massacred. Philoctète chose to dramatize the cruelty of this operation by focusing on the relationship between the Dominican Pedro and the Haitian Adèle, whose loving marriage is interrupted by Adèle's death at the hands of the soldiers.

Instead of "the river running with blood" Danticat had imagined before she made that journey to get a feeling of the place, she found "a tiny braid of water" with the sand of the riverbed close to the surface (Danticat 2005b, 8). She was also impressed by an atmosphere of closeness and vicinity among the people she saw on the banks of the river, "the living people of the river" (8, 9), "people who though haunted by a gory history still live, sometimes peacefully and sometimes uneasily, side by side" (9). However, on the bridge she also saw "Dominican soldiers in camouflage uniforms with rifles on their shoulders" (9) reminding the people that their lives are under political control. Nonetheless, Danticat leaves the place with a hopeful note, wishing that "the spiritual children of the river" will "continue to challenge the meaning of community and humanity in all of us" (9). And, I would say, Danticat also continues to challenge interdiction to reenact the possibility of inter-diction—communication among peoples within and across borders. After all, the ideology of racial or ethnic discrimination is inscribed in the idea of the border as boundary, but the border may also contain the ideas of contiguity and vicinity.

The tragic episode that inspired Danticat in *The Farming of Bones* is also known as the Parsley Massacre.[15] As mentioned above, Kreyòl-speaking Haitians were supposedly identified by their inability to correctly pronounce the Spanish word *perejil* (parsley), Spanish being the native language of the Dominicans.[16] The centrality of this detail in Danticat's novel reveals the brutality of a system of power built upon such perverse methods just to exclude migrants on racial grounds. Ironically, interdiction is imposed on the basis of diction. The mispronunciation (misdiction?) of a common word like *perejil* became a death sentence; a complex set of factors based on the politics of discrimination and exclusion—historical, cultural, economic, colonial, racial, class-biased—was condensed and translated into an insignificant, senseless act turned into an act of national identification. Danticat's choice of the biblical passage Judges 12:4–6 for the epigraph of *The Farming of Bones*—the killing of the Ephraimites by the men of Gilead as determined by the former's inability to pronounce the word *shibboleth*[17]—emphasizes the transversal and transhistorical discrimination against the Other reinforced by political propaganda targeting any so-called threat against the security of a nation. After all, it just reiterates the logic of exclusion expressed by Toni Morrison in her interview with the *Washington Post* quoted above, an exclusion that is informed by a sense of exclusivity (Streitfeld 1998). I see in both Morrison's and Danticat's way of relating to the Other an analogy with Jacques Derrida's depiction of the stranger (*l'étranger*) in his essay *Of Hospitality*. The aspect of his reflection that I find clarifying in this context is the defenselessness of the stranger before the language of the host, which is also the latter's power of hospitality. Demanding from the stranger the use of the host's language is an act of violence:

> [T]he foreigner, [if] inept at speaking the language, always risks being without defense before the law of the country that welcomes or expels him; the foreigner is first of all foreign to the legal language in which the duty of hospitality is formulated, the right to asylum, its limits, norms, policing, etc. He has to ask for hospitality in a language which by definition is not his own, the one imposed on him by the master of the house, the host, the king, the lord, the authorities, the nation, the State, the father, etc. This personage imposes on him translation into their own language, and that's the first act of violence. (Derrida 2000, 15)

The narrative strategy in *The Farming of Bones* subtly debunks the brutal logic of power and its radical reversal of hospitality (Derrida 2000). Haitian workers cross the border to mainly work in the cane fields on the Dominican side. The novel's protagonist, Amabelle Désir, a dark-skinned Haitian domestic worker living in the Dominican Republic, refers to cane life as "travay te pou zo," or the farming of bones, because after harvest the cane stalks resemble bones. Besides the hardship of work in the fields, cane and the machete scars mark the workers' bodies. On the first page of the novel, we are introduced to Sebastien Onius, Amabelle's lover. Through her eyes, we see that Sebastien "is lavishly handsome [. . .] even though the cane stalks have ripped apart most of the skin on his shiny black face, leaving him with crisscrossed trails of furrowed scars." And his "palms have lost their lifelines to the machetes that cut the cane" (Danticat 1998, 1).[18] Brutal cane field work leaves inscriptions written on the flesh for us to read the text of neocolonial exploitation.[19] Father Romain, a Haitian priest and community leader, puts the cane work in its proper colonial context; referring to the nearest town, he says: "Alegría, a name to evoke joy. [. . .] Perhaps this is what its founders—those who named it—had in mind. Perhaps there had been joy for them in finding that sugar could be made from blood" (FB, 271).

The fierce conditions accepted by migrant workers in the Dominican cane fields also dehumanize and devalue them in the eyes of the Dominicans. Don Ignacio (Papi) and his daughter, Señora Valencia, had found little Amabelle on the riverside after her parents had drowned, and they took her as a maid in their residence, where she stayed until her adult life. When Señor Pico, Señora Valencia's husband and a loyal supporter of Rafael Trujillo, inadvertently bumps his car against one of the workers, Joël, and kills him, he does not even care to stop and check on the body. When Amabelle records Sebastien's reaction to how Joël, his coworker and friend, was killed and discarded without the slightest respect, the irony in his articulation is the measure of his moral empowerment: "His friend had died. He could have died. We were in the house of the man who had done it. Sebastien could go in and kill him if he really wanted to—'Señor Pico has rifles,' I reminded him, 'and we are on his property'—'Is the air we breathe his property?' he asked" (FB, 53). Bodies may be scarred, tortured, and killed, but Danticat's characters still find dignity in their spirit and their mind to resist.

Sylvie, the young Haitian servant whom Señora Valencia in the absence of her husband had hidden in the house to protect her and her family from the slaughter, asks her: "Why parsley? Why did they choose parsley?" The story Señora Valencia tells her to justify the massacre contains the ingredients of a foundational myth for a fascist and racist ideology, a neutralizing justification for a politics of exclusion and ethnic cleansing. In Señora Valencia's story, the Generalissimo, when he was a young man, had a moment of epiphany when he realized that Haitians did not trill their r's or pronounce the jota the way Dominicans did: "You can never hide as long as there is parsley nearby, the Generalissimo is believed to have said. On this island, you walk too far and people speak a different language. Their own words reveal who belongs on what side" (FB, 304).

In her visit to Alegría years after the massacre—which is now euphemistically called El Corte by the Dominicans and Kout Kouto (a stabbing) by the

Haitians—Amabelle notices several signs of new boundaries and interdictions: "The border had lost a number of its trees. Holes were still too evident where the trees had been plucked out and replaced with poles that held up doubled strands of barbed wire" (FB, 284–85); "Alegría was now a closed town, a group of haciendas behind high walls cemented with metal spikes and broken bottles at the top. Flamboyants[20] towered over these walls and old men crouching in cane-back chairs guarded the gates. Every house was a fortress, everyone an intruder" (FB, 288–89). And in the people's behavior Amabelle can sense fear, as in Señora Valencia's servants' attitudes: "Her jaws were tightly drawn. [. . .] She gave the girl and older boy a nod of recognition, then kept her eyes on the path behind us, as if waiting for someone to ambush her through the grill in the gate" (FB, 292).

To counterbalance the negativity of the traumatic experience, Danticat offers several signs of common people's capacity to live together, mix together, help each other, and overcome the ruptures caused by the authorities' political measures, a possible balance found between oppression and resistance, interdiction and disobedience. The Dominicans Doctor Javier and Father Vargas and the Haitian Father Romain, who attempt to build bridges between Dominicans and Haitians, are sacrificed for their disobedience. The novel includes several examples of stable lives that relatively prosperous Haitians have been able to build on the Dominican side of the border, having lived there for generations, intermarried, learned Spanish, and mixed it with Kreyòl. However, even they are not safe: "To them we are always foreigners, even if our granmèmès' granmèmès were born in this country" (FB, 69). And even parsley is more than once described as a familiar and beneficent presence in people's everyday life, in whatever language or diction: "We used pèsi, perejil, parsley, the damp summer morningness of it [. . .] for our food, our teas, our baths, to cleanse our insides as well as our outsides of old aches and griefs, to shed a passing year's dust as a new one dawned, to wash a new infant's hair for the first time and—along with boiled orange leaves—a corpse's remains one final time" (FB, 62). This reference to the presence of parsley both in the most common and the most significant activities of everyday life adds to the tragic irony of its use to target people for slaughter.

Other positive elements in the novel serve to counterbalance the negativity of oppression. The most important in symbolic terms are water and light. Danticat later wrote a new text to celebrate these two elements: *Claire of the Sea Light* (2013). In *The Farming of Bones*, the memory of Amabelle's lover, Sebastien Onius, who disappears during the massacre, keeps her alive. At the end of the novel, she goes back to Alegría, namely to see again the waterfall where she believes his spirit must be. They made love for the first time in "the narrow cave behind the waterfall, at the source of the stream where the cane workers bathe. [. . .] When the night comes, you don't know it inside the cramped slippery cave because the waterfall, Sebastien says, holds on to some memory of the sun that it will not surrender. On the inside of the cave, there is always light, day and night" (FB, 100). Sebastien also taught her that "[i]t takes patience [. . .] to raise a setting sun" (FB, 283). The water of the river has twice been tainted with blood; it entombs so many corpses of innocent victims, and it buries so many bones, including those of Amabelle's parents. Notwithstanding, by the end of the novel, Amabelle will be there in the water, naked and patiently waiting for the dawn to bring back the sun. If any hope is left for us to assert our humanity, it lies in the imperishable human capacity to imagine paradise, however small the chances are to find it.

DISOBEDIENT WRITING, DISOBEDIENT READING

Going back to the way Toni Morrison and Edwidge Danticat reflect on the myth of Eden, we are led to think that to adopt as a foundational myth a story of punishment and exclusion gives meaning to the power structure that keeps human lives in such profound imbalance and vulnerability. When power defines itself as absolute and unquestionable—power defined, again, by "*my* way, *my* land, *my* borders, *my* values"—the chance of resistance may be reduced to a simple expression of disobedience at the last living moment. Although Danticat underlines resistance against oppression, the imbalance is still too dramatic between the blind forces of authority and the capacity of the most vulnerable to fight back. In a most eloquent and empathic passage of *The Farming of Bones*, when Odette, a Haitian woman who tries to escape from the Dominican Republic alongside Amabelle and a group of other evacuees, is dying after the dramatic crossing of the Massacre River, her voice of resistance and disobedience is sounded but barely heard:

> As we sat there with Odette under a canopy of trees in the middle of a grassy field, she spat up the chest full of water she had collected in the river. With her parting breath, she mouthed in Kreyòl "pèsi," not calmly and slowly as if she were asking for it at a roadside garden or open market, not questioning as if demanding of the face of Heaven the greater meaning of senseless acts, no effort to say "perejil" as if pleading for her life. (FB, 202–3)

Regardless of that imbalance, the text implies a creative reading of the act of disobedience—first enacted by the writer, then filtered through Amabelle's thoughts as narrator:

> The Generalissimo's mind was surely as dark as death, but if he had heard Odette's "pèsi," it might have startled him, not the tears and supplications he would have expected, no shriek from unbound fear, but a provocation, a challenge, a dare. To the devil with your world, your grass, your wind, your water, your air, your words. You ask for perejil, I give you more. (*FB*, 203)

Having lost track of Sebastien, Amabelle decides to embark on a journey of escape through the mountains accompanied by Sebastien's friend, Yves. From the group that joined them along the way, Amabelle and Yves are the only ones who survive the dangerous crossing of the Massacre River. Once they reach Haiti, Yves offers to take Amabelle to his home, but she never ceases to search for Sebastien. When Yves tells Amabelle years later that the priests at the cathedral are collecting testimonials of the slaughter, Amabelle doesn't want to give hers. Instead, she fantasizes about going back with Odette and saying her "pèsi" to the Generalissimo, thus reenacting her act of moral resistance. The dedication of the novel, not signed by the author as would be expected but by her character—"In confidence to you, Mètres Dlo, Mother of the Rivers, Amabelle Désir"—may also be read as an expression of resistance. To open the book with the protagonist's utterance of faith and confidence in the Mother of the Rivers appeals to the superiority of a spiritual order over the musings of earthly powers and celebrates the spiritual empowerment of the Haitian characters.

Not only is the story in *The Farming of Bones* centered around the episode at the Massacre River; the episode and all its meanings frame it. Although the first scene's setting is Sebastien's cot, where he sleeps with Amabelle, the emphasis is on her frequent haunting nightmare that brings her to the moment she lost her parents, who drowned in the Massacre River. She survived but could never liberate herself from this defining moment, which left her an orphan, forever undefined. This circumstance elects her as a protagonist, capable of understanding the most vulnerable in the world. Although her scars were not caused by the lashes of the sugarcane, her "deep black skin" is marked by "all the shades of black" (*FB*, 3); rescued and brought to live a protected life at Señora Valencia's property, she nevertheless keeps dreaming of being called back to her homeland. Despite the fact that her tragic experience has made her a "a living dead," she still has a name to be engraved on her stone marker. And it is because of all this that she is entitled to give us her testimonial, the one she denies the authorities: "But it must be known that I understood. I saw things too. [. . .] Only when Mimi and Sebastien were taken did I realize that the river of blood might come to my doorstep, that it had always been in our house, that it is in all our houses" (*FB*, 265). This note of wisdom is followed by a crucial message at the end of the novel. The imbalance of power distribution may be too tough to fight, but human beings still resist, if not with weapons then with words: "It is perhaps the great discomfort of those trying to silence the world to discover that we have voices sealed inside our heads, voices that with each passing day, grow even louder than the clamor of the world outside" (*FB*, 266). "Pito nou lèd, nou la."[21] First the writer, then the fictional voices she creates, last her readers—all build a community of interposers who speak truth to power by learning to disobey.

NOTES

1. The essay "Create Dangerously" that lends this collection its title was delivered as part of a 2008 lecture series at Princeton University in honor of Toni Morrison. Danticat takes her title from a lecture by Albert Camus that had impressed her (originally delivered at the University of Uppsala in December 1957 and entitled "L'artiste et son temps").

2. In an interview with Maxine Lavon Montgomery in 2016, Danticat explicitly refers to her indebtedness to Toni Morrison: "I find the ways Ms. Morrison engages history very [. . .] powerful, both in her fiction and her nonfictional work. [. . .] Her work inspires me in many ways" (Montgomery 2017, 206).

3. Cf. Morrison: "Exclusivity however [. . .] is still an attractive, even compelling feature of paradise because so many people—the unworthy—are not there. Boundaries are secure, watchdogs, security systems, and gates are there to verify the legitimacy of the inhabitants" (2014). I believe that this craving has been intensified in our global world by threats of terrorism and by US propaganda to justify politics of surveillance. But the real danger lies when the fear propelled by these threats is manipulated against other so-called threats such as undocumented immigrants.

4. See my articles "Toni Morrison and Edwidge Danticat: Writers-as-Citizens of the African Diaspora; or, 'The Margin as a Space of Radical Openness'" (2017); and "'What Moves at the Margin': As vozes insurretas de Toni Morrison, bell hooks e Ntozake Shange" (2017).

5. Spivak is alluding to the distinction Jacques Derrida makes between *répondre à* and *répondre de* ("give an answer to," "answering to," "being answerable for"). And she is also in dialogue with Emmanuel Levinas and his conception of the Other as being ungraspable, beyond comprehension by the self. For more elaboration, see my article "Who Has the Right to Claim America?" (2012).

6. The book was published right after the earthquake of January 2010 and was dedicated to the two hundred thousand victims of the tragedy.

7. Danticat is addressing the case of women who seek refuge in the United States and "receive a cold welcome" (Danticat 2005a), placed as they are in the so-called iceboxes before being deported (Danticat 2010, 161). The expression she uses in a *Nation* article, "a crime to dream," comes from a poem by the Haitian activist Marleine Bastien, executive director of Haitian Women of Miami, an organization located in the heart of Little Haiti. As Danticat tells us, Bastien wrote a poem to honor the hundreds, if not thousands, of women who are in detention and are unable to speak for themselves: "[W]e are the women of the world / in search of a safe haven [. . .] / Is it a crime to want a future? [. . .] / Is it a crime to dream?" (Danticat 2005a).

8. Interposer: from the Latin *inter* (between) + *ponere* (to put, place).

9. I delve into "Children of the Sea" in a forthcoming article, "Liquid Grave or Route to Freedom? Edwidge Danticat's 'Children of the Sea.'"

10. Shemak's method in playing with the word "interdiction" is visible in the diachronic meaning change of the word. In its etymology in Latin, *interdictum* is the past participle of *interdicere*, where *inter* means between and *dicere*, to say. Over time, the noun *interdict* gained the meaning of a prohibition in a legal as well as an ecclesiastical sense.

11. For Danticat, the word *dyaspora* carries a charge of stigma and shame, because it implies taking advantage of good conditions in times of stability, but abandoning the country in times of crisis (see McLemee 2010).

12. In *Create Dangerously*, Danticat says that she intends to be "an echo chamber" for Haitians (2010a, 159).

13. Ironically, the machete, which is a cane-cutting tool and representative of the Haitian peasantry, is used as a weapon to slaughter them.

14. The island, which had once belonged to indigenous people, the Taíno, was divided in two by colonial powers—the Spanish and the French—and later occupied by the US Americans. The present reality is represented by Philoctète as inevitably mixed.

15. A story included in *Krik? Krak!*—"Nineteen Thirty-Seven"—also refers to this episode. Its focus is on the vulnerability of women but also their resilience, and the 1937 massacre is a painful memory in the lives of the protagonist and her mother.

16. Kreyòl—*kreyòl ayisyen*—is a French-based language, so the pronunciation of the letter *r* is completely different from its pronunciation in Spanish. From the various sources I could access, I could not conclude with rigor that the pronunciation of *perejil* was really used to detect Haitians during the 1937 massacre, although the term "Parsley Massacre" was used frequently in the English-speaking media for many decades after the event. Michele Wucker (the US author of *Why the Cocks Fight: Dominicans, Haitians, and the Struggle for Hispaniola*), in her article "The River Massacre" (1998), argues that at the time of the slaughter most residents of the border were bilingual, which would make the *perejil* test as a way to tell Haitians from Dominicans of no avail. However, Richard Lee Turits (2003), a US historian of the Caribbean and Latin America, gives us an interpretation that I think is very convincing. On the border, local authorities had long been in the habit of using the Spanish pronunciation of various words to try to identify who was Haitian, either to collect taxes or to conduct prison interrogations. Although fallible, it

is to be expected that the same method was used at the time of the massacre. Due to a politics of silence and fear so typical during the Trujillo dictatorship, the massacre was obliterated from the official discourse, and for several generations it has never been mentioned in Dominican schools. This surely contributes to the shadow that hovers around this subject and the factual imprecisions we encounter.

17. *Shibboleth* means "ear of corn" in Hebrew.

18. Henceforth, references to *The Farming of Bones* will be indicated in the text as *FB* followed by the page number.

19. Hortense Spillers (1987) uses the metaphor "hieroglyphics of the flesh" to describe the marks inflicted on captive bodies, which retell the history of African Americans in the New World.

20. The flamboyant tree (*Delonix regia*), also called the royal poinciana and renowned for its bright red flowers, is native to Madagascar. It requires a tropical or near-tropical climate and grows throughout the Caribbean (https://www.vinow.com/blog/nature/brilliant -royal-poinciana-flamboyant/).

21. This Haitian proverb means, "Better that we are ugly, but we are here" (Danticat, 2010, 147).

BIBLIOGRAPHY

André, Richard. 2014. "The Dominican Republic and Haiti: A Shared View from the Diaspora; A Conversation with Edwidge Danticat and Junot Díaz." *Americas Quarterly*, July 28. https://www.americasquarterly.org/content/dominican-republic-and-haiti -shared-view-diaspora.

Balaguer, Joaquín. 1983. *La isla al revés: Haití y el destino domicano*. Santo Domingo: Fundación José Antonio Caro.

Caldeira, Isabel. 2012. "Who Has the Right to Claim America?" In *America Where? Transatlantic Views of the United States in the Twenty-First Century*, edited by Isabel Caldeira, Maria José Canelo, and Irene Ramalho Santos, 173–96. Amsterdam: Peter Lang.

Caldeira, Isabel. 2017a. "Toni Morrison and Edwidge Danticat: Writers-as-Citizens of the African Diaspora; or, 'The Margin as a Space of Radical Openness.'" In *The Routledge Companion to Inter-American Studies*, edited by Wilfried Raussert, 207–18. Abingdon, Oxon., England: Routledge.

Caldeira, Isabel. 2017b. "'What Moves at the Margin': As vozes insurretas de Toni Morrison, bell hooks e Ntozake Shange." In *The Edge of One of Many Circles: Homenagem a Irene Ramalho Santos*, edited by Isabel Caldeira, Graça Capinha, and Jacinta Matos, 140–62. Coimbra: Imprensa da Universidade de Coimbra, 2017.

Caldeira, Isabel. Forthcoming. "Liquid Grave or Route to Freedom? Edwidge Danticat's 'Children of the Sea.'" In *American Studies OverSeas*, edited by Dulce M. Scott et al. Amsterdam: Peter Lang.

Chen, Karissa. 2019. "Edwidge Danticat Wants More Haitian Storytellers." *Electric Lit*, September 30. https://electricliterature.com/edwidge-danticat-wants-more-haitian -storytellers/.

Danticat, Edwidge. 1996. *Krik? Krak!* London: Abacus.

Danticat, Edwidge. 1998. *The Farming of Bones*. London: Abacus.

Danticat, Edwidge. 2005a. "A Crime to Dream: Women Seeking Refuge in the United States Receive a Cold Welcome." *The Nation*, April 14. https://www.thenation.com /article/crime-dream/.

Danticat, Edwidge. 2005b. Preface to *Massacre River*, by René Philoctète. New York: New Directions.

Danticat, Edwidge. 2010. *Create Dangerously: The Immigrant Artist at Work*. Princeton, NJ: Princeton University Press.

Danticat, Edwidge, ed. 2011. *Haiti Noir*. Brooklyn: Akashic Books.

Danticat, Edwidge. 2013. *Claire of the Sea Light*. London: Quercus.

Dhar, Nandini. 2005–2006. "Memory, Gender, Race and Class: Edwidge Danticat's *The Farming of Bones*." *Obsidian III* 6, no. 2; 7, no. 1 (Fall/Winter–Spring/Summer): 185–202.

Derrida, Jacques. 2000. *Of Hospitality: Anne Dufourmantelle Invites Jacques Derrida to Respond*. Translated by Rachel Bowlby. Stanford, CA: Stanford University Press.

Farnsworth, Elizabeth. 2008. "Conversation: Toni Morrison." In *Toni Morrison: Conversations*, edited by Carolyn C. Denard, 155–58. Jackson: University Press of Mississippi.

McLemee, Scott. 2010. "Edwidge Danticat Creates Dangerously." *The National*, Arts and Culture, November 4. https://www.thenational.ae/arts-culture/books/edwidge -danticat-creates-dangerously-1.488706.

Montgomery, Maxine Lavon, ed. 2017. *Conversations with Edwidge Danticat*. Jackson: University Press of Mississippi.

Morrison, Toni. 1992. *Playing in the Dark: Whiteness and the Literary Imagination*. Cambridge, MA: Harvard University Press.

Morrison, Toni, ed. 2009. *Burn This Book: PEN Writers Speak Out on the Power of the Word*. New York: Harper.

Morrison, Toni. 2014. "Can We Find Paradise on Earth?" *Telegraph*, May 27. https://www .telegraph.co.uk/culture/hay-festival/10848569/Toni-Morrison-can-we-find-paradise -on-Earth.html.

Morrison, Toni. 2017. *The Origin of Others*. Cambridge, MA: Harvard University Press.

Morrison, Toni. 2019. *The Source of Self-Regard: Selected Essays, Speeches, and Meditations*. New York: Alfred A. Knopf.

Phillip, Abby. 2015. "The Bloody Origins of the Dominican Republic's Ethnic 'Cleansing' of Haitians." *Washington Post*, June 17. https://www.washingtonpost.com/news/world views/wp/2015/06/16/the-bloody-origins-of-the-dominican-republics-ethnic-cleansing -of-haitians/.

Shemak, April. 2011. *Asylum Speakers: Caribbean Refugees and Testimonial Discourse*. New York: Fordham University Press.

Spillers, Hortense J. 1987. "Mama's Baby, Papa's Maybe: An American Grammar Book." *Diacritics* 17, no. 2 (Summer): 65–81.

Spivak, Gayatri Chakravorty. 1988. "Can the Subaltern Speak?" In *Marxism and the Interpretation of Culture*, edited by Cary Nelson and Lawrence Grossberg, 271–313. Urbana: University of Illinois Press.

Spivak, Gayatri Chakravorty. 1994. "Responsibility." *boundary 2* 21, no. 3 (Autumn): 19–64.

Spivak, Gayatri Chakravorty. 1999. *A Critique of Postcolonial Reason: Toward a History of the Vanishing Present.* Cambridge, MA: Harvard University Press.

Streitfeld, David. 1998. "The Novelist's Prism." Interview with Toni Morrison. *Washington Post*, January 6. https://www.washingtonpost.com/archive/lifestyle/1998/01/06/the -novelists-prism/6ff53e27-cfaf-45e1-b4af-14f0f12b0178/.

Strongman, Roberto. 2006. "Reading through the Bloody Borderlands of Hispaniola: Fictionalizing the 1937 Massacre of Haitian Sugarcane Workers in the Dominican Republic." *Journal of Haitian Studies* 12, no. 2 (Fall): 21–45.

Turits, Richard Lee. 2003. "Un mundo destruido, una nación impuesta: La masacre haitiana de 1937 en la República Dominicana." Translated by Victoria Ferreira and Lenny A. Ureña Valerio. *Estudios Sociales* 36, no. 133 (July–September). https://quod.lib.umich .edu/l/lacs/12338892.0002.001/--un-mundo-destruido-una-nacion-impuesta-la -masacre-haitiana?rgn=main;view=fulltext.

Wucker, Michele. 1998. "The River Massacre: The Real and Imagined Borders of Hispaniola." Windows on Haiti. https://windowsonhaiti.com/windowson haiti.com/wucker1 .shtml.

Chapter Fourteen

MORE THAN A PHRASE

Fighting Silence and Objectification in Danticat's *Claire of the Sea Light*

DELPHINE GRAS

In *Claire of the Sea Light* (2013), Edwidge Danticat offers readers a novel anchored in Haitian history and culture. This return to the past is all the more pressing in the aftermath of the 2010 earthquake. Indeed, the media coverage of this tragic event brought Haiti visibility, yet it obscured its history prior to what came to be known as "year zero" and stigmatized Haiti as "the Poorest Nation in the Western Hemisphere."[1] Laurent Dubois rightly points out: "When Haiti appears at all in the media, it registers largely as a place of disaster, poverty, and suffering."[2] The dehumanizing phrase, "the Poorest Nation in the Western Hemisphere"—aptly described by Joel Dreyfuss as a "metaphorical prison"[3]—criminalizes Haitians for having transformed a once lucrative island into a catastrophic nation.[4] In the words of Dubois, "many seemed all too ready to believe that the fault must lie with the Haitians themselves."[5] Danticat's novel instead encourages readers to grapple with the ways Haiti's past as a French colony has far-reaching effects on its contemporary ecological and sociopolitical landscapes.[6] What emerges throughout *Claire of the Sea Light* is that Haiti is not inherently home to disasters. Rather, centuries of exploitation have left an indelible mark on Haiti's economy, environment, and social relations.[7] This chapter thus explores how Danticat combats the mediatic vilification of Haiti and its inhabitants. On the one hand, exploring the connections between historical, social, and natural disasters allows readers to get a more complex understanding of the challenges Haitians currently face. On the other, Danticat also humanizes Haitians by presenting them as characters with a voice and a role to play in bringing together their community and putting an end to a cycle of injustices.[8]

In recounting the hardships that widowed fisherman Nozias and his seven-year-old daughter Claire Limyè Lanmè Faustin experience in the Haitian sea town of Ville Rose, Danticat portrays a world in which no one is immune to suffering. As the narrative unfolds, it sheds light on the ways French colonialism had an irreversible impact on Haiti. Instead of reinforcing the stigmatization of the island and its inhabitants, Danticat showcases the connection between Haiti's past as a French colony and its current natural disasters. In this way, readers become better equipped to understand the factors that prompt Nozias to consider entrusting his only daughter to the wealthy fabric vendor, Gaëlle Lavaud.

From the beginning of the story, the landscape is described as bearing the marks of exploitation. There is a subtle but strikingly visual representation of the correlation between dilapidation and French colonialism. Landmarks such as the Abitasyon Pauline (Pauline's Dwelling), a castle built "as a gift for Napoleon Bonaparte's sister Pauline" and "left unfinished in 1802,"[9] point to the literal and metaphorical ruins of French colonialism. Pauline Bonaparte's sudden departure after her husband's death exemplifies how France exploited this territory for its resources, abandoning the territory when it could no longer maintain control. Haiti is a place whose history most French ignore or would rather forget. This amnesia disavows France's participation in the slave trade, its reinstatement of slavery after the practice had been abolished, and its imposition of an outrageous treaty condemning Haiti to endless debt for fighting for the same universal rights that were at the center of the French Revolution yet apparently did not apply to all.[10]

Moreover, whereas affluent fabric vendors Laurent and Gaëlle Lavaud, who would drive by the Abitasyon Pauline during their romantic car rides in their youth, never reflected on its history, the narrator notes the proximity of the castle to the sugarcane fields. The escapades of their youth hence bring to the fore the connection between French grandeur under Bonaparte, cane cutting, and slavery, as well as what Danticat calls "communal and historical amnesia."[11] The Abitasyon Pauline stands as a symbol of French involvement in Haiti, and a reminder of its role in enslaving Haitians and exploiting their resources. As Paul Farmer explains, it was the French who moved the slave trade into high gear: "Haiti was the Americas' chief port of call for slavers. [...] It brought more income for the French, noted Moreau de St-Méry (the chief French chronicler of the era), than all of their colonial possessions combined."[12] Haiti, long before it became a country that outsiders only know by the phrase "the Poorest Nation in the Western Hemisphere," was France's most prized possession.[13]

Throughout *Claire of the Sea Light*, Danticat destigmatizes poverty in Haiti by suggesting interconnections between local issues and broader historical forces. Just as the narrative connects landmarks to French imperialism, it also prompts readers to look at the colonial origins of child servitude within the *restavèk* system. In fact, the French root of the term *restavèk* (*rester avec*, to stay with) speaks to the ways this modern form of slavery subsists as a remnant of French colonialism. Whereas stressing the high numbers of *restavèks* and the illiteracy rate in Haiti brings awareness to this pressing issue, it can also stigmatize Haitians.[14] By contrast, Danticat advocates against this practice while providing a more complex understanding of the causes of child slavery in Haiti.[15] Her approach is doubly important when, as Lucía Suárez suggests, "three-fourths of the *restavèks* are girls, but the most prominent story is of a boy."[16] Indeed, apart Jean-Robert Cadet's 1998 autobiography *Restavec: From Haitian Slave Child to Middle-Class American*, very few works tackle this important issue, and Danticat is one of the first to focus on a girl.

Under Danticat's pen, readers discover not an abusive parent willingly participating in child servitude, but a widower whose trade brings in little profit and could leave his daughter an orphan. They learn about the dangers of fishing in "the most unpredictable waters of the Caribbean Sea" (*CSL*, 5). Living in a town "home to eleven thousand people, five percent of them wealthy or comfortable," Nozias belongs to the majority, characterized as "poor, some dirt-poor" (*CSL*, 5). Hence, Danticat depicts the harsh living conditions in Ville Rose to offer a nuanced view of the limited options parents, and single parents in particular, confront in a system of entrenched poverty. Nozias is a hard-working single father, and fishing, as dangerous as it is in Ville Rose, is among the only jobs available. As she stresses how year after year Nozias considers yet cannot bring himself to give Claire away to Gaëlle, Danticat urges readers to examine the causes of poverty on the island and highlights the endurance of a people fighting against harsh working conditions to offer a better future for their offspring.

Nozias's story illustrates the ecological factors that prevent many Haitians from earning a decent living.[17] From its first sentence, the novel underscores the danger of working at sea. It describes "a freak wave, measuring between ten and twelve feet high," with its "giant blue-green tongue, trying, it seemed, to lick a pink sky," "pummeling a cutter called Fifine, sinking it and Caleb, the sole fisherman onboard" (*CSL*, 3). The personification of the wave depicts the violent life fishermen experience. Caleb and his boat seem equally insignificant before the godlike ocean that takes more than it gives. This environment has become unnatural because of a history of overexploitation now worsened by climate change. There are even "jokes about the town eventually becoming a cemetery" (*CSL*, 4). This opening description of an unforgiving environment vividly illustrates the perilous conditions in which fishermen have to work. In this way, the narrative neither blames nor excuses Haitians for practicing child labor. Instead, it prompts readers to examine the life-threatening challenges fishermen daily face to eke out a living—a reality that a widower like Nozias has to take into consideration as his child's sole guardian.

Danticat thus associates Caleb's and Nozias's tragedies to historical and climatic changes in the region. As the narrator reveals: "You could no longer afford to fish in season, to let the sea replenish itself [. . .] even as the seabed was disappearing, and the sea grass that used to nourish the fish was buried under silt and trash" (*CSL*, 9). Overfishing and pollution are directly related to Nozias's heartbreaking resolution. He is not a neglectful parent. He is a widower who fears dying at sea and leaving his daughter without protection. His letter to Claire makes that clear: "I am not doing this for money. I did not sell you. I am giving you a better life" (*CSL*, 203). After witnessing Caleb's death, the need to find a guardian appears more understandable. Furthermore, Nozias thinks about Gaëlle as a potential surrogate because of her socioeconomic position as well as their shared experience as parents who lost their spouses the day their children were born.

Their connection also extends to the ways they are affected by a precarious environment. Despite their economic privileges, Gaëlle and her late husband Laurent could lose their property due to the increasing risk of flash floods—an ecological threat exacerbated by overexploitation initiated under French colonialism. Across class, Haitians fear the perils posed by a changing climate, but, unlike their wealthier compatriots, fishermen and peasants are often forced to participate in overfishing and deforestation because their options are more limited.[18] As one farmer responds to Laurent's warning about erosion, "If I have to kill a tree to save my child [. . .] I'll do it" (*CSL*, 52). Just as Nozias considers entrusting Gaëlle with his daughter, so too are farmers forced to make painful choices. Danticat suggests that their actions are motivated not by laziness or irresponsibility but by the struggle to survive in circumstances not of their own making.[19] With no alternative, peasants overuse the little resources still available, while formerly rural families end up in slums like Cité Pendue.

Danticat denounces how French colonialism left a mark not just on Haiti's environment but also on social relations.[20] The past of slavery is inscribed in the creation of the town Ville Rose, named after Gaëlle's ancestor, Sò Rose, the daughter of a "slave mother and French father" (*CSL*, 55). Though not directly addressing the conditions of Sò Rose's birth, Danticat warns against the legacy of the slave system and its use of sexual "terrorism."[21] The violence today's women experience betrays what Chantal Kalisa calls "the double legacy of historical and patriarchal rape."[22] This is what, in Danticat's novel, fictional radio host Louise George exposes in her show *Di Mwen* (Tell Me): affluent Haitians still perpetuate systemic sexual abuse. Louise invites Flore Voltaire, a domestic worker in the home of a wealthy family, to denounce how Max Junior, the son of her employer, raped her. This abuse, which Max Senior, the father of the perpetrator, calls "Droit du Seigneur" (the right of the lord) (*CSL*, 185), is shockingly still seen as a common right centuries after the abolition of slavery.[23] Additionally, the use of the French term *droit du seigneur* locates rape at the heart of French imperialism, illustrating how abuse is tied with colonial history—a legacy that outlasted the French presence in Haiti.

Flore and Louise, however, refuse victimhood and reject this remnant of the slave economy. Louise is a modern storyteller who has dedicated her life to condemning injustices. In her role as a part-time teacher in Max Senior's school, she teaches children how maroons used to escape slavery by running to the ironically named Mòn Initil (Useless Mountain). Further, after years not standing up to Max Senior and accepting her role as his lover and guest teacher whenever he summons her, Louise finally sees him for the town patriarch he always was. The epiphany she experiences after he allows a disgruntled parent to hit her marks a turning point for Louise. It is a "slap back to life" (*CSL*, 143), which inspires her to broaden her audience from schoolchildren to the rest of the community (132). In the words of scholar Iliana Rosales Figueroa, "the women assume the role of protectors and defenders of the whole town."[24] Interviewing Flore is a means to fight the silencing and objectification of women and thus take down the town patriarch and his son. In this way, Louise empowers herself, her guest Flore, and other women who suffer a similar fate. The radio program unearths hidden histories in order to respond to unpunished injustices. For Danticat, it is "a medium of justice," "the most democratic form of justice where people can be heard."[25] Flore is a rape survivor who will not let her past define or silence her. She refuses for her or her son to be "not worthy" and claims their right to live: "I'm still here," "*nou la*" (we're here) (*CSL*, 179). Her testimonial marks an important step in eradicating sexual abuse because it empowers other women (182).[26]

Claire of the Sea Light illuminates how the patriarchal heteronormative system inherited from French colonialism is one of the major causes of violence on the island. Max Junior, the man who raped Flore, is a product of this system. He admits that "he had foolishly wanted to prove something to his father" (*CSL*, 109). Rather than confessing his love for aspiring radio host Bernard Dorien to his homophobic father, Max participates in the very imposition of a system he seeks to escape. He rapes Flore in a vain attempt to reclaim his masculinity. Yet Max Junior cannot forget his guilt, even as he tries to do so by leaving for Florida. Returning home after years of exile, he attempts to commit suicide by throwing himself into the sea when he realizes the impossibility of undoing the pain he caused. The fact that self-destruction seems easier than confronting his father and attempting to end the cycle of toxic masculinity speaks to the difficulty of dismantling the mechanisms of colonial abuse that live on in unacknowledged ways through the continued imposition of norms that trigger violence.

Ironically, Bernard wanted to move away from these inherited norms and to encourage empathy by redefining masculinity. Unfortunately, he dies prematurely after he is mistakenly punished for the murder of Gaëlle's husband. Through Bernard and Louise, Danticat subtly pays tribute to Jean Dominique, the famous journalist who was shot in front of his radio station and to whom she dedicates *The Butterfly's Way* and *Create Dangerously*.[27] All three want to use the radio to bring about a better future. Describing the idea for his show, Bernard explains that "the gang members were also called *chimè*, chimeras or ghosts, and were, for the most part, street children who couldn't remember ever having lived in a house" (*CSL*, 65).[28] Instead of portraying *chimè* as born criminals, Bernard pictures them as suffering children. He wants to bring his community together by stressing their shared humanity: "We can't move forward as a neighborhood, as a town, or as a country [. . .] unless we know what makes these men cry. They cannot remain *chimè*" (*CSL*, 68). The novel functions as a mirror of Bernard's project to give life to these ghosts.

Through Bernard's eyes, readers discover multifaceted characters who desperately try to reclaim their masculinity. He underscores how poverty and trauma have transformed them:

> He would open *Chimè* with a discussion of how many people in Cité Pendue had lost arms, legs, or hands. He would go from limbs to souls—to the number of people who had lost siblings, parents, children, and friends. These were the real ghosts, he would say, the phantom limbs, phantom minds, phantom loves that haunted them because they were used, then abandoned, because they were out of choices, because they were poor. (*CSL*, 82)

Bernard strives to be a voice for those who live in the slums and are constantly misrepresented. Although he never gets his own show, his vision stays with the reader, now better equipped to challenge the vilification of Haitian men. When Bernard is killed by the Special Forces who murdered Laurent, Danticat provides insight into the brutality of a system that condones physical punishment. The problem is not gang violence but systemic violence, once sanctioned under the Black Code and still claiming lives to this day.[29] This violence is also epistemic, given how the media negate the very humanity of these men. Bernard is a murder victim, yet he appears as "another bandit" in the news (*CSL*, 83), a telling reflection of mediated misrepresentations of Haitians. To outsiders, and sometimes to Haitians themselves, it is not just the gang members who are *chimè* but everyone on and from the island.

The characters of *Claire of the Sea Light* are not just ghosts, criminals, or victims. They are complex characters whose voices need to be heard. In sharing their stories, Danticat complicates the mediatic representation of Haitians. At first, it seems that tragedies take center stage in this text. However, this arrangement of tragic stories, which corresponds to what Silvia Martínez-Falquina describes as a "strategic representation of grief," fights invisibility and appropriation in order to "denounce the continuing effects of colonial trauma."[30] Moreover, what eventually emerges is the characters' capacity to love one another as a means to end a cycle of violence. Through the story of Gaëlle, readers learn how love can bring about change. At first drowning in sorrow, Gaëlle issues orders to kill Bernard, whom she mistakenly blames for her husband's murder. It is only with her daughter's death that she comes to the conclusion that violence begets violence. When Rose dies in a motorcycle accident, Gaëlle cannot help but think that this might be a "terrible cosmic design" (*CSL*, 146), a punishment for killing Bernard. This realization helps her reconnect with the rest of her community. It is only by breaking the chain of violence and replacing it with an act of generosity that she can recover from loss. Hence, it is this epiphany that prompts Gaëlle to show affection toward Claire. In doing so, she responds to the kindness of Claire's mother, who first modeled how women could support each other by bringing presents for Rose's birth and providing emotional support when Laurent dies. Her words stay with Gaëlle: "Fòk nou voye je youn sou lòt" (We need to look after each other) (164). Gaëlle understands the necessity for women to be there for one another. It is partly to repay Claire Narcis's gesture of solidary that Gaëlle contemplates the idea of adopting Claire. With this new chain of kindness, Danticat breaks class boundaries and calls for empathy toward characters who all belong to "the human family" (85).

A similar epiphany happens to Claire. When she realizes that her father is about to entrust her to Gaëlle, she runs away. She follows in the footsteps of the maroons who hid on Mòn Initil to escape life as slaves. However, as she reaches the top of the mountain, she sees the rest of her community gathered around a stranger who has washed ashore (*CSL*, 236). Faced with a choice between personal freedom and communal responsibility, she chooses to put her community before herself and decides to go back. She knows that her return could mean becoming a *restavèk*, the very situation she has tried to escape. Yet, she wants to rejoin her community in their attempt to rescue this man—who is probably Max Junior after he tried to drown himself. As with Claire Narcis and Gaëlle, it is the less fortunate characters who first demonstrate compassion. In this way, the narrative complicates the equation between poverty and victimhood and uncovers the need for communal action across class boundaries.

Through the evolution of her *wonn* song, Claire emerges as the voice of her community. She changes the lyrics of her song from an individual act of rebellion into a song of reunion:

> Yo t ap chèche li . . .
> They were looking for her
> Like a pebble in a bowl of rice
> They were looking for her
> But no, no, no she didn't want to be found (*CSL*, 233)

> Fòk li retounen
> She has to go back
> [. . .]
> She has to go home
> To see the man
> Who'd crawled half dead
> Out of the sea (*CSL*, 238)

What starts as an individual farewell song, a *wonn* song "for a circle of one" because "she didn't want to be found," transforms into a communal song, "a good song of *wonn*." As the story closes, Claire intones a coming home chant that evokes how she will rejoin her community, forming a circle with other people as in traditional *wonn* songs. Hence, this song depicts Claire's change from not wanting to be found as she is running away, emphasized by the repeated negation in the first verse, to feeling the need to go back, stressed by the repetition of "has to" in the second verse. What could have been a tragedy—Claire wandering alone in the mountains or Max Junior drowning—turns into a renewed sense of belonging. This song connects Claire, the child who risks becoming a *restavèk*, to Max, the tormented man who assaulted Flore. Neither of them can be understood as victims or oppressors.

In her interview with Rachel Martin, Danticat explains that "the healing comes through their coming together as a community."[31] As Claire goes back to the village to see if Max survived, so too the reader is encouraged to look beyond labels to better understand the complex lives of the characters and the ways they are still affected by the legacy of slavery.

At a time when media coverage of Haiti criminalizes the poor and overwhelmingly depicts them as looters, it is crucial to share stories of generosity.[32] Since the 2010 earthquake, scholars, activists, and artists have denounced what Haitian filmmaker Raoul Peck calls "media violence."[33] As if to answer writer Michel Le Bris's call for accounts that would speak to "the courage of the people, their dignity, their solidarity in misfortune,"[34] Danticat provides corrective accounts of Haiti. Her fictional and nonfictional works alike seek to address the mediatic vilification of her homeland. As she relates in her essay "Lòt Bò Dlo: The Other Side of the Water," "I was surprised to learn that fewer than two hundred people had been rescued by professional rescuers. The rest, like Maxo's wife and children, had been saved by their Haitian friends and neighbors."[35] In this essay, Danticat comments on the pivotal role Haitians played post-earthquake and stresses their courage: "Haiti[,] which is often referred to as the poorest country in the western hemisphere, had yet another lesson to teach the world: a lesson in resilience."[36] This picture of strength resurfaces in Danticat's fiction, where her characters persevere against the odds and, more pointedly, against the expectation created by the media that the only hope for Haiti comes from the outside. *Claire of the Sea Light* showcases this sense of unity in order to dispel dehumanizing stereotypes about Haitians. Without ignoring violence, Danticat sheds light on its roots and points to solidarity as a way to undo trauma. It comes as no surprise, then, that the story concludes with Claire sharing this sense of responsibility.

The use of personal tales shared by distinct storytellers merges the poor and the rich, the local and the global, the personal and the historical, prompting readers to reflect on the confining parameters used to interpret current and past events in Haiti. There cannot be a single account of what it means to live in Haiti, nor a single Haitian voice to overturn centuries of objectification and misrepresentation of Haiti. As Bonnie Thomas contends, finding a balance between distance and proximity is integral for healing and renewal.[37] This is what Danticat creates through her multivoiced narrative. This structure mirrors the *wonn*, the song game that Claire and other children play throughout the novel. In the spirit of the game, in which children hold hands, Danticat imagines "the reader joining that circle, if you will, as he or she tries to understand what is happening in the town."[38] It seems fitting that Claire's final song urges the characters as well as readers to assume personal responsibility. When tragedy affects so many, as it did in 2010, traumatic events should prompt us to see each other's humanity and come together to build a better future. Throughout *Claire of the Sea Light*, Danticat becomes the genealogist of the forgotten and misunderstood. In her words, "I hope my work has made those contributions, made Haitians seem more complex, more present."[39] Similarly, when journalist Robert Birnbaum asks Danticat what she wishes North Americans knew about Haiti, she provides a mini history lesson that contrasts with the ossified stories and repeated fallacies ordinarily used to describe her birthplace. She voices pride for her home, a country that emerged as a trailblazer in creating a republic in the hemisphere, in eradicating slavery, in helping America become the land it is today, and in defeating Napoleon, one of the most admired French figures in history.[40] Danticat also celebrates Haitian heroes such as John James Audubon and Jean Baptiste Point du Sable, as well as the more famous Toussaint L'Ouverture and Jean-Jacques Dessalines. As she explains, it is too easy to focus on the current status of Haiti without taking into consideration its past successes and the global factors that hindered its growth, especially the role that France and the United States played in sabotaging the stability of this nation.[41] In *Claire of the Sea Light*, Danticat does not directly mention these historical events. However, she infuses the narrative with the complex history and rich culture of Haiti in order to undermine the metaphorical prison of narratives that entrap her homeland and its inhabitants.[42] She neither criminalizes nor idealizes her birth country. Instead, she becomes a cultural mediator who allows for Haitians to not seem as foreign, and therefore unrelatable, to non-Haitian readers.[43] The result is a multivoiced text that is both a requiem for what was lost and a renewed national anthem for a country that can come together in times of adversity. Like the sculptors of ancient Egypt whom she describes in *Create Dangerously*, Danticat is "one who keeps things alive."[44] As demonstrated throughout *Claire of the Sea Light*, she plays the role of a modern bard who connects the past, the present, and the future in all its richness—a time-binding act all the more necessary to undo the damage of French colonialism and resist the mediatic silencing of Haiti's resilient people.

NOTES

1. On the media coverage of the earthquake and the overuse of this phrase, see Bonnie Thomas, "Narrating Trauma: Distance and Proximity in the Haitian Earthquake of 2010," *Australian Journal of French Studies* 53, no. 1 (2016): 71; Nadège T. Clitandre, "Silence and False Starts in Times of Disaster," *Afro-Hispanic Review* 32, no. 2 (Fall 2013):

105–6; Edwidge Danticat, "Lòt Bò Dlo: The Other Side of the Water," in *Haiti after the Earthquake*, ed. Paul Farmer (New York: Public Affairs, 2011), 255–58; Laurent Dubois, *Haiti: The Aftershocks of History* (New York: Picador, 2012), 3; Thomas C. Spear, "Point of View," in *Haiti Rising: Haitian History, Culture, and the Earthquake of 2010*, edited by Martin Munro (Mona, Jamaica: University of the West Indies Press, 2010), 39; J. Michael Dash, "Rising from the Ruins," in Munro, *Haiti Rising*, 63; Maryse Condé, "Haïti Chérie," in Munro, *Haiti Rising*, 153; and Beverly Bell, "7.0 on the Horror Scale: Notes on the Haitian Earthquake," in Munro, *Haiti Rising*, 157.

2. Dubois, *Haiti: The Aftershocks of History*, 3.

3. Joel Dreyfuss, "A Cage of Words," in *The Butterfly's Way: Voices from the Haitian Dyaspora in the United States*, ed. Edwidge Danticat (New York: Soho Press, 2001), 57.

4. Laura Wagner, "Salvaging," in Munro, *Haiti Rising*, 23; and Marlène Rigaud Apollon, "Manman, Pa Kite Yo Koupe Janm Mwen! Mommy Don't Let Them Cut My Leg," in Munro, *Haiti Rising*, 12. On the earthquake as a curse, see Leslie G. Desmangles and Elizabeth McAlister, "Religion in Post-Earthquake Haiti," in Munro, *Haiti Rising*, 71; Deborah Jenson, "The Writing of Disaster in Haiti: Signifying Cataclysm from Slave Revolution to Earthquake," in Munro, *Haiti Rising*, 104; and Condé, "Haïti Chérie," 152.

5. Dubois, *Haiti: The Aftershocks of History*, 3.

6. On the lack of complexity and erasure of history in depictions of Haiti, see Dash, "Rising from the Ruins," 63; Raoul Peck, "Dead-End in Port-au-Prince," in Munro, *Haiti Rising*, 46; John D. Garrigus, "The Legacies of Pre-Revolutionary Saint-Domingue," in Munro, *Haiti Rising*, 115; Paul Farmer, ed., *Haiti after the Earthquake* (New York: Public Affairs, 2011), 36–37, 122; and Nathalie Handal, "We Are All Going to Die," in *Conversations with Edwidge Danticat*, ed. Maxine Lavon Montgomery (Jackson: University Press of Mississippi, 2017), 125. Although not within the scope of this chapter, *Claire of the Sea Light* also addresses US interventions and occupations in Haiti.

7. Wagner, "Salvaging," 15, 18.

8. Maxine Lavon Montgomery, ed., *Conversations with Edwidge Danticat* (Jackson: University Press of Mississippi, 2017), xiii; and Rachel Martin, "Haitian Youth Illuminated in *Claire of the Sea Light*," in Montgomery, *Conversations*, 149.

9. Edwidge Danticat, *Claire of the Sea Light* (New York: Vintage Books, 2013), 47. Henceforth, references to *Claire of the Sea Light* will be indicated in the text as *CSL* followed by the page number.

10. On French amnesia, see Françoise Vergès, *La mémoire enchaînée: Questions sur l'esclavage* (Paris: Albin Michel, 2006), 32, 35–36, 51; and Bonnie Thomas, *Connecting Histories: Francophone Caribbean Writers Interrogating Their Pasts* (Jackson: University Press of Mississippi, 2017), 13. For exclusionary Enlightenment ideals, see Vergès, *La mémoire enchaînée*, 40–41.

11. Edwidge Danticat, Create Dangerously: The Immigrant Artist at Work (New York: Vintage Books, 2011), 64.

12. Farmer, *Haiti after the Earthquake*, 124.

13. Dubois, *Haiti: The Aftershocks of History*, 4, 19; and Jéhane Sedky, "Building Back Better," in Farmer, *Haiti after the Earthquake*, 358.

14. For more information, see Restavek Freedom, https://restavekfreedom.org/issue/; "'Restavek' Children in Haiti: A New Form of Modern Slavery," Humanium, September 5, 2016, https://www.humanium.org/en/restavek-children-in-haiti-a-new-form-of-modern -slavery/; Corey Adwar, "Why Haiti Is One of the Worst Countries for Child Slavery," *Business Insider*, September 3, 2014, http://www.businessinsider.com/flawed-arrangement -turns-haitian-restaveks-into-slaves-2014-8; Elizabeth Cohen, "Painful Plight of Haiti's 'Restavec' Children," CNN, January 29, 2010, http://www.cnn.com/2010/HEALTH/01/29 /haiti.restavek.sende.sencil/index.html; and Vlad Sokhin and the Restavek Freedom Foundation, "Restaveks: Haitian Slave Children," End Slavery Now, n.d., https://www .endslaverynow.org/blog/articles/restaveks-haitian-slave-children.

15. This approach is crucial when imperialist powers like France and the United States deploy infantilizing rhetoric to justify intervention (Dash, "Rising from the Ruins," 67).

16. Lucía M. Suárez, *The Tears of Hispaniola: Haitian and Dominican Diaspora Memory* (Gainesville: University Press of Florida, 2006), 144.

17. Georg Zipp, "Selling Poverty: Junot Díaz's and Edwidge Danticat's Assessments of Picturesque Stereotypes of Poverty in the Caribbean," *Zeitschrift für Anglistik und Amerikanistik* 63, no. 2 (2015): 234.

18. Farmer, *Haiti after the Earthquake*, 35–36; and Dubois, *Haiti: The Aftershocks of History*, 4.

19. Garrigus, "The Legacies of Pre-Revolutionary Saint-Domingue," 117.

20. Paula Morgan and Valerie Youssef, *Writing Rage: Unmasking Violence through Caribbean Discourse* (Mona, Jamaica: University of the West Indies Press, 2006), 10–12; and Garrigus, "The Legacies of Pre-Revolutionary Saint-Domingue," 124.

21. bell hooks, *Ain't I a Woman: Black Women and Feminism* (Boston: South End Press, 1981), 27.

22. Chantal Kalisa, *Violence in Francophone African and Caribbean Women's Literature* (Lincoln: University of Nebraska Press, 2009), 121.

23. On sexual violence, see Régine Michelle Jean-Charles, "Shaken Ground, Strong Foundations: Honoring the Legacy of Haitian Feminism after the Earthquake," in Munro, *Haiti Rising*, 83; and Suárez, *The Tears of Hispaniola*, 61–90.

24. Iliana Rosales Figueroa, "(Re)Imagining Haiti through the Eyes of a Seven-Year-Old Girl," *Journal of International Women's Studies* 17, no. 3 (2016): 179.

25. Kima Jones, "A Conversation with Edwidge Danticat," in Montgomery, *Conversations*, 170.

26. On speaking out, see Silvia Martínez-Falquina, "Postcolonial Trauma Theory in the Contact Zone: The Strategic Representation of Grief in Edwidge Danticat's *Claire of the Sea Light*," *Humanities* 4, no. 4 (2015): 838; Aitor Ibarrola-Armendáriz, "Broken Memories of a Traumatic Past and the Redemptive Power of Narrative in the Fiction of Edwidge Danticat," in *The Splintered Glass: Facets of Trauma in the Post-Colony and Beyond*, ed. Dolores Herrero and Sonia Baelo-Allué (Amsterdam: Rodopi, 2011), 16; and Suárez, *The Tears of Hispaniola*, 61–90.

27. Jean Dominique's legacy appears in multiple characters: Louise, Bernard, and Laurent. Like them, Jean Dominique and his wife spent their lives broadcasting "the

voices of those who are never heard." See Michèle Montas-Dominique, "*Sim Pa Rele* (If I Don't Shout)," in Farmer, *Haiti after the Earthquake*, 259–60, 270.

28. The word *chimè* does not put the blame on parents, as the term *malélevé* ("ill brought up") or *sansmaman* ("the motherless ones") might (Farmer, *Haiti after the Earthquake*, 137).

29. Morgan and Youssef, *Writing Rage*, 225.

30. Martínez-Falquina, "Postcolonial Trauma Theory in the Contact Zone," 834–35.

31. Martin, "Haitian Youth Illuminated," 149. See also Figueroa, "(Re)Imagining Haiti," 186.

32. Dubois, *Haiti: The Aftershocks of History*, 12; Wagner, "Salvaging," 18; Spear, "Point of View," 37; Peck, "Dead-End in Port-au-Prince," 46–47; Nancy Dorsinville, "Goudou Goudou," in Farmer, *Haiti after the Earthquake*, 275; Yanick Lahens, "Haiti; or, The Health of Misery," in Munro, *Haiti Rising*, 10; and Michel Le Bris, "Finding the Words," in Munro, *Haiti Rising*, 29–30.

33. Peck, "Dead-End in Port-au-Prince," 47.

34. Le Bris, "Finding the Words," 30.

35. Danticat, "Lòt Bò Dlo," 255.

36. Danticat, "Lòt Bò Dlo," 256–57.

37. Thomas, "Narrating Trauma," 70. See also Figueroa, "(Re)Imagining Haiti," 178.

38. Brendan Dowling, "Maneuvering Myself around a Scene: A Conversation with Edwidge Danticat," in Montgomery, *Conversations*, 164.

39. Opal Palmer Adisa, "Up Close and Personal: Edwidge Danticat on Haitian Identity and the Writer's Life," *African American Review* 43, nos. 2–3 (Summer–Fall 2009): 347.

40. Robert Birnbaum, "Edwidge Danticat," in Montgomery, *Conversations*, 12. See also Clitandre, "Silence and False Starts," 100.

41. Birnbaum, "Edwidge Danticat," 2–15.

42. Handal, "We Are All Going to Die," 118.

43. Figueroa, "(Re)Imagining Haiti," 177.

44. Danticat, *Create Dangerously*, 20.

BIBLIOGRAPHY

Adisa, Opal Palmer. "Up Close and Personal: Edwidge Danticat on Haitian Identity and the Writer's Life." *African American Review* 43, nos. 2–3 (Summer–Fall 2009): 345–55.

Adwar, Corey. "Why Haiti Is One of the Worst Countries for Child Slavery." *Business Insider*, September 3, 2014. http://www.businessinsider.com/flawed-arrangement -turns-haitian-restaveks-into-slaves-2014-8.

Bell, Beverly. "7.0 on the Horror Scale: Notes on the Haitian Earthquake." In *Haiti Rising: Haitian History, Culture, and the Earthquake of 2010*, edited by Martin Munro, 7–20. Mona, Jamaica: University of the West Indies Press, 2010.

Birnbaum Robert. "Edwidge Danticat." In *Conversations with Edwidge Danticat*, edited by Maxine Lavon Montgomery, 7–20. Jackson: University Press of Mississippi, 2017.

Clitandre, Nadège T. "Silence and False Starts in Times of Disaster." *Afro-Hispanic Review* 32, no. 2 (Fall 2013): 99–110.

Cohen, Elizabeth. "Painful Plight of Haiti's 'Restavec' Children." CNN, January 29, 2010. http://www.cnn.com/2010/HEALTH/01/29/haiti.restavek.sende.sencil/index.html.

Condé, Maryse. "Haïti Chérie." In *Haiti Rising: Haitian History, Culture, and the Earthquake of 2010*, edited by Martin Munro, 147–54. Mona, Jamaica: University of the West Indies Press, 2010.

Danticat, Edwidge, ed. *The Butterfly's Way: Voices from the Haitian Dyaspora in the United States*. New York: Soho Press, 2001.

Danticat, Edwidge. *Claire of the Sea Light*. New York: Vintage Books, 2013.

Danticat, Edwidge. *Create Dangerously: The Immigrant Artist at Work*. New York: Vintage Books, 2011.

Danticat, Edwidge. *Krik? Krak!* New York: Vintage Books, 1996.

Danticat, Edwidge. "Lòt Bò Dlo: The Other Side of the Water." In *Haiti after the Earthquake*, edited by Paul Farmer, 261–70. New York: Public Affairs, 2011.

Dash, J. Michael. "Rising from the Ruins." In *Haiti Rising: Haitian History, Culture, and the Earthquake of 2010*, edited by Martin Munro, 63–69. Mona, Jamaica: University of the West Indies Press, 2010.

Desmangles, Leslie G., and Elizabeth McAlister. "Religion in Post-Earthquake Haiti." In *Haiti Rising: Haitian History, Culture, and the Earthquake of 2010*, edited by Martin Munro, 70–78. Mona, Jamaica: University of the West Indies Press, 2010.

Dorsinville, Nancy. "Goudou Goudou." In *Haiti after the Earthquake*, edited by Paul Farmer, 273–81. New York: Public Affairs, 2011.

Dowling, Brendan. "Maneuvering Myself around a Scene: A Conversation with Edwidge Danticat." In *Conversations with Edwidge Danticat*, edited by Maxine Lavon Montgomery, 163–66. Jackson: University Press of Mississippi, 2017.

Dreyfuss, Joel. "A Cage of Words." In *The Butterfly's Way: Voices from the Haitian Dyaspora in the United States*, edited by Edwidge Danticat, 57–59. New York: Soho Press, 2001.

Dubois, Laurent. *Haiti: The Aftershocks of History*. New York: Picador, 2012.

Farmer, Paul, ed. *Haiti after the Earthquake*. New York: Public Affairs, 2011.

Figueroa, Iliana Rosales. "(Re)Imagining Haiti through the Eyes of a Seven-Year-Old Girl." *Journal of International Women's Studies* 17, no. 3 (2016): 177–87.

Garrigus, John D. "The Legacies of Pre-Revolutionary Saint-Domingue." In *Haiti Rising: Haitian History, Culture, and the Earthquake of 2010*, edited by Martin Munro, 115–25. Mona, Jamaica: University of the West Indies Press, 2010.

Handal, Nathalie. "We Are All Going to Die." In *Conversations with Edwidge Danticat*, edited by Maxine Lavon Montgomery, 117–27. Jackson: University Press of Mississippi, 2017.

hooks, bell. *Ain't I a Woman: Black Women and Feminism*. Boston: South End Press, 1981.

Humanium. "'Restavek' Children in Haiti: A New Form of Modern Slavery." September 5, 2016. https://www.humanium.org/en/restavek-children-in-haiti-a-new-form-of-modern-slavery/.

Ibarrola-Armendáriz, Aitor. "Broken Memories of a Traumatic Past and the Redemptive Power of Narrative in the Fiction of Edwidge Danticat." In *The Splintered Glass: Facets* of Trauma in the Post-Colony and Beyond, edited by Dolores Herrero and Sonia Baelo-Allué, 3–27. Amsterdam: Rodopi, 2011.

Jean-Charles, Régine Michelle. "Shaken Ground, Strong Foundations: Honoring the Legacy of Haitian Feminism after the Earthquake." In Haiti Rising: Haitian History, Culture, and the Earthquake of 2010, edited by Martin Munro, 79–86. Mona, Jamaica: University of the West Indies Press, 2010.

Jenson, Deborah. "The Writing of Disaster in Haiti: Signifying Cataclysm from Slave Revolution to Earthquake." In Haiti Rising: Haitian History, Culture, and the Earthquake of 2010, edited by Martin Munro, 102–11. Mona, Jamaica: University of the West Indies Press, 2010.

Jones, Kima. "A Conversation with Edwidge Danticat." In Conversations with Edwidge Danticat, edited by Maxine Lavon Montgomery, 167–74. Jackson: University Press of Mississippi, 2017.

Kalisa, Chantal. Violence in Francophone African and Caribbean Women's Literature. Lincoln: University of Nebraska Press, 2009.

Lahens, Yanick. "Haiti; or, The Health of Misery." In Haiti Rising: Haitian History, Culture, and the Earthquake of 2010, edited by Martin Munro, 9–11. Mona, Jamaica: University of the West Indies Press, 2010.

Le Bris, Michel. "Finding the Words." In Haiti Rising: Haitian History, Culture, and the Earthquake of 2010, edited by Martin Munro, 29–34. Mona, Jamaica: University of the West Indies Press, 2010.

Martin, Rachel. "Haitian Youth Illuminated in Claire of the Sea Light." In Conversations with Edwidge Danticat, edited by Maxine Lavon Montgomery, 148–51. Jackson: University Press of Mississippi, 2017.

Martínez-Falquina, Silvia. "Postcolonial Trauma Theory in the Contact Zone: The Strategic Representation of Grief in Edwidge Danticat's Claire of the Sea Light." Humanities 4, no. 4 (2015): 834–60.

Montas-Dominique, Michèle. "Sim Pa Rele (If I Don't Shout)." In Haiti after the Earthquake, edited by Paul Farmer, 259–72. New York: Public Affairs, 2011.

Montgomery, Maxine Lavon, ed. Conversations with Edwidge Danticat. Jackson: University Press of Mississippi, 2017.

Morgan, Paula, and Valerie Youssef. Writing Rage: Unmasking Violence through Caribbean Discourse. Mona, Jamaica: University of the West Indies Press, 2006.

Munro, Martin, ed. Haiti Rising: Haitian History, Culture, and the Earthquake of 2010. Mona, Jamaica: University of the West Indies Press, 2010.

Peck, Raoul. "Dead-End in Port-au-Prince." In Haiti Rising: Haitian History, Culture, and the Earthquake of 2010, edited by Martin Munro, 43–48. Mona, Jamaica: University of the West Indies Press, 2010.

Restavek Freedom. https://restavekfreedom.org/issue/.

Rigaud Apollon, Marlène. "Manman, Pa Kite Yo Koupe Janm Mwen! Mommy Don't Let Them Cut My Leg." In Haiti Rising: Haitian History, Culture, and the Earthquake of 2010, edited by Martin Munro, 12–14. Mona, Jamaica: University of the West Indies Press, 2010.

Sedky, Jéhane. "Building Back Better." In *Haiti after the Earthquake*, edited by Paul Farmer, 351–60. New York: Public Affairs, 2011.

Sokhin, Vlad, and the Restavek Freedom Foundation. "Restaveks: Haitian Slave Children." End Slavery Now, n.d. https://www.endslaverynow.org/blog/articles/restaveks -haitian-slave-children.

Spear, Thomas C. "Point of View." In *Haiti Rising: Haitian History, Culture, and the Earthquake of 2010*, edited by Martin Munro, 35–42. Mona, Jamaica: University of the West Indies Press, 2010.

Suárez, Lucía M. *The Tears of Hispaniola: Haitian and Dominican Diaspora Memory.* Gainesville: University Press of Florida, 2006.

Thomas, Bonnie. *Connecting Histories: Francophone Caribbean Writers Interrogating Their Past.* Jackson: University Press of Mississippi, 2017.

Thomas, Bonnie. "Narrating Trauma: Distance and Proximity in the Haitian Earthquake of 2010." *Australian Journal of French Studies* 53, no. 1 (2016): 67–78.

Vergès, Françoise. *La mémoire enchaînée: Questions sur l'esclavage.* Paris: Albin Michel, 2006.

Wagner, Laura. "Salvaging." In *Haiti Rising: Haitian History, Culture, and the Earthquake of 2010*, edited by Martin Munro, 15–23. Mona, Jamaica: University of the West Indies Press, 2010.

Zipp, Georg. "Selling Poverty: Junot Díaz's and Edwidge Danticat's Assessments of Picturesque Stereotypes of Poverty in the Caribbean." *Zeitschrift für Anglistik und Amerikanistik* 63, no. 2 (2015): 229–46.

Chapter Fifteen

BLACK BUTTERFLIES

Survival, Transformation, and the Invention of Home in Edwidge Danticat's Fiction and Nonfiction

MARION CHRISTINA ROHRLEITNER

> You can't go home again except in writing . . .
>
> —EDWIDGE DANTICAT

Loss and death figure prominently in most of Edwidge Danticat's fiction and nonfiction. While tragic death due to mental and physical illness, environmental catastrophe, a genocidal history, abject poverty, and an inhumane immigration system occupies a central place in Danticat's work, her narratives never end with victimization; instead, Danticat highlights the survivors' resilience and focuses on their turn to writing, art, and social activism in an effort to resist and eventually transform the environment that has produced and caused these losses, and to create a notion of home that is fluid and mobile.

In Danticat's work, home is never a safe, stable place of unperturbed childhood innocence and joy; instead, it is often the source of thinly veiled violence and silenced family narratives. As Viet Thanh Nguyen has pointed out in "At Home with Race," "Even as a metaphor, home is not always safe. . . . [H]ome is also where one's pathologies are. . . . [T]he home we find will provide not only chances for love and new futures but also the opportunity to inflict pain and to repeat our forebears' mistakes."[1] In *The Dew Breaker*, for example, the father of artist Ka turns out to be a former member of the Tonton Macoutes; in *The Farming of Bones*, the home of migrant worker Amabelle Désir on the Dominican-Haitian border becomes the site of a massacre; and in *Breath, Eyes, Memory*, the young Haitian immigrant Sophie Caco is subjected to humiliating and painful "testing" of her virginity in her mother's home in Brooklyn. In Danticat's fictional universe, home can thus not be found in a nostalgic and romanticized past on the island, but is often collectively created by sharing stories of survival in the dyaspora—even if the dyaspora, too, can be a profoundly unsafe space.

From Sophie Caco's life-affirming response to her mother Martine's suicide in *Breath, Eyes, Memory*, to Amabelle Désir's embodied *testimonio* of El Corte in *The Farming of Bones*, to Danticat's moving engagement with the deaths of her beloved father and of her Uncle Joseph in the memoir *Brother, I'm Dying* and the passing of her mother Rose from cancer in *The Art of Death: Writing the Final Story*, the author develops a theory of resilience and survival best expressed in philosopher Jonathan Lear's concept of "radical hope." According to Lear, radical hope can be described as "a daunting form of commitment to a goodness in the world that transcends one's current ability to grasp it."[2] Junot Díaz, a personal friend and frequent collaborator of Danticat, draws on Lear's definition of radical hope, stating in a piece published in the *New Yorker* a week after the 2016 US presidential election: "Radical hope is our best weapon against despair, even when despair seems justifiable; it makes the survival of the end of your world possible. Only radical hope could have imagined people like us into existence."[3] As I have written elsewhere, Danticat's work shows how such acts of the creative imagination are part and parcel of the immigrant experience.[4] In this chapter, I argue that the same radical hope lies at the heart of Danticat's artistic vision when it comes to the creation of affective and ever-changing homeplaces beyond national borders and even beyond death. Home, to Danticat, is never confined to the nation-state; instead, it is found in many unexpected sites and locations. Home can originate in an imaginary, deterritorialized space in flux, it can manifest in an ancestral presence that allows for reconciliation with history, it can emerge in dyasporic movements, after leaving one's birthplace, and it can be created in language, in the very process of writing.

Home is an elusive and often fraught concept, especially in postcolonial literatures in which home is simultaneously a site of loss and of potential reinvention.[5] Home, as a tangible or imagined space where we ideally feel at ease, loved, understood, comfortable, and safe, gains added significance for a people in exile or in a dyaspora; cultural identities are inextricably linked to one's place of origin, regardless of whether we embrace or reject said origin—and perhaps especially if it rejects us. As Stuart Hall has argued in "Cultural Identity and Diaspora," the diasporic individual home, like cultural identity itself, is forever in flux, a constant back and forth movement shifting between "being" and "becoming."[6] Throughout Danticat's fiction and nonfiction, the figures of the immigrant, the refugee, and the exile are linked to mobility and to the concept of the *vwayajé*,[7] whose home is not a specific geographic or even cultural location but a movable, malleable affect associated with fellow travelers and a life grounded in movement and constant transformation.

Even though migration offers countless opportunities for transformation and reinvention, it is also a dangerous endeavor for many Haitians. From the perilous crossing of the Mona Strait on fragile boats, described in "Children of the Sea," to the treacherous abyss of an indifferent immigration bureaucracy, highlighted in *Brother, I'm Dying*, transnational movement is associated not only with freedom of mobility but also with the omnipresence of death. Always already criminalized and pathologized, Haitian migrants and refugees often escape one lethal threat, such as earthquakes, poverty, or the Tonton Macoutes, only to be met with other dangers, from violent racism to illness and persecution in the dyaspora. And yet Danticat does not consider death an ultimate silencing, but a transformative process that invites a creative confrontation. In a 2010 interview with Nathalie Handal, Danticat suggests: "It's a lot of work to die. . . . Art is about life as much as it is about death. Art is a way, I think, of acknowledging that we are alive, but also a way of leaving our imprints because we know that we will die one day and we hope that the work will outlive us."[8] Death, as the ultimate journey and transformation, is often represented by black butterflies in Danticat's fiction.

In many indigenous cultures, black butterflies are seen as bad omens and often as harbingers of death. In a Caribbean context in particular, black butterflies also symbolize rebirth, the transformation of life through death into a new and perhaps freer form of being. Semia Harwabi, for example, has persuasively argued that "both the butterfly and the kite are versatile manifestations of an emblematic impulsion towards resistance as a locus of transformation."[9] In what follows, I show how Danticat's fiction and non-fiction contribute to a new ethics of belonging that is characterized by a "radical hope" for a home not grounded in a specific geographic location but in a shared affective culture of belonging, a culture that is characterized by constant movement and transformation and extends into the continuity between life and death in the dyaspora. The visual symbol for this notion of home in Danticat's narrative universe is the black butterfly. In an interview with Sandy Alexandre and Ravi Y. Howard, Danticat describes her affinity for butterflies:

> My favorite kind of butterfly is the monarch butterfly. It is a butterfly that travels 3,000 miles each year from colder climates to warmer ones. The butterfly that leaves the cold climate is not the one that returns the following spring. Along the way it gives life to offsprings

which somehow know how to go back to the same place its mother
or grandmother came from. The original butterfly dies, but the off-
springs continue the journey and then return.[10]

The genetic memory of the monarch butterflies, which allows a new generation to return to the precise location of their progenitors' origins, has clearly
provided ample inspiration to the author. *Breath, Eyes, Memory*, Danticat's
1994 debut novel, is based on the MFA thesis she submitted at Brown University. At the end of the novel, Martine, the narrator's mother, commits
suicide after a lifelong battle with depression. Her daughter Sophie finds
out that she is the product of rape by a member of the Tonton Macoutes
during the regime of François Duvalier. Unable to accept her mother's death
as final and irredeemable, Sophie turns to Haitian folklore at the end of the
novel and reimagines her mother's tragic death as a spiritual and physical transformation that liberates her. When Martine's grieving lover, Marc,
worries that "Saint Peter won't allow your mother into Heaven" in the loud
crimson dress her daughter chose for the burial, Sophie defiantly asserts,
"She is going to Guinea . . . or she is going to be a star. She's going to be a
butterfly or a lark in a tree. She's going to be free."[11] Sophie intuitively connects her mother's self-liberation from pain with Guinea, the mythological
homeland of members of the African diaspora in the Americas, many of
them descendants of slaves. She concludes, on the last page of the novel: "My
mother was like that woman who could never bleed and then could never
stop bleeding, the one who gave in to her pain, to live as a butterfly."[12] Even
though Martine's suicide is devastating to her daughter, Sophie imagines a
future for her mother in death that allows her the kind of freedom she never
had in life. In so doing, Sophie neither romanticizes Martine's suicide nor
succumbs to the utter pain of losing her mother; instead, Sophie articulates
radical hope for her mother's transformed self.

In "Children of the Sea," the opening story of Danticat's award-winning
1995 collection *Krik? Krak!*, an unnamed couple of young lovers are separated
by the turmoil in the aftermath of the first coup d'état against the democrati-
cally elected president Jean-Bertrand Aristide in 1991. The young woman's
father locks her up in his house in a desperate effort to protect her from
violence and abuse by marauding Tonton Macoutes, while the young man
is aboard a tiny, sinking raft in the ocean trying to cross the Mona Strait and
seek political asylum in Puerto Rico or Florida. Unable to communicate, they
each write a series of letters to each other knowing that the letters will never
be read. And yet, the letters create a sense of emotional home to both these
victims of political unrest, even in the face of death. An epistolary romance,

the young woman concludes her final unsent letter to her beloved: "[N]ow there are always butterflies around me, black ones that I refuse to let find my hand. . . . [B]ehind these mountains are more mountains and more black butterflies still and a sea that is endless like my love for you."[13] The young woman initially resists the inevitability of death but eventually concludes that the butterflies are omnipresent and are perhaps even a powerful symbol of her love for the young man on the raft. In an act of radical hope, Danticat's narrator rises above paralyzing fear and desperation and acknowledges the inevitability of her lover's eventual death, without allowing this fact to dim her emotional attachment to him. The young couple find solace and a sense of home in their unsent and imaginary letters to each other. Home, in this short story, is deterritorialized and encompasses the vast and uncertain space that connects the two lovers in the face of violence.

The Farming of Bones, Danticat's historical novel about the notorious 1937 Parsley Massacre, begins and ends near Dajabón on the Dominican-Haitian border. In the novel's final chapter, the main narrator, Amabelle Désir, returns "home" to the Haitian-Dominican border region. Amabelle is a former domestic servant and midwife in the home of Pico and Valencia, Dominican plantation owners; she barely survived the massacre and has spent her life as a living memorial to those who lost their lives. She returns to Massacre River in October, the very site and month of her parents' drowning, her lover's disappearance, the deaths of many of her close friends, and her own traumatic injury during El Corte. In the concluding passage of the novel, Amabelle immerses herself in the soothing waters of the stream:

> The water was warm for October, warm and shallow, so shallow that I could lie on my back in it with my shoulders only half submerged, the current floating over me in a less than gentle caress, the pebbles in the riverbed scouring my back. I looked to my dreams for softness, for a gentler embrace, for relief from the fear of mudslides and blood bubbling out of the riverbed, where it is said the dead add their tears to the river flow.[14]

In this passage, Amabelle turns to her creative imagination to make the ever-present memory of death at Massacre River bearable and find solace in "a place to lay it down now again, a safe nest."[15] In her focus on death as transformation and a form of home, Amabelle also reveals a spirituality strikingly akin to the Zen Buddhist notion of "birthdeath" and the Akan concept of Sankofa (🔣). Sankofa stresses the importance of knowing one's past while still looking into the future. Death and life are two sides of the same coin; they mutually condition each other and eventually merge in the final transformation from life to death. Drawing on Barbara Christian's critical reading of the presence of ghosts in Toni Morrison's *Beloved*,[16] I propose to read the presence of the spirits of the victims of the massacre neither as morbid symbolism nor as an instance of the Freudian uncanny; instead, I suggest that the haunting Amabelle experiences is an example the ancestral presence of *lo real maravilloso* in the Americas, which connects the living and the dead in the realm of the fluidity of water.

Early in the novel, Amabelle acknowledges the intimate link between being born and dying. Recalling her parents' midwifery services to the community, she observes: "Births and deaths were my parents' work."[17] In "Transition," the final chapter in *Brother, I'm Dying*, Danticat viscerally connects her going into labor to give birth to her first child with her father's dying: "There's a stage in labor called transition, when the baby, preparing to separate from the mother, twists and turns to pass through the birth canal. I am sure there is a similar stage for exiting life. . . . [E]ach time I wish for an easy transition for my daughter and myself, I wish the same for my father."[18] After her daughter Mira safely enters the world, Danticat is able to capture a series of photos of her father holding his newborn granddaughter named after him. Her father passes away three days later, shortly after Danticat leaves Brooklyn for Miami. Danticat speculates that her "father had waited for me to leave. That he did not want me to hold Mira with one hand and his corpse with the other."[19] While the living are but a connecting point between those not yet born and those who have passed on into a different spiritual realm, Danticat's father seems to suggest they still need to be separated into mutually respected spaces, to ensure the dead a peaceful resting place, a home beyond the familiar.

In "Bodies on the Move: A Poetics of Home and Diaspora," Susan Stanford Friedman observes: "A poetics of dislocation may begin for some in recognizing 'home' as no place they want to be, as a place where the heart may be, but a place that must be left, as a place whose leaving is the source of speech and writing."[20] To Danticat, home is thus simultaneously embodied and deterritorialized; an immigrant herself, and the daughter of refugees from the political and economic havoc the Duvalier regimes had wreaked on Haiti, Danticat finds home in her close personal relationships with family members and other Haitian Americans in the dyaspora, as well as in the deterritorialized space of writing.

In "Have You Enjoyed Your Life?," the opening chapter of *Brother, I'm Dying*, Danticat recalls a conversation with her father, who's suffering from end-stage pulmonary fibrosis:

"How can you leave New York?" he asked. . . . "Your mother's here in Brooklyn, I'm here, two of your three brothers are here. You have no family in Miami. What if this man you're moving there for mistreats you? Who are you going to turn to?"[21]

The concern of Danticat's father stems from a sense of home associated with security through kinship. Miami may have a significant Haitian American population, but are they kin and will they protect this daughter if need be? Not every dyaspora, to Danticat's father, is created equal.

When faced with her father's ill health, Danticat feels a pang of guilt for having left. When they visit a Caribbean herbalist together, the woman reads her iris and assures Danticat that she may be pregnant, a diagnosis Danticat confirms later. Her father's impending death—the pulmonologist suggests six months to two years should resistance to the treatment persist—is countered with Danticat's first pregnancy. Overwhelmed, as if in a trance, Danticat keeps repeating the phrase "My father is dying and I'm pregnant."[22] As in her fictional treatment of the 1937 massacre, Danticat's foray into the genre of the memoir continues to link the simultaneity of birth and death. Rather than being presented as bracketing our lives, the two phenomena constantly intersect, overlap, and disrupt each other in Danticat's work. Death, one could argue, is but one of many transformations in Haitian immigrants' lives.

In her recent collection of essays, *The Art of Death: Writing the Final Story* (2017), Danticat concludes that in the absence of a stable geographic homespace or a singular fixed national identity, she finds herself most at home in her writing. Citing Toni Morrison's 1993 Nobel lecture, Danticat, too, believes that "we die. That may be the meaning of life. But we do language. That may be the measure of our lives."[23] "Doing language" thus becomes a site not only of struggle but also of comfort. The language Danticat chooses to write her fiction and nonfiction also tells us about the ongoing process of shaping a cultural identity and creating a home in the dyaspora. By using English as the main vehicle to tell her stories, Danticat both claims for herself the most powerful language in publishing and distributing literature in the United States, yet also, in this process of transculturation,[24] alters standard American English to reflect French and, even more importantly, Kreyòl influences. English, which has provided a home to so many of Danticat's narratives, is on its way to being transformed into a multicultural language that also includes the experiences of Haitian Americans, whose mother tongue is Kreyòl. In the aforementioned interview with Sandy Alexandre and Ravi Y. Howard, Danticat expresses her admiration for fellow Caribbean American writers such Julia Alvarez and Junot Díaz for "introducing another language into English,"[25] and she emphasizes how her prose, too, strives to transform both English and Kreyòl in the cross-cultural encounters that result from exile and immigration. Danticat cites Cuban American writer Gustavo Pérez Firmat's well-known poem from his 1995 collection *Bilingual Blues* as part of her location as a Haitian American author writing in English:

> My subject:
> how to explain to you that I
> don't belong to English
> though I belong nowhere else.[26]

This sense of belonging to neither only Haiti nor only the United States, of a bifurcated identity that claims both spaces as home, is reflected in Danticat's fiction and nonfiction alike. Danticat has described this diasporic sense of home as follows: "Haiti is and always will be one of the two places, the United States being the other, that I call home. Haiti is where I was born and Haiti was my first home. I am like most Haitians living with my feet in both worlds."[27] Her family is one part of this bridge between Haiti and the United States; Kreyòl and her historical consciousness as a Haitian American woman are other parts of the bridge.

The epigraph to Danticat's moving memoir on the deaths of her father and late uncle Joseph, who died at the age of eighty-one while being detained by US Immigration and Customs Enforcement (ICE) after being refused treatment for an ailment, is taken from Paul Auster's *The Invention of Solitude:*

> To begin with death, To work my way back into life,
> And then, finally, to return to death.
> Or else: the vanity of trying to say anything about anyone.

In her fiction and nonfiction, Danticat has often "worked her way back into life," but perhaps never as immediately and heartbreakingly as in her two memoirs, *Brother, I'm Dying* and *The Art of Death*, a text concerning the death of her beloved uncle Joseph and her mother, Rose.

For Danticat, home, and the radical hope necessary for creating a home in the dyaspora, is associated with the lettered word early on. When her parents leave Danticat and her older brother, Bob, in the care of their uncle Joseph when emigrating to New York City, Danticat's only connection to her parents, in the absence of access to affordable and functioning phone lines, is the letters they write.

Scribbled in his minuscule scrawl . . . my father's letters were composed in stilted French, with the first paragraph offering news of his
and my mother's health, the second detailing how to spend the money
they had wired for food, lodging and school expenses for Bob and
myself, the third section concluding abruptly after reassuring us that
we'd be hearing from him again before long. Later I would discover in
a first-year college composition class that his letters had been written
in a diamond sequence, the Aristotelian Poetics of correspondence,
requiring an open greeting, a middle detail or request, and a brief
farewell at the end.[28]

Danticat's extraordinary attention to detail in this passage hints at the great
significance these letters continue to hold for her, and yet how they were
never quite able to provide the feeling of home she was longing for. Her
father, many decades later, confirms this sentiment and asserts, "I was no
writer. . . . What I wanted to tell you and your brother was too big for any
piece of paper and a small envelope."[29] While her father's letters often proved
too scarce, too pragmatic, too rushed to provide a sense of love and feeling
at home, her uncle Joseph's public performance of reading the letters turned
them into a communal event very much capable of providing a sense of
community and home: "Whatever restraint my father showed in his letters
was easily compensated for by Uncle Joseph's reactions to them."[30] Home
is thus not only found in the individual reading and writing of letters but
also in public readings and affective communal responses to such readings,
a process that showcases the ongoing presence and influence of the art of
Haitian storytelling in the dyaspora.

Danticat is a highly effective chronicler of family and national history and
astutely aware of the processes Diana Taylor has summarized in the terms
"the archive and the repertoire."[31] Taylor highlights the importance of the
repertoire, especially in the colonized context of the Americas, and defines
it as that which "enacts embodied memory . . . all those acts usually thought
of as ephemeral, nonreproducible knowledge."[32] In her fiction and nonfiction, Danticat listens to these fleeting forms of knowledge and translates
them, via her writing, into the realm of the archive. In *Brother, I'm Dying*,
Danticat lets us know:

I write these things now, some as I witness them and today remember them, others from official documents, as well as the borrowed
recollections of family members. . . . [W]hat I learned from my father
and uncle, I learned out of sequence and in fragments. This is an

attempt at cohesiveness, and at re-creating a few wondrous and terrible months when their lives and mine intersected in startling ways,
forcing me to look forward and back at the same time.[33]

Witnessing in writing is one key role the dyasporic Haitian author can and
perhaps must perform, in an effort to help create a sense of home in a shared
history. Personal and family histories become inseparable from historical
events; in Haiti, nobody has the luxury to separate the personal from the
political, since political decisions and events, often made outside of Haiti,
have a direct impact on Haitians living on the island and in the dyaspora.
    When Danticat recalls the location of her uncle's family home in Bel Air,
a fairly affluent neighborhood in Port-au-Prince, the house is inextricably
intertwined with a history of conquest, slavery, and revolution:

The hill in Bel Air on which the house was built had been the site of
a famous battle between mulatto abolitionists and French colonists
who'd controlled most of the islands since 1697 and had imported
black Africans to labor on coffee and sugar plantations as slaves. A
century later, slaves and mulattoes joined together to drive the French
out, and on January 1, 1804 formed the Republic of Haiti.[34]

Home is thus also the shared knowledge of a past grounded in abolition and
anticolonial revolution. As Danticat observes in her memoir, not only are the
vast majority of Haitians and Haitian Americans very knowledgeable about
the Haitian Revolution, they also feel intimately connected to this history.
In a 2009 interview with Opal Palmer Adisa, Danticat asserts: "History is
very present in Haiti. We're always talking about the past because the present is either a recycling of the past or an echo of it or is too painful itself to
discuss as much as the victories, or hindsight failures, of the past."[35] Danticat
confronts Haitian history especially in her short fiction and novels. In "1937,"
a short story included in Krik? Krak!, Danticat dives into the aftermath of
the Parsley Massacre and tells the story of a survivor, who, like Amabelle
Désir in The Farming of Bones, is brutally marked by the traumatic ordeal. In
contrast to Amabelle, however, this survivor does not flee to safety to Haiti,
her supposed home. Instead of being protected and healed, the woman is
accused of being a soucouyant,[36] and is incarcerated in a decaying prison
and left to die there. The woman saves herself by diving into the river, running with the blood of the victims of the massacre, and emerging on the
Haitian side with a back that has turned a deep crimson. Shunned by her
family and her fellow inmates as a witch, only her daughter, the narrative

consciousness of the story, is willing to provide her with food and affection. Imprisonment has taken its toll, and the woman dies in solitude. And yet, in spite of the horrific fate of the innocent woman, her daughter's story rejects the silencing of the archive, adding her voice to a repertoire critical of the abuses of folklore in the name of nationalism, offering radical hope in the most hopeless of circumstance.

In Danticat's work, home is a work in progress, an aspiration sustained by radical hope. In her fiction and nonfiction, painful histories need to be confronted, told, and shared via narrative and art in order to create the possibility for creating home in the dyaspora. Nationalist, territorial definitions of home are replaced with fluid, transnational, and diachronic narratives of home, which allow for multiple affiliations, simultaneities, and contradictions and require shifting movements to thrive. This concept of home is perhaps best embodied in Kamau Brathwaite's "tidalectics," which, rejecting Western dialectics, refuses neat synthesis and instead is embodied in "the ripple and the two tide movement."[37] It describes a creative process of "becoming," initiated by an often violent impetus for emigration from the protagonists' country of birth, a ripple with a complex and long-standing impact on formations of home in the dyaspora in target countries with their own troubled histories. In Danticat's fiction and nonfiction, tidalectic movements toward home are propelled by a radical hope that is confined neither by national or linguistic boundaries nor by strict divisions between past and present, nor are such movements divided between the realms of the living and the dead. Danticat's Haitian and Haitian American protagonists, like black butterflies, move away from their places of origin only to revisit, confront, reclaim, reinvent, and constantly readjust "home" to their shifting politics of location via the creative imagination and in writing.

NOTES

1. Viet Thanh Nguyen, "At Home with Race," *PMLA* 123, no. 5 (October 2008): 1563.

2. Jonathan Lear, *Radical Hope: Ethics in the Face of Cultural Devastation* (Cambridge, MA: Harvard University Press, 2006), 103.

3. Junot Díaz, "Under President Trump, Radical Hope Is Our Best Weapon," *New Yorker*, November 21, 2016, https://www.newyorker.com/magazine/2016/11/21/under -president-trump-radical-hope-is-our-best-weapon.

4. Marion Christina Rohrleitner, "'Create Dangerously': Immigration as Radical Hope in Edwidge Danticat's Fiction and Creative Nonfiction," in *The Immigrant Experience: Critical Insights*, edited by Maryse Jayasuriya (Ipswich, MA: Salem Press, 2018), 134.

5. I am drawing on Nadia Ragbar's understanding of the role of postcoloniality in Danticat's work here: "As such, 'postcoloniality' signals a reformist view of history—the position of Danticat's female narrators standing in contradistinction to the status quo— so that postcolonialism operates simultaneous to colonialism (and neocolonialism) as a parallel movement of resistance. There are many who would hesitate to employ the term 'post-colonial' usually for one of two reasons: as a reaction against the diachronic version of history, which would see colonialism displaced." Nadia Ragbar, "Post-Colonialism as a Revolutionary Reality: Edwidge Danticat's Opus as a Testimony of Haitian Women's Survival through Narration," *Journal of Haitian Studies* 7, no. 2 (Fall 2001): 122.

6. Stuart Hall, "Cultural Identity and Diaspora," in *Identity: Community, Culture, Difference*, edited by Jonathan Rutherford (London: Lawrence and Wishart, 1990), 222.

7. *Vwayajé* is Kreyòl for "to travel" or "the voyager." The term has rich connotations for Haitians who have migrated north and live in the dyaspora.

8. Nathalie Handal, "We Are All Going to Die," in *Conversations with Edwidge Danticat*, ed. Maxine Lavon Montgomery (Jackson: University Press of Mississippi, 2017), 123.

9. Semia Harwabi, "Writing Memory: Edwidge Danticat's Limbo Inscriptions," *Journal of West Indian Literature* 16, no. 1 (November 2007): 45.

10. Sandy Alexandre and Ravi Y. Howard, "An Interview with Edwidge Danticat," *Journal of Caribbean Literatures* 4, no. 3 (Spring 2007): 162.

11. Edwidge Danticat, *Breath, Eyes, Memory* (New York: Vintage Books, 1994), 228.

12. Danticat, *Breath, Eyes, Memory*, 234.

13. Edwidge Danticat, "Children of the Sea," in *Krik? Krak!* (New York: Vintage Books, 1996), 28–29.

14. Edwidge Danticat, *The Farming of Bones* (New York: Penguin Books, 1998), 310.

15. Danticat, *The Farming of Bones*, 266.

16. Barbara Christian, "Beloved, She's Ours," *Narrative* 5, no. 1 (January 1997): 36–49.

17. Danticat, *The Farming of Bones*, 5.

18. Edwidge Danticat, *Brother, I'm Dying* (New York: Vintage Books, 2007), 252.

19. Danticat, *Brother, I'm Dying*, 263.

20. Susan Stanford Friedman, "Bodies on the Move: A Poetics of Home and Diaspora," *Tulsa Studies in Women's Literature* 23, no. 2 (Fall 2004): 205.

21. Danticat, *Brother, I'm Dying*, 4.

22. Danticat, *Brother, I'm Dying*, 15.

23. Toni Morrison, quoted in Edwidge Danticat, *The Art of Death: Writing the Final Story* (Minneapolis: Graywolf Press, 2017), 7.

24. Diana Taylor defines transculturation as "the transformative process undergone by all societies as they come in contact with and acquire foreign cultural material, whether willingly or unwillingly." Diana Taylor, *The Archive and the Repertoire: Performing Cultural Memory in the Americas* (Durham, NC: Duke University Press, 2003), 10.

25. Alexandre and Howard, "An Interview with Edwidge Danticat," 167.

26. Gustavo Pérez Firmat, quoted in Alexandre and Howard, "An Interview with Edwidge Danticat," 167.

27. Alexandre and Howard, "An Interview with Edwidge Danticat," 345.

28. Danticat, *Brother, I'm Dying*, 22.

29. Danticat, *Brother, I'm Dying*, 22.

30. Danticat, *Brother, I'm Dying*, 22.

31. Taylor, *The Archive and the Repertoire*, 19–20.

32. Taylor, *The Archive and the Repertoire*, 20.

33. Danticat, *Brother, I'm Dying*, 25–26.

34. Danticat, *Brother, I'm Dying*, 29.

35. Opal Palmer Adisa, "Up Close and Personal: Edwidge Danticat on Haitian Identity and the Writer's Life," *African American Review* 43, nos. 2–3 (Summer–Fall 2009): 352.

36. Monica A. Coleman defines the *soucouyant* as follows: "With roots in the African Fula and Sonyinke, the Soucouyant is a mythical woman who strips off her skin at night and roams the streets looking for the blood of babies and animals to survive. . . . The legend says that she leaves her skin at home at night and she can be defeated if her skin is salted while she is away. Akin to the European vampire, she can also be defeated if she is exposed to sunlight before returning to her body." Monica A. Coleman, "Serving the Spirits: The Pan-Caribbean African-Derived Religion in Nalo Hopkinson's *Brown Girl in the Ring*," *Journal of Caribbean Literatures* 6, no. 1 (Summer 2009): 10. See also Lucie Pradel, *African Beliefs in the New World: Popular Literary Traditions of the Caribbean*, trans. Catherine Bernard (Trenton, NJ: Africa World Press, 2001), 151–52.

37. Quoted in Paul Naylor, *Poetic Investigations: Singing the Holes in History* (Evanston, IL: Northwestern University Press, 1999), 145.

BIBLIOGRAPHY

Adisa, Opal Palmer. "Up Close and Personal: Edwidge Danticat on Haitian Identity and the Writer's Life." *African American Review* 43, nos. 2–3 (Summer–Fall 2009): 345–55.

Alexandre, Sandy, and Ravi Y. Howard. "An Interview with Edwidge Danticat." *Journal of Caribbean Literatures* 4, no. 3 (Spring 2007): 161–74.

Brathwaite, Kamau. *The Arrivants: A New World Trilogy*. Oxford: Oxford University Press, 1988.

Christian, Barbara. "Beloved, She's Ours." *Narrative* 5, no. 1 (January 1997): 36–49.

Coleman, Monica A. "Serving the Spirits: The Pan-Caribbean African-Derived Religion in Nalo Hopkinson's *Brown Girl in the Ring*." *Journal of Caribbean Literatures* 6, no. 1 (Summer 2009): 1–13.

Danticat, Edwidge. *The Art of Death: Writing the Final Story*. Minneapolis: Graywolf Press, 2017.

Danticat, Edwidge. *Breath, Eyes, Memory*. New York: Vintage Books, 1994.

Danticat, Edwidge. *Brother, I'm Dying*. New York: Vintage Books, 2007.

Danticat, Edwidge, ed. *The Butterfly's Way: Voices from the Haitian Dyaspora in the United States*. New York: Soho Press, 2001.

Danticat, Edwidge. "Children of the Sea." In *Krik? Krak!*, 1–30. New York: Vintage Books, 1996.

Danticat, Edwidge. *Create Dangerously: The Immigrant Artist at Work*. Princeton, NJ: Princeton University Press, 2010.

Danticat, Edwidge. *The Dew Breaker*. New York: Vintage Books, 2005.

Danticat, Edwidge. *The Farming of Bones*. New York: Penguin Books, 1998.

Díaz, Junot. "Under President Trump, Radical Hope Is Our Best Weapon." *New Yorker*, November 21, 2016. https://www.newyorker.com/magazine/2016/11/21/under-presi dent-trump-radical-hope-is-our-best-weapon.

Friedman, Susan Stanford. "Bodies on the Move: A Poetics of Home and Diaspora." *Tulsa Studies in Women's Literature* 23, no. 2 (Fall 2004): 189–212.

Hall, Stuart. "Cultural Identity and Diaspora." In *Identity: Community, Culture, Difference*, edited by Jonathan Rutherford, 222–37. London: Lawrence and Wishart, 1990.

Handal, Nathalie. "We Are All Going to Die." In *Conversations with Edwidge Danticat*, edited by Maxine Lavon Montgomery, 117–27. Jackson: University Press of Mississippi, 2017.

Harwabi, Semia. "Writing Memory: Edwidge Danticat's Limbo Inscriptions." *Journal of West Indian Literature* 16, no. 1 (November 2007): 37–58.

hooks, bell. "Homeplace: A Site of Resistance." In *Yearning: Race, Gender, and Cultural Politics*, 41–50. Boston: South End Press, 1999.

Lear, Jonathan. *Radical Hope: Ethics in the Face of Cultural Devastation*. Cambridge, MA: Harvard University Press, 2006.

Marxsen, Patti M. "The Map Within: Place, Displacement, and the Long Shadow of History in the Work of Edwidge Danticat." *Journal of Haitian Studies* 11, no. 1 (Spring 2005): 140–55.

Morrison, Toni. "Nobel Lecture." December 7, 1993. https://www.nobelprize.org/prizes /literature/1993/morrison/lecture/.

Naylor, Paul. *Poetic Investigations: Singing the Holes in History*. Evanston, IL: Northwestern University Press, 1999.

Nguyen, Viet Thanh. "At Home with Race." *PMLA* 123, no. 5 (October 2008): 1557–64.

Pérez Firmat, Gustavo. *Bilingual Blues: Poems, 1981–1994*. Tempe, AZ: Bilingual Press, 1995.

Pradel, Lucie. *African Beliefs in the New World: Popular Literary Traditions of the Caribbean*. Translated by Catherine Bernard. Trenton, NJ: Africa World Press, 2001.

Ragbar, Nadia. "Post-Colonialism as a Revolutionary Reality: Edwidge Danticat's Opus as a Testimony of Haitian Women's Survival through Narration." *Journal of Haitian Studies* 7, no. 2 (Fall 2001): 110–26.

Rohrleitner, Marion Christina. "'Create Dangerously': Immigration as Radical Hope in Edwidge Danticat's Fiction and Creative Nonfiction." In *The Immigrant Experience: Critical Insights*, edited by Maryse Jayasuriya, 134–50. Ipswich, MA: Salem Press, 2018.

Rushdie, Salman. *Imaginary Homelands: Essays and Criticism 1981–1991*. New York: Penguin Books, 1992.

Taylor, Diana. *The Archive and the Repertoire: Performing Cultural Memory in the Americas*. Durham, NC: Duke University Press, 2003.

Trouillot, Michel-Rolph. *Silencing the Past: Power and the Production of History*. Boston: Beacon Press, 1995.

Vega-González, Susana. "Metaphor and Symbolism in Edwidge Danticat's *The Farming of Bones*." *Polish Journal for American Studies* 1 (January 2004): 55–65.

AFTERWORD

To Breathe a Collective Air

THADIOUS M. DAVIS

Looking back at the publication of Edwidge Danticat's first book, *Breath, Eyes, Memory* (1994), I am struck by how prescient the young writer was to focus on breath. Breath comes even before eyes/sight and memory/remembrance. The concept of breathing as living takes precedence over seeing and vision, and is the antecedent of remembering the past. To breathe is so obviously a necessary part of the process of living, yet it is almost indiscernible under ordinary circumstances when breathing shows no outward sign of laboring or movement. At the same time, however, so much of the body is involved in the act of breathing, that taking in and letting out of air, the necessary oxygen fueling the entire body.

Oxygen, in the era of COVID-19 and the resulting pandemic, has become an all too familiar topic. The virus's attack on breathing has made clear the importance of oxygen and its connection to breath. That knowledge, now circulating in public discourse and on social media, is painful in what it has revealed about the vulnerable human body and its limited capacity to keep breathing while under physical assault. The ability to take a breath, whether independently or artificially assisted, is currently linked more explicitly with living and escaping death. That fact has reverberated in the unprecedented number of lives lost to the virus.

Breath, as Edwidge Danticat discerned in her first visionary novel, is inextricably linked to life and its converse, death. In *Breath, Eyes, Memory*, she renders breath revelatory in its ordinary necessity and its inescapable price. She brings into dramatic focus the meaning of breath in its internal and external functioning. To breathe is, in and of itself, a prediction of life, a motion of enabling that is predicated upon the functioning of bodily parts working in an all-knowing clairvoyance about what constitutes life. Shortness of breath signals trouble. A deep breath indicates fullness, inflating and bringing air fully through the lungs.

In *Breath, Eyes, Memory*, Danticat has imagined the coexistence of deep breaths in Sophie's affirmation of life and the shortness of breath in her mother Martine's acceptance of death by suicide. The essays in *Narrating History, Home, and Dyaspora* confront this duality in reading Danticat's text. Marion Christina Rohrleitner points out in "Black Butterflies: Survival, Transformation, and the Invention of Home in Edwidge Danticat's Fiction and Nonfiction" that *Breath, Eyes, Memory* resonates with the complex interrelationship between life-giving and life-destroying forces at work in the existences of Haitian émigrés living in the United States and attempting to live with the reality of their inherited traditions and customs. Tammie Jenkins and Akia Jackson also take up this tension in *Breath, Eyes, Memory* by considering the imbricated past and the embodied memories in Danticat's characters that induce set ways of creating identity and responding to living. In a sense, breath becomes from the start of Danticat's career a sign of overcoming or succumbing to the trauma of Haitian people living as exiles or immigrants outside of Haiti but who cannot fully leave Haiti behind.

Breath and breathing are terms that have come to mark so much public life since the appearance of Danticat's first book. In the age of the coronavirus and a renewed awareness of what it means to be able to breathe, and the political implications of addressing the right to breathe and have life, her early vision materializes as even more profound. Woven into all the essays in *Narrating History, Home, and Dyaspora* is a cognizance of Danticat's boundless ability to live and write within the ever widening and deepening dimensions of that vision. The contributors understand that Edwidge Danticat, in her seamlessly breathing the literary, social, and political spaces of the human body into her texts, has brought her readers along with her. They show the extent to which, in tackling her own history and antecedents in Haiti and beyond, she has moved with a bodily grace and intellectual force into being fully alive and breathing a collective air in what she has identified as "the floating homeland" that connects all Haitians existing outside of Haiti. The metaphor of breath and the act of breathing push back against notions of structural confinement in native economic, social, or political states. Danticat positions the innate freedom of the body in its simplest functioning form of breathing as a counter to state or familial political oppression. If the body can see and breathe, then it can necessarily move in memory toward exits from structures of confinement (structural suppression and containment) and from concomitant pressures that the body whether still or in motion experiences. This countervalence symbolizes the possibility of egress for even the most vulnerable or entrapped.

Danticat processes the intricacy and intimacy of life and death, of living and dying, as acts unfolding and attenuated over time and not in a single moment or event. She is able, therefore, to express the truth of very human actions by individuals who while living fully also recognize the inextricable nearness of death. Her elegiac imagination and poetic vision strip down to the inevitability of death yet epitomize the reality of life in the making of personal (private) or national (public) identity. Despite her recognition of bodily trauma whether experienced directly or inherited from tragic historical assaults, Danticat articulates hope as resident within the resilient human spirit. The will to live in freedom abides within even those of her characters facing certain death. Dying, separation, and change are part of living that carry an element of sadness, and sometimes regret. In her memoir *Brother, I'm Dying* (2007), however, the prevailing elegy is rich in looking back to inform the future, and not merely to make sense of the present. Her elegiac is then a celebration of lives lived, not simply of suffering endured, but also of accomplishments and connections, and especially of loving relationships.

Concomitantly, Laura Dawkins and Maria Rice Bellamy in their essays well understand that the power of writing about state violence and endangered lives is also a call for political action, for mobilizing in the face of deliberate dispersal and separation and death. It is a form of textual witnessing, as Jennifer Lozano recognizes in her focus on Danticat's *Create Dangerously: The Immigrant Artist at Work* (2010), an essay collection that is a political statement expressing an aesthetic vision fully accepting the civic duties and moral responsibilities of the artist to protest state overreaches of power and to protect the citizenry against political tyranny. Quietly extolling freedom as a natural state and insistently rebuking oppression, Danticat deploys her distinctive embodied voice to breathe life into the necessary struggles of the artist and her readers.

This aspect of breath and breathing in Danticat resonates with the political apparent in its recent social connotations: "I can't breathe." That simple statement has become a rallying cry for justice, mercy, and change in the sociopolitical sphere. Breathing is political in its leveling of all living beings to the simplest common denominator of aliveness, that is, taking breath. Breathing is the requirement for staying alive. It is the demand that has been heard in Black voices most insistently in the past few years, as breathing itself has become a demand to recognize the validity of Black life. To be allowed to breathe, to be permitted to continue to breathe, that simple insistence is at once a political statement and a social force. The enactment of the crushing out of breath has emerged as the metaphor for the ultimate oppression of the human. Relegation to the inhuman now not merely references the unbreathing dead but also specifies the one who stifles the breath, who denies the right to breathe and therefore the ability to live.

"I can't breathe," said eleven or twelve times by a dying man in New York's Staten Island, brought unprecedented public attention to a sad reality. Eric Garner's death on Bay Street from a choke hold by a police officer on July 17, 2017, caused an outcry for the right to breathe free from deliberate brutality leading to death. Two years earlier almost to the day, Michael Sabbie died in his Bi-State Jail cell in Texarkana, Arkansas. On the morning of July 22, 2015, Sabbie was found dead in his cell after having cried "I can't breathe" in asking for help the evening before. Guards threw him to the floor and ignored his pleas, "I can't breathe, I have pneumonia." When he cried out for water, they dragged him into a shower; when he passed out, they threw him into his cell. These events all were captured on video. This history has repeated again in the more recent videotaped death of George Floyd on May 25, 2020, on a Minneapolis street with a police officer's knee on his neck while he cried out, "Please, I can't breathe." For eight minutes and forty-six seconds, that officer of the law kept his knee on Floyd's neck even though life was slipping away as he called in anguish for his dead mother and pleaded for release, repeating, "Please, please, please I can't breathe. Please, man," until all breath was gone. But even in the aftermath of Floyd's death, the horrible echo of the familiar words "I can't breathe" have continue to circulate in incidents that still shock. Elijah McClain, stopped by police in Aurora, Colorado, on August 24, 2019, uttered those same words after being placed in a choke hold: "I can't breathe, please." The videotape of the incident would emerge in the aftermath of the protest surrounding George Floyd's death. McClain's now all too familiar plea for compassion and breath made no difference in the outcome. Administered ketamine, McClain went into cardiac arrest and died on August 30, 2019.

These videotaped incidents, linking breath, life, Blackness, and death, add a poignant urgency to the political undertones in Danticat's socially conscious writing. She documents in words, and often in the very language and patterns of speech used by Haitians, the claims to the sanctity of Black life so often under siege or restraint as videos have witnessed. Ever aware of the tenuous position not merely of the very endangered nature of Black body but especially of the Black diasporic body endangered for its visible difference, Danticat has written of the pain experienced by Black people in simply trying to live. *Brother, I'm Dying* may be an overt example, but so much of her work calls out for both an understanding of and a reckoning with the all too avoidable deaths of Black people. "I have been writing about death for as long as I have been writing," she reveals in her introduction to *The Art of Death: Writing the Final Story* (2017). That admission is all the more poignant because in this critical memoir she writes about her mother's death from cancer, and she contemplates how a myriad of other authors have dealt with the subject of death. Danticat infuses that text with her personal sense of loss and grief, but she leaves the reader and all those left behind to grieve with an unmistakable collective understanding of the enormity and nearness of death. She ends this exquisite book with a prayer offered up in the voice of her beloved mother.

Danticat's *matière* in this work and throughout her writing is a personal evocation of her own life and the lives of those nearest to her, and the felt presence of those now at a distance. The pressures that the mobile body faces stand out most starkly in the representations of diaspora that she brings to all her writing. Her gift is making intimate that vast, spread-out cacophony of voices and diasporic experiences. Language and meaning cohere in her treatment of the everyday as profound and global. That point Cécile Accilien makes by means of reading Danticat's children's book *Mama's Nightingale: A Story of Immigration and Separation* (2015) and her earlier young adult novel *Anacaona: Golden Flower, Haiti, 1490* (2005), in which she visualizes Haitian near and far history and inserts Kreyòl and Taíno words to make that history and her own as a child of the diaspora palpable and audible particularly for girls and women. Erika Serrato and Shewonda Leger understand that work of attending to the young as a means of both defining identity and healing subjectivity.

With a clear-sighted maturity and an empathy for ritual, Danticat reaches into the Haiti of her childhood and the New York of her youth to glean stories of ordinary life and extraordinary people. She breathes out forgiveness and wisdom for the next generations to be able to exercise their full humanity on the soil of their homeland or in their settlement homeplace—whichever allows for their growth in productive and meaningful living. Her broad evocations of girlhood are rich in narrative truth and symbolic hope. In work such as *Behind the Mountains* (2002), *The Last Mapou* (2013), and *Untwine* (2015), she bestows grace to younger readers and future generations in the form of love along with hope and forgiveness. At the same time, Danticat as a visionary seer tells stories that remind us all what is at stake in the present and in the between spaces involuntarily inhabited and occupied.

A creative force mirroring the complexities and achievements of our time, Edwidge Danticat is one of the great writers of the turn into the twenty-first century. Coming into her own just as the twentieth century was ending, she was in the vanguard of talented authors, such as Zadie Smith and Chimamanda Ngozi Adichie, who would come to prominence with a focus on their immigrant status, their bicultural upbringing, and their double vision. In the decade of the 1990s, Danticat completed a BA at Barnard College, an MFA at Brown University, her first novel, and her first collection of short stories, *Krik? Krak!* (1995). She launched a remarkable writing career, one marked from this very beginning by wisdom, grace, beauty, and strength. Most remarkably as seen now in retrospect, she began publishing writing that was nothing short of visionary for the ending of one century and the beginning of the next. In microcosm writ large, she engaged her present and the coming future of those extended others in a new dynamic the world over: migration and immigration and with them the accompanying displacement and mobility of millions of people across the globe; the dispersal of family and separation of blood kin; the search for an embracing homeplace; the desire for familial safety; the need for sanity in the midst of ever encroaching disasters (natural and man-made); the desperate effort to ward off hunger and food scarcity; the struggle for political and social justice—these and so many more of the issues that began to thread their way through the literature that would dominate the twenty-first century and its reckoning with resurgent meanings of diaspora and globalism.

Danticat has, however, from the beginning specifically tackled what it means to live as Haitian within a changed and changing family, environment, language, and culture. Successively, in confronting the traumatic splits and violent upheavals of the Haitian diaspora, she never loses sight of the human person, the individual no better and no worse than circumstances and relations allow. Her intergenerational stories have drawn acclaim for their clarity of voice and vision regarding journeying into a cultural past as not simply an aspect of mobility but as a sign of freedom or an actualization of choice to reunite with Haiti, its places, people, customs, and traditions on the ground where they originate. Those realities haunt the diasporic person returning who is not completely an insider and yet not an outsider either. In *After the Dance: A Walk through Carnival in Jacmel, Haiti* (2002), for example, Danticat both joins in the cultural revels in active reportage but also maintains the distance that from her childhood she was warned to maintain for propriety. Intersubjective, intercultural, and intersectional identities all come together in the subjective space and conscious awareness that she offers. This balancing act is the kind of tightrope of existence that Danticat mediates and records in her creations that attempt to get at the essence of diasporic identity.

Her narratives display her understanding of the complexities of her own life and those adjacent to hers. A calm, serenely confident storyteller, she acknowledges the grace and art of her craft and the beauty and necessity of her history. She makes orality seamless in writing so exquisitely true that it seems effortless, much like breath itself. Yet, any examination, as in the essays presented here in *Narrating History, Home, and Dyaspora*, ultimately has accentuated her craftsmanship and underscored the painstaking thought and dedicated artistry that go into all that she produces and sends forth into the world.

From her first book, she emphasized the body, historically and metaphorically, in a positionality located within the family, specifically the racial and immigrant family. Utilizing the conception of "Marassa" or the double that is the same and inseparable, she explored the hidden and off-limits secrets of women's matrilineal cultural legacies. Mother-daughter relationships form not merely the core of familial bonds but the basis of cultural ones as well. Those bonds become representations, too, of the mobility or movement that like breath is necessary for living yet also forced and traumatic, as in separation. Mothers and daughters configure so much of Danticat's vision, not only in her remarkable fiction but also in her meticulous nonfiction, and increasingly in her forceful topical essays. In these relationships, she remember her own mother and visualizes her own self in her representations of mother-daughter interactions that, while not mirroring her own, take their cue from what she knows about the cultural ties between mother and daughter that go beyond blood links and interpersonal connections.

With that knowledge, she leans into the heart of diasporic existence from a feminist perspective. Whether cultural oppression, systemic racism, gender bias, color prejudice, or language discrimination, Danticat renders the legible, audible, muted, or subdued signs that have impacted Haitians whether at home or abroad. She does not back away from the pain, the grief, the longing, and the loneliness of the displaced or from the cruelty, the hatred, and the irrational supporting regimes of terror and fear and the agents of corruption and genocide. Often, too, she traces in personal, womanist essays the onslaught of everyday living, as in "Mourning in Place" (2020) with its elegant expression of what loss has meant to her as a woman, daughter, wife, mother, and neighbor living in Miami's Little Haiti during the COVID pandemic. The feminine in Danticat's work, much like an easy softness of breath in inhaling and exhaling, stems from within the hard muscles of the body and the mind strengthened by willful sight and memory.

It is her unblinking willingness to look, to observe, to listen, to record, and, above all, to imagine that has given her readers the gift of *The Farming of Bones* (1998) and *The Dew Breaker* (2004). These intricate texts, alongside her two edited anthologies, *Haiti Noir* (2011) and *Haiti Noir 2: The Classics* (2013), signify that her sight is ever focused on understanding Haiti, its history and heritage, and her vision is always evolving to encompass the human effect of the many transgressions and the multiple joys she sees in its people and culture. Each book has been unfailingly textured in drawing upon the complex history and rich culture of Haiti, but each has also been distinctly and deeply personal in revealing the human face of Haitian people in myriad locations or contortions and in probing nuance or residue in what she calls "a darker place."

Danticat has not overlooked attention to political regimes and state governments that impact individual lives. Moreover, she has represented the migrating body with a forward motion and a back-looking movement. Both are inevitable, yet both are painful. The process involves reckoning and recompense, letting go and holding on: in other words, dual actions and perhaps even contradictory ways of attempting to actualize being at home in the literal world and of understanding the figurative one.

That dual action references Danticat's situating of diaspora as structuring her identity as both Haitian and American. The work of understanding that the "dyasporic" body is not landless but living between breaths in a dimension rarely identified as real and actual. Recognizing the danger of literally breathing the air in the in-between spaces and places of identity, body, and significance, she tells in a unique and wise voice the costs, sacrifices, and losses as well as the gains, benefits, and advances accrued in the risk-taking of diaspora subjects.

Danticat's *Everything Inside: Stories* (2019), for instance, presents a trenchant epigraph from Cindy Jiménez-Vera: "Being born is the first exile. / To walk the earth / is an eternal diaspora." It straightforwardly indicates what is so significant about the eight stories in *Everything Inside* in the context of Danticat's oeuvre. Moving into and out of spaces is, for her, a way of marking life. The markings, however, are even more dramatic when the resonances of the term "diaspora" come into play. Here, the genius of Danticat's everyday movement about the earth becomes extraordinary in her stories of the ways in which the displacements and the disruptions of the human heart become the measure of what it means to live in the world today. This book, like those preceding it, is a testimony to the urgency of her voice and vision and of her visceral diasporic aliveness.

The editors and contributors to *Narrating History, Home, and Dyaspora* rightly use Danticat's term "dyaspora" with its evocation of Haitian Kreyòl.

That term allows access to the layered implications within any discussion of Danticat's oeuvre, as the first part of the collection, "Another County: Nation and Dyaspora," makes plain in establishing the intersections of identity, creativity, and spatiality. The editors, Maia Butler, Joanna Davis-McElligatt, and Megan Feifer, in opening with a nod to James Baldwin, specifically to his novel *Another Country* but simultaneously to his prodigious perceptive essays on race, nation, and being, place the contributors in a significant line of salient writings on the complexities of identity for people of color in the United States. Theirs is an eloquent reminder of why the essay form and critical analysis have become so important for understanding not merely the present moment but also the near past and their combined gateway to a future.

These essays offer a deep dive into the very air that Danticat breathes. They reveal the Kongo cosmology from the African past that infuses her being in the diasporic present, as Joyce White, Olga Blomgren, and Gwen Bergner emphasize in explicating *lò bò dlo* (across the water) in essays exploring diasporic place, identity, and relations. The essays help readers comprehend that present in which Danticat has absorbed New York, Miami, and the culture of the United States as a backdrop and filter for her rendering of life, of the everyday of ordinary women and men who, in the enormous richness of her understanding and the simplicity of her vision, emerge as extraordinary. These concepts and ideas flow from her dynamic writing and demand our attention to the meaning and significance of their lives, as Isabel Caldeira and Delphine Gras maintain in their essays that explain Danticat's determined ethical stance against the silencing of dissident voices especially in the twenty-first century, whether explicitly historical and political as in *The Farming of Bones* and *The Dew Breaker* or in the reflective historicity and personal language of *Behind the Mountains, Claire of the Sea Light*, and *Untwine*. Lucía Stecher and Thomás Rothe further utilize that ethical and aesthetic lens to move between Danticat's fiction and nonfiction, especially *Claire of the Sea Light* and *The Art of Death: Writing the Final Story*, in order to unpack how she both traces a dual Haitian and African American literary heritage and develops a communal voice to embrace the languages and perspectives she shares with those writers and intellectuals who have gone before her.

The breadth of *Narrating History, Home, and Dyaspora* is a testimony not only to Danticat's own prolific and prodigious work but also to the critical acumen and analytic brilliance of these readers of her work and their intellectual and communal commitment to shedding more light on an incomparable contemporary artist. Herein is a succinct yet expansive articulation of an aesthetic breathing room within Danticat's texts as well as a welcoming invitation to enlarge the critical approaches to her writing and messages. Eschewing any superficial nod to Danticat's reputation, these essays proceed knowingly and expertly. With a clear sense of the standing of their subject in the wider public world and of their own expertise in approaching her work, the authors coalesce into an impressive voice for taking heed, listening, understanding, and apprehending Danticat's vision and for reading her canon deeply, compassionately, and comprehensively.

Narrating History, Home, and Dyaspora forwards the work of *Edwidge Danticat: A Reader's Guide*, edited by Martin Munro, that served as an introduction to Danticat in 2010. Now a decade later, this new edited collection of critical essays takes full advantage of the astonishing, rich forward motion of Danticat's artistic production and gives full range to the modes of articulating the significant reach and intellectual force of that production. *Narrating History, Home, and Dyaspora* comes at a moment when political and personal intersections abound in the public world and in the artistic milieu. It brings together in a necessary time of reckoning a mature body of eloquent work that offers much across the spectrum of readers and the divides of beliefs. The breadth and depth of this collection and the scope and seriousness of the attentive essays make clear how much Danticat offers to diverse readers and critics. Its succinct yet expansive sense of the breathing room within Danticat's work for myriad readers and its magnification of multiple theoretical conceptions of how to breathe in and absorb her writing have together issued an important call to all.

The three editors and sixteen contributors engage the entire span of Danticat's career and breathe fresh insights into approaching and appraising her texts. They attest that her storytelling, across genres and formats, audiences and ages, has brought her much-deserved national and international recognition and praise. They recognize her achievements and acknowledge the early accolades for her work, her writing, and her vision: a Pushcart Prize for fiction, an American Book Award, a National Book Critics Circle Award, and an Oprah's Book Club selection; awards from *Seventeen* magazine, *Essence* magazine, and *Granta*, and from *Harper's Bazaar* as one of the "20 in their 20s to watch," then from the *New York Times* as one of the "30 under 30 creative people to watch," and from *Jane* as one of their "15 gutsiest women"; and, of course, a MacArthur Foundation "Genius" Award, followed by many more honors, including the Neustadt International Prize for Literature. The scholars writing here know that, given Danticat's expanding canon with its inimitable social and political impact created by her powerful words and diasporic vision, these honors, recognitions, and awards will surely continue.

They celebrate her stature in the literary world and in the public sphere in which artists and scholars alike herald her. They speak directly to the amazing presence that is Edwidge Danticat, writer, storyteller, visionary, and intellectual who is a Haitian woman and a US American woman, and truly an unparalleled voice of this age and for these current hemispheric landscapes.

ABOUT THE CONTRIBUTORS

Cécile Accilien is chair of the Department of Interdisciplinary Studies and professor of African and African diaspora studies in the Department of Interdisciplinary Studies at Kennesaw State University. She is the author of *Rethinking Marriage in Francophone African and Caribbean Literatures* (Lexington Books, 2008). She has coedited and coauthored several volumes including *Francophone Cultures through Film* (Focus Publishing, 2013), *English-Haitian Creole Phrasebook* (McGraw-Hill, 2010), *Just Below South: Intercultural Performance in the Caribbean and the U.S. South* (University of Virginia Press, 2007), and *Revolutionary Freedoms: A History of Strength, Survival and Imagination in Haiti* (Caribbean Studies Press, 2006). She is currently working on a coedited volume, *Teaching Haiti beyond Literature: Intersectionalities of History, Literature and Culture* (under contract with University Press of Florida), and a book project manuscript on the Haitian Hollywood movement (under contract with the State University of New York Press).

Maria Rice Bellamy is an associate professor of English and the director of African and African diaspora studies at the College of Staten Island of the City University of New York. She recently coedited a special issue of *Women's Studies Quarterly* on the theme of inheritance (Spring 2020) and is the author of *Bridges to Memory: Postmemory in Contemporary Ethnic American Women's Fiction* (University of Virginia Press, 2015). Maria is currently editing volume 17: 2000–2020 of the Cambridge University Press series *African American Literature in Transition*. Her next book project explores contemporary representations of slavery in fiction, memoir, and popular culture. Maria is a member of the Advisory Board for the Edwidge Danticat Society.

Gwen Bergner is an associate professor of English at West Virginia University. She is the author of *Taboo Subjects: Race, Sex, and Psychoanalysis* (University of Minnesota Press, 2005), coeditor with Zita Nunes of a special issue of *American Literature* titled "The Plantation, the Post-Plantation, and the Afterlives of Slavery" (November 2019), and author of articles on race, US imperialism, and transnational feminism in *PMLA*, *American Quarterly*, and *American Literary History*, among others. Her essay on Douglas Sirk's racial melodrama *Imitation of Life* is forthcoming in *Signs: Journal of Women in Culture and Society*.

Olga Blomgren's research encompasses language hierarchies, master narratives, pedagogy, and access to literary studies in higher education. She is a Dissertation Fellow in the Department of Black Studies at the University of California, Santa Barbara, and a doctoral candidate in the Department of Comparative Literature at Binghamton University, State University of New York. She has taught literature and composition in California, where she participated in grant-funded research in retention and engagement at Hispanic-Serving Institutions. These experiences motivated her to enter doctoral study. Working to articulate the ways multilingual authors' English-language texts trouble the divisions of existing academic disciplines, Olga's current research in the Caribbean engages literary and translation studies, and archipelagic and spatial studies to examine how and where "new" world literatures might emerge. She is preparing a dissertation, "Reading Dangerously: Cannibalizing Languages, Creolizing Texts and Archipelagic Thinking in Writings by Rosario Ferré and Edwidge Danticat," accentuating the relations between mobility and citizenship, language and power, and the creolized use of English to destabilize the state and its narratives. Researching the movement of language in the Caribbean, Olga's dissertation addresses reverberations of post/mono-lingualism and globalization, advancing the interpretative possibilities opened by "archipelagic thinking."

Maia L. Butler is assistant professor of African American literature at the University of North Carolina Wilmington, where she is also affiliate faculty in women's and gender studies and Africana studies. She is a literary geographer researching and teaching in African American/diasporic, Anglophone postcolonial, and American (broadly conceived) studies, with an emphasis on Black women's literature and feminist theories. She has chapters in the collections *Approaches to Teaching the Work of Edwidge Danticat* (Routledge, 2019), *Revisiting the Elegy in the Black Lives Matter Era* (Routledge, 2019), and *The Bloomsbury Handbook to Edwidge Danticat* (Bloomsbury, 2021). She has collaborative work in a colloquium section of *Frontiers: A Journal of Women's Studies* called "Sowing the Seeds: Decolonial Practices and Pedagogies" (September 2020) as well as an interview with and a coauthored article about Stephanie Powell Watts in *North Carolina Literary Review* (2019, 2020). She is the cofounding vice president of the Edwidge Danticat Society.

Isabel Caldeira is associate professor of American studies at the Faculty of Letters and Senior Research Fellow of the Center for Social Studies, University of Coimbra, Portugal. Her research fields are African American studies, comparative studies of the African diaspora, inter-American studies, postcolonial studies, and feminist studies. Her most recent publications include: "Black Women Writers in the Americas: The Struggle for Human Rights in the Context of Coloniality" (in *Human Rights in the Americas*, edited by María Herrera-Sobek, Francisco A. Lomelí, and Luz Angélica Kirschner; Routledge, 2021); "Entre a dessexualização e a hipersexualização dos corpos de mulheres negras: Roxane Gay: *Fome, uma autobiografia do (meu) corpo*" (Between Desexualization and Hypersexualization of the Bodies of Black Women: Roxane Gay: *Hunger, A Memoir of [My] Body*) (in *Intersexualidades/Interseccionalidades: Saberes e sentidos do corpo*, edited by Paulo César Garcia and Emerson Inácio; O Sexo da Palavra, 2019); and "Toni Morrison and Edwidge Danticat: Writers-as-Citizens of the African Diaspora" (in *The Routledge Companion to Inter-American Studies*, edited by Wilfried Raussert; Routledge, 2017). She is president of the International Association of Inter-American Studies.

Nadège T. Clitandre is currently associate professor in the Department of Global Studies at the University of California, Santa Barbara, where she holds affiliate appointments in the Departments of Black Studies and Comparative Literature. She is the author of *Edwidge Danticat: The Haitian Diasporic Imaginary* (2018) and coeditor of two volumes: *The Bloomsbury Handbook to Edwidge Danticat* (2021) and *Remembrance: Loss, Hope, Recovery after the Earthquake in Haiti* (2016). Clitandre received her BA in English literature from Hampton University, an MA in the humanities from the University of Chicago, and a PhD in African diaspora studies with a designated emphasis in women, gender, and sexuality from the University of California, Berkeley. Clitandre works on theoretical frameworks of the African diaspora and issues concerning the linked relationship between migration, displacement, and transnationalism with a particular focus on Haiti and Haitian diasporic literature. Her teaching interests include diaspora studies, anticolonial literature, postcolonial Caribbean women's literature, globalization, and NGO and humanitarian intervention in Haiti post-earthquake. Clitandre is the recipient of the University of California President's Postdoctoral Fellowship (2009) and the Ford Foundation Predoctoral Fellowship (2004). She is also the founder of Haiti Soleil, a nonprofit organization that focuses on engaging youth and building community through the development of libraries and cultural centers in Haiti.

Thadious M. Davis is the Geraldine R. Segal Professor of American Social Thought, emerita, and professor of English at the University of Pennsylvania. She is the author of *Understanding Alice Walker*; *Southscapes: Geographies of Race, Region, and Literature*; *Games of Property: Law, Race, Gender, and Faulkner's "Go Down, Moses"*; *Nella Larsen, Novelist of the Harlem Renaissance: A Woman's Life Unveiled*; and *Faulkner's "Negro": Art and the Southern Context*. She has warm memories of the honor of teaching Edwidge Danticat at Brown University.

Joanna Davis-McElligatt is an assistant professor of Black literary and cultural studies in the Department of English at the University of North Texas. She is coeditor of *Narratives of Marginalized Identities in Higher Education: Inside and Outside the Academy* (Routledge, 2019) and *BOOM! Splat: Comics and Violence* (University Press of Mississippi, under contract). She is currently at work on her first monograph, entitled *Black and Immigrant: Belonging, Diaspora, and Time in American Literature after 1965*, a critical exploration of representations of immigrants of African descent to the United States from Afropolitans to Wakandan Americans. Her scholarly work appears or is forthcoming in *South: A Scholarly Journal*; *Mississippi Quarterly*; *A History of the Literature of the U.S. South* (Cambridge University Press, 2021); *The Cambridge Companion to New Faulkner Studies* (Cambridge University Press, forthcoming); *The Cambridge Companion to the American Graphic Novel* (Cambridge University Press, under contract); *Small-Screen Souths: Region, Identity, and the Cultural Politics of Television* (Louisiana State University Press, 2017); and *Critical Insights: American Multicultural Identity* (Salem Press, 2014), among other places. Her work on comics has appeared in the *Comics Journal*; *Graphic Novels for Children and Young Adults* (University Press of Mississippi, 2017); and *The Comics of Chris Ware: Drawing Is a Way of Thinking* (University Press of Mississippi, 2010). Before joining UNT, she spent nine years at the University of Louisiana at Lafayette.

Laura Dawkins received her PhD in English from Indiana University in 1999. She is currently professor of American literature at Murray State University. Her research interests include African American literature, gender studies, American modernism, and race theory. Her articles on American literature and culture have appeared in *Callaloo*, *Literature Interpretation*

Theory, *South Atlantic Review*, *49th Parallel*, *Short Story*, and seven edited collections including *Resistance and Reform: Modernist Women Writers and American Social Engagement*, edited by Jody Cardinal, Deirdre Egan-Ryan, and Julia Lisella (Lexington Books, 2019); *Emmett Till in Literary Memory and Imagination*, edited by Harriet Pollack and Christopher Metress (Louisiana State University Press, 2008); and *The American Child: A Cultural Studies Reader*, edited by Caroline Levander and Carol Singley (Rutgers University Press, 2003).

Megan Feifer is one of the inaugural resident teacher-scholars at the bell hooks center at Berea College. She earned her BA and MA from the University of Wisconsin and PhD at Louisiana State University. Her research and teaching addresses Afro-Caribbean diasporas in the United States, multiethnic literatures, postcolonial literature and theory, and feminist theories. Her dissertation research examines the collective counter-archival project created in the essays, fiction, and nonfiction work of authors Julia Alvarez, Edwidge Danticat, and Junot Díaz. She is the author of the article "The Remembering of Bones: Working through Trauma and the Counter-Archive in Edwidge Danticat's *The Farming of Bones*" in *Palimpsest: A Journal on Women, Gender, and the Black International*; and has chapters in *Revisiting the Elegy in the Black Lives Matter Era* (Routledge, 2019) and *The Bloomsbury Handbook to Edwidge Danticat* (Bloomsbury, 2021). She is a cofounding president of the Edwidge Danticat Society.

Delphine Gras, an associate professor at Florida Gulf Coast University, teaches a variety of language and literature courses. In her research, Dr. Gras specializes in twentieth-century literature of the Americas and the African diaspora. She was a finalist for the 2011 Vanderbilt ICI Book Competition on the African diaspora and has published on various topics including service learning, Shay Youngblood, Nicolás Guillén, and Toni Morrison.

Akia Jackson is currently a reading and writing specialist at Trinity Washington University in Washington, DC, and a senior tutor in the Writing Center at Washington University in St. Louis, Missouri. She completed her PhD in English literature in August 2019 at the University of Iowa. Her dissertation was entitled "The Mobility of Memory and Shame: African American and Afro-Caribbean Women's Fiction 1980s–1990s," and her research focuses primarily on women's diaspora studies, affect theory, and critical race studies. In the early portion of her matriculation at the University of Iowa, she worked with the university's Rhetoric Department as a Speaking Center tutor helping domestic and international students improve their linguistic understanding of the English language, as well as building their listening and speaking acumen. During her time at the University of Iowa, she also served as a graduate writing tutor in the Frank Business Center. In her time as a graduate instructor in both the English and Rhetoric Departments, she mentored several domestic minority and international minority undergraduate students, helping them gain early leadership prowess in their young academic careers. In the final year of her program to sharpen her teaching and mentoring background, she was awarded a Dissertation Fellowship in the English Department at Middle Tennessee State University in Murfreesboro, Tennessee, for the 2018–2019 academic year. Dr. Jackson, at her current university, continues to work toward equitable writing and speaking solutions for the Minority-Serving Institution (MSI) and population at her college.

Tammie Jenkins received her doctorate degree in curriculum and instruction from Louisiana State University. Dr. Jenkins's research interests are gender studies, Black Atlantic studies, and African American history. Her recent publications include "Reading, Singing, and Viewing Rape: Uncovering Hidden Messages of Womanhood and Manhood in Popular Culture" (*Taboo*, Spring 2020); "(Re)Writing the Black Female Body or Cleansing Her Soul: Narratives of Generational Traumas and Healing in Edwidge Danticat's *Breath, Eyes, Memory*" (in *Approaches to Teaching the Works of Edwidge Danticat*, edited by Celucien L. Joseph, Suchismita Banerjee, Marvin E. Hobson, and Danny M. Hoey Jr.; Routledge, 2020); and "Culture, Identity, and Otherness: An Analysis of Kino's Songs in John Steinbeck's *The Pearl* and Pilate's Melody in Toni Morrison's *Song of Solomon*" (in *Critical Insights: "The Pearl,"* edited by Laura Nicosia and James F. Nicosia; Salem Press, 2020). She serves as an associate editor for the *Criterion* and is on the editorial board of *Epitome*. She currently works as a special education teacher in her local public school system.

Shewonda Leger is an assistant professor of multilingual writing and pedagogy in the Department of English at Florida International University. As a Black feminist Haitian filmmaker, her research areas are Caribbean rhetorics, cultural rhetorics, digital rhetorics, and multimodal composition—emphasizing Haitian women of the diaspora cultural identities and practices. She received her doctorate (2019) from Michigan State University in rhetoric and writing with a graduate specialization in women's and gender studies, where she also received her MA (2015) in digital rhetoric and professional writing.

Jennifer M. Lozano is assistant professor of English and affiliate faculty in the Gender Studies and Resource Center at the University of North Carolina Wilmington (UNCW). Her primary research focuses on spirituality, neoliberalism, and transnational Latino/a identity and experience in contemporary Latina/o literature and culture. She is also interested in women of color feminism, women and gender studies, digital media studies, "global" literature, and twentieth- and twenty-first-century American literature and culture, especially literature of the Southwest.

Marion Christina Rohrleitner is an associate professor of English at the University of Texas at El Paso, where she researches and teaches twentieth- and twenty-first-century ethnic American literatures with a focus on Chicanx/Latinx and Caribbean diasporic fiction and poetry. Her coedited collection *Dialogues across Diasporas: Women Writers, Scholars, and Activists of Africana and Latina Descent in Conversation* was published by Lexington Books in 2012. Her scholarship has appeared, for example, in *American Quarterly, Antipodas, Latino Studies Symbolism,* the *European Journal of American Studies,* and *The Palgrave Handbook of Magical Realism in the Twenty-First Century* (Palgrave Macmillan, 2020). Her coauthored and coedited book *Haitian Revolutionary Fictions: An Anthology* is forthcoming with the University of Virginia Press in 2022, and she is currently completing *Transnational Latinidades,* a monograph on the politics and poetics of translating Latinx literatures in the European Union.

Thomás Rothe holds a PhD in literature from the Universidad de Chile and teaches at several universities in Santiago, Chile. His research focuses on Caribbean and Latin American literature, with an emphasis on translation, cultural magazines, and literary history. His work has appeared in *Anales del Caribe, Meridional, Mutatis Mutandis, Revista de Estudios Hispánicos,* and *Sargasso,* among other academic journals. He has translated several volumes of poetry into English, including Jaime Huenún's *Fanon City Meu,* Rodrigo Lira's *Testimony of Circumstances,* and Emma Villazón's *Expendables.* With Lucía Stecher, he translated into Spanish Edwidge Danticat's *Create Dangerously,* published by Banda Propia in 2020, and he is currently working on a translation of Danticat's *Claire of the Sea Light.*

Erika V. Serrato holds a PhD in French from Emory University. She is currently a Carolina Postdoctoral Fellow in the Department of Romance Studies at the University of North Carolina at Chapel Hill. Her research focuses on intellectual and aesthetic exchanges between voices, texts, and figures from the Francophone, Hispanic, and Anglophone Caribbean. Her main questions concern what Édouard Glissant calls "l'Autre Amérique," indigeneity, language, aesthetics, "l'entour," and intersectional subjectivities. She has published in *Women in French* and *SX Salon* and has a forthcoming chapter on Afro-Cuban poet Jesús Cos Causse's Haitian influence. She is currently working on an article regarding commemoration practices in the Caribbean as well as on a book manuscript regarding indigeneity in the Francophone Caribbean.

Lucía Stecher is an associate professor at the Universidad de Chile. Her research areas cover Caribbean and Latin American literature, women's writing, and feminist criticism. She is the author of *Narrativas migrantes del Caribe: Michelle Cliff, Jamaica Kincaid y Edwidge Danticat* (Ediciones Corregidor, 2016) and coeditor of *Aimé Césaire desde América Latina: Diálogos con el poeta de la negritud* (2011) and *Frantz Fanon desde América Latina: Lecturas contemporáneas de un pensador del siglo XX* (2013). She has published many articles in academic journals, including *Tulsa Studies in Women's Literature, Revista de Estudios Filológicos, Revista de Estudios Hispánicos, Revista Chilena de Literatura, Callaloo*, and *Revista de Crítica Literaria Latinoamericana*. With Thomás Rothe, she translated into Spanish Edwidge Danticat's *Create Dangerously*, published by Banda Propia in 2020, and she is currently working on a translation of Danticat's *Claire of the Sea Light*.

Joyce White is an assistant professor of English in African American literature at Winthrop University. She received her PhD in humanities with a primary focus on African American studies from Clark Atlanta University and earned a BA and MA in English, with a focus on creative writing and literature, from Florida State University. Her research interests include nineteenth-, twentieth-, and twenty-first-century African American and diasporic literature as well as African cosmological and spiritual continuities in diasporic literature.

INDEX

CPSIA information can be obtained
at www.ICGtesting.com
Printed in the USA
BVHW070008210522
637573BV00002B/7

9 781496 839886